Amakudari

Amakudari
The Hidden Fabric of Japan's Economy

RICHARD A. COLIGNON
and
CHIKAKO USUI

ILR PRESS
an imprint of
CORNELL UNIVERSITY PRESS
Ithaca & London

First published 2003 by Cornell University Press

Printed in the United States of America

Library of Congress Cataloging-in-Publication Data
Colignon, Richard A., 1951–
  Amakudari : the hidden fabric of Japan's economy / Richard A. Colignon and Chikako Usui.
    p. cm.
Includes bibliographical references and index.
  ISBN 0-8014-4083-1 (cloth : alk. paper)
  1. Bureaucracy—Japan. 2. Japan—Economic conditions—1989– 3. Power (Social sciences)—Japan. I. Usui, Chikako, 1953– II. Title.
  JQ1631 . C65 2003
  322'.3'0952—dc21

                                         2002152814

Cornell University Press strives to use environmentally responsible suppliers and materials to the fullest extent possible in the publishing of its books. Such materials include vegetable-based, low-VOC inks and acid-free papers that are recycled, totally chlorine-free, or partly composed of nonwood fibers. For further information, visit our website at www.cornellpress.cornell.edu.

Cloth printing   10 9 8 7 6 5 4 3 2 1

Contents

Acknowledgments   vii
1. *Amakudari* and the Political Economy of Japan   1
2. *Amakudari* as an Institution   29
3. *Amakudari*: Movement to the Private Sector   57
4. *Yokosuberi* and Public Corporations   82
5. *Wataridori* and Private and Public Corporations   112
6. *Seikai Tensin*: Movement to the Political World   135
7. *Amakudari* as a Power Structure   164
Appendix   187
Notes   191
References   205
Index   217

Acknowledgments

After we published our first article on *amakudari*, we received timely encouragement to pursue a book from Henry Tom. In the end this book took us on a long intellectual quest. We collected the bulk of our data in Japan in 1997–98 when Richard Colignon received the Fulbright Fellowship to Tokyo University and Kyoritsu Women's University and Chikako Usui took a visiting researcher position at Tokyo University during her sabbatical leave. We express our gratitude to a number of people who assisted us along the journey. Eizaburo Toyoshima and Chikio Hayashi educated us about *amakudari* and public corporations. Members of the Fulbright Association, staff at the Tokyo Fulbright office, Yutaka Tsujinaka, Kieko Suehiro, Shigemichi Endo, Yasuo Endo, Ichiro Fujita, Hirohisa Kishino, Michiyuki Inukai, and Yoshisuke Iinuma helped us collect data in Japan.

We presented our preliminary papers at Tohoku University Seminar and at the annual meetings of the Association of Japanese Business Studies and the American Sociological Association. We are grateful to Yoshimichi Sato, Masato Kimura, Tom Roehl, Kiyohiko Ito, Leonard Lynn, David Plath, Midwest Japan Seminar members, Herman Smith, and Marlis Buchmann for spirited discussions of our papers and helpful comments.

Our warm appreciation goes to Hiromi Ishida, Chisato Usui, Kuniko Nihira, Joel Glassman, Kathy Cochrane, Robert Baumann, and the staff at the interlibrary loan desk at the University of Missouri-St. Louis for their continuing support of our research activities. We owe special thanks to T. J. Pempel and one anonymous reviewer for Cornell University Press for their detailed comments and constructive criticisms for the revision of the entire manuscript. We thank Martha Walsh, Karen Laun, and Julie Nemer for their help in editing the manuscript, and Frances Benson for her advice and encouragement.

The financial support for this manuscript came from various sources. They include the University of Missouri Research Board, a University of Missouri-St. Louis Small Research Grant, the Japan Foundation, the Center for International Studies at the University of Missouri-St. Louis, and a Duquesne University Presidential Grant. We also received travel assistance from the Center for East Asian Studies at the University of Chicago, the Center for Japanese Studies at the University of Michigan, and the Graduate Programs in Gerontology at University of Missouri-St. Louis.

We did the data collection, coding, analysis, and writing of the manuscript on our own. Any errors of facts or judgment are our sole responsibility.

We dedicate this book to Tony and Margaret Colignon and to Shizuo and Akiko Usui.

Amakudari

1 *Amakudari* and the Political Economy of Japan

A sense of frustration pervades Japan. Since the bubble burst in 1990, the Japanese economy has continued to stagnate. What has happened to Japan's economic miracle? How could the world's most acclaimed economic success have collapsed so badly? Some observers characterize the 1990s as the era of the unraveling of the old system—the elements that made Japan the second largest economy in the world have outlived their usefulness and are no longer effective. To revive the economy, they argue, fundamental reforms are necessary. And although Japan has initiated a series of administrative and electoral reforms and the deregulation of the economy since the mid-1980s, debates continue over their real significance. Whereas some believe old elements of the system are starting to break up, others maintain the changes that have occurred are more apparent than real and that the old system is still in place.[1]

As the recession drags on, some authors contend that the ability of the bureaucracy to guide the nation has deteriorated and that no political leader has been capable of effecting fundamental reforms amid increasingly robust centrifugal forces. Reformers and conservatives, for example, divide over supporting deregulation and favoring the internationally competitive sectors or continuing the protections and subsidies of the domestic sectors. The political system fractured in the 1990s as it struggled to adjust to changing domestic and international challenges. The electoral defeat of the dominant Liberal Democratic Party (LDP) in 1993 was the result of a split among its own party members. Although debates continue on the real significance of the changes, many believe the power structure of vested interests is so strong that Japan will continue to muddle through the foreseeable future.

The issue, we believe, is a matter of the framework of discussion. Authors who apply a free market framework to Japan focus on issues of efficiency in the current economic and social arrangements. They point to the relations among institutions, define them as pathological, and contend the solution to the recession is independent institutions oriented to market efficiency. Critics of these economic interpretations (Dore 2000; Hamilton and Biggart 1988; Lincoln Gerlach, and Takahashi 1992; Stark 1996; Usui and Colignon 1996), however, indicate that market structures include a wide variety of social structures based on repeated interactions, forms of governance, and relations to the state. They suggest that Japan's economy is more oriented to stability facilitating the effectiveness and survival of corporations (Dore 1983, 2001a). Changes are proceeding slowly in a measured way to avoid the chaos anticipated from the implementation of drastic reform measures advanced by many economists.

The power structure in Japan represents both a mechanism of change and resistance to reform with a preference for more stability. The alliance of top bureaucrats, leading LDP politicians, and corporate elites created through the institution of *amakudari* is one fundamental nexus of such resistance to change and orientation toward stability. Literally translated, *amakudari* means "descent from heaven" and refers to the reemployment of top-level bureaucrats in high-level positions in private and public corporations as well as their movement to national political office. Reforms that restructured the bureaucracy and electoral system, in addition to the deregulation of banking and security markets, have had minimal impact on the interinstitutional alliances and the old policymaking structure. Observers of regulatory reform report that close ties between private firms and the bureaucracy protect the interests of firms in particular industries and promote compensating arrangements in other policy areas, frustrating and complicating the issues of deregulation (Carlile and Tilton 1998; Cottingham-Streater and Konishi 1999; Miyajima 1998; Norville 1998). Opaque and elusive bureaucratic control and manifold informal ties bind government and private interests and account for the tenacity and adaptability of the political-bureaucratic-business (iron triangle) alliances[2] and the difficulties of reform (Carlile and Tilton 1998, 211). Networks created by *amakudari* alliances resist change at a subterranean or foundational level, meaning they are impervious to the formal dictates of reform and restructuring. "The broadest process of deregulation will continue to be hindered by the strength of institutions nested in the regulatory environment. The essential problem remains one of political and bureaucratic resistance to change" (Mulgen 1997, 10). In short, *amakudari* networks provide underlying structural continuity and stability in a context of dramatic events, pressures, and formal policy changes.[3] In this book we examine change and continuity in the paths of *amakudari* that create the complex interinstitutional cooperation distinguishing Japan from other political economies.

The Roles of *Amakudari*

Bureaucrats in Japan are recruited exclusively from select universities, primarily the University of Tokyo (Todai). Career bureaucrats compete for up or out promotion that is strictly age determined. These meritocratic elites are forced to retire by their early fifties and, through *amakudari*, move to the boards of directors of public- and private-sector corporations and to political office. This reemployment of high-level officials in the firms and industries they once regulated generates pervasive *amakudari* networks and alliances among numerous elements of Japanese business, politics, and the bureaucracy. In moving to their new positions, the former bureaucrats take with them invaluable insider knowledge about a ministry's policies and procedures, as well as the contacts and personal relationships developed during their careers. With *amakudari*, this wealth of information transfers to the firms employing the ex-bureaucrats and helps them maintain smoother relations with the ministries that license, subsidize, guide, and regulate their industry.

Amakudari is an institutionalized form of human resource management that developed in rebuilding the postwar economy. One of numerous interinstitutional ties, *amakudari* can mobilize bureaucratic resources and coordinate institutions for long-term economic planning and lower interinstitutional transaction costs. *Amakudari* provides channels of information and negotiations across legislative, bureaucratic, and business institutions. In this sense, *amakudari* is itself a root social institution operating beneath the formal institutions involving bureaucrats, politicians, and corporate leaders, representing an alliance of Japan's elite power structure. Arranged by the ministry, not the individual, it in effect provides private corporations with lobbyists to ministries with windows to private corporations (Prestowitz 1988).

The social institution of *amakudari* is pervasive, unique, and enigmatic. *Amakudari*-like processes exist everywhere in Japan, binding large firms and smaller firms in the private and public sectors. High-ranking employees of large organizations retire to important positions in their smaller counterparts, just as central ministry bureaucrats descend to local political offices and industry associations to act as pipelines of communication between the administrative center and provincial localities. Local governments, in turn, move their high-ranking officials to lucrative jobs in affiliated companies. The Tokyo metropolitan government, for example, has more than seventy affiliated organizations that guarantee its senior officials *amakudari*-like positions. *Keiretsu* alliances (industrial groups) maintain not only the cross-shareholding, overlapping boards of directors, and exchanges of personnel, but also *amakudari*-like arrangements among corporate affiliates. In education, bureaucrats descend to important positions at universities and research institutions. Similarly, high-ranking public university professors (they are public employees) retire to positions at private universities. These examples illustrate not only the pervasiveness of institutional alliance building, but also the hierarchical nature of Japanese society. This is but one of the many reasons why Japanese society is referred to as a network society distinguished by institutionalized alliances that underpin political and economic actions. In addition to these networks, there are informal, even more obscure links created by school ties (*gakubatsu*), marriage alliances (*keibatsu*), study groups, friendships developed in the course of government-industry contacts, and other connections. These overlapping and mutually reinforcing networks provide stability and multiple bases for group identity, the webs of mutual support and elite unity as well as a bulwark against change.

Amakudari is a comparatively unusual institutionalized element of the Japanese power structure. Societies differ in the extent to which institutional arrangements separate the political, economic, and bureaucratic spheres of activities or fuse them together in cohesion, cooperation, and negotiation (Funaki 1997; Muramatsu 1994; Samuels 1987; Pempel 1998). For example, many observers see the

United States as separating the executive bureaucracy from markets and legislative processes with the conviction that separate institutions produce the best outcomes for everyone. This separation is celebrated in principles of checks and balances, the laissez-faire tradition, an open market economy, and a weak state bureaucracy with strict limits on government regulation. Of course, the United States has the revolving-door syndrome, in which top private-sector personnel move in and out of government office. Private defense contractors often hire retired politicians and armed forces personnel. Richard B. Cheney, a high-profile example, moved from secretary of defense to a lucrative position with an oil-equipment company and then went back to government service as vice president of the United States. *Amakudari* is distinctive because of the unidirectional movement of personnel from the bureaucracy to other sectors of society and its institutional character that fuses diverse spheres of society. Japan creates a myriad of formal and informal relationships in an apparent belief that such institutional cooperation produces the best outcome for all. Personnel movements across institutions are the rule and not an exception.

France is often compared to Japan because it has the *grandes écoles*, which supply most personnel to the bureaucracy, and *pantouflage*, whereby civil servants join the private sector and politics. The most important differences between *amakudari* and *pantouflage* are that French students are defined as civil servants upon entrance to university and most bureaucrats leave the civil service early in their careers (by their mid-thirties).[4] Further, French bureaucrats often are in conflict with politicians (in part, this may be related to multiparty French politics), whereas Japanese bureaucrats rarely come into conflict with the dominant political party, the LDP, which ruled from 1955 to 1993 and has regained the helm through coalitions with the opposition parties since 1996.

Amakudari is enigmatic in that it is neither a formal nor an informal process. It follows strict but unwritten institutional rules. Patterns of *amakudari* movements are routinized and standardized but not codified. There are important informal features to these relationships, but they are not based on individual arrangement nor are they spontaneous. In many ways, *amakudari* grows out of a bureaucratic culture of rules, codes, and norms that are nowhere transcribed. It contains elements of loyalty and alliance, but is dictated by rank and status; it is an institutionalized part of a power elite in Japan. As an elite institution, it lacks transparency—the extent and nature of its influence are not well known.[5] This book presents a systematic analysis of *amakudari* to bring a measure of transparency to the phenomenon.

Our analysis follows the tradition of power structure research. Writing about elites, societal power, and the prospects for democracy, C. Wright Mills notes that elites are not simply those with a greater share of money, power, and prestige. Rather, they have the most of those things because of their positions at the top of the major institutions of society. Mills sees societal power as rooted in the relations among large-scale institutions and examines the ways institutional leaders coalesce to form a power structure in society (Mills 1956). *Amakudari*, which distributes elites to key positions in different institutions of Japanese society, is part of a unified elite power structure with influence over Japanese society.

Three features of *amakudari* provide unity in the Japanese power structure. First, a shared culture among elites results from a similarity of origin, education, career experience, and life style. In a sense, a shared culture unites *amakudari* officials with a similar policy-making orientation. Second, behind the cultural basis of unity are the structures over which these elites preside. The social organization of the private sector, Diet (Japan's parliament), and ministries and the ways these institutions relate to one another govern the patterns of *amakudari* movements. Following *amakudari*, former officials tend to form a coherent grouping because of their many interconnections and concurrent interests. Finally, the unity of *amakudari* at times is a unity of explicit coordination. Institutional structures and processes allow *amakudari* officials to pursue shared interests, with the recognition that such interests can be realized more easily by working together.

Amakudari networks fuse the private and public sectors and political office to the ministries through the movement of personnel and through the shared culture of these personnel. By material and administrative means, the retired bureaucrats link diverse institutional sectors, but relations between ministry and corporation also have a cultural component based on the rules and norms of shared socialization, experience, status, and national goals. This is seen through the regular, intimate, and reciprocal negotiations and renegotiations of government goals and policy across these networks created by *amakudari*. Norms, rules, and commitments set the parameters of negotiation. The function of *amakudari* is to "ensure 'smooth communication' between industry and the ministries" and to "mingle and busily monitor the economy and maintain social control" (van Wolferen 1989, 45). This configuration of personnel relations and shared cultural orientation creates a network of consensus around policy commitments among Japan's institutional elites.

A meaningful treatment of this institutional fusion requires mapping *amakudari* paths (the movement of retiring officials from ministries to other positions in the public and private sectors) and identifying how they are structurally and culturally embedded in society. These administrative and cultural features provide an environment between ministries and the private sector that blurs the distinction between government and business. Without such a sensitive and expanded view, it is impossible to fully grasp the changing degree of integration between government and business.

Different Paths of *Amakudari*

The pressures of the seniority system within ministries drive *amakudari*. Entering bureaucrats, upon passing the civil service exam and being selected by a ministry, go through extensive training and advance as a cohort. By the time these bureaucrats reach their forties, their career-mobility options begin to narrow. In each ministry, there are few section-chief positions, fewer bureau-chief positions, and only one vice ministership. Those promoted to bureau chief are still in the running for the vice ministership. The usual retirement age for the vice minister is slightly over fifty. Of course, not everyone competes for the vice ministership—many bureaucrats retire before they reach the level of bureau chief—but everyone must ultimately descend because of the unremitting pressure from new cohorts advancing from below. The process of separating those who will resign early from those who will stay in the ministry is called *kata-tataki* (the tap on the shoulder) or *mabiki* (thinning out). The final weeding out comes at the vice-ministerial level. One member of the next cohort is chosen by the outgoing vice minister as his replacement, and all the new vice minister's classmates must resign to insure his absolute seniority. The new vice minister and the chief of the secretariat are responsible for finding the retiring officials (and fellow classmates) good positions in different sectors of society.

Table 1.1 Ministries and Agencies of the Japanese Government

Ministry/Agency	Number Employed	Subagencies
National Personnel Authority (Jinjiin)		
Prime Minister's Office (Sorifu)	52,402	National Police Agency (Keisatsu Cho)
		Imperial Household Agency (Kunai Cho)
		Management and Coordination Agency (Somu Cho)
		Hokkaido Development Agency (Hokkaido Kaihatsu Cho)
		Defense Agency (Boei Cho)
		Defense Facilities Administration Agency (Boei Shisetsu Cho)
		Economic Planning Agency (Keizai Kikaku Cho)
		Science and Technology Agency (Kagaku Gijutsu Cho)
		Environment Agency (Kankyo Cho)
		Okinawa Development Agency (Okinawa Kaihatsu Cho)
		National Land Agency (Kokudo Cho)
Ministry of Justice (Homu Sho)	51,025	Public Security Investigation Agency (Koan Chosa Cho)
		Supreme Public Prosecutor's Office
Ministry of Foreign Affairs (Gaimu Sho)	4,889	
Ministry of Finance (Okura Sho)	72,016	National Tax Agency (Kokuzei Cho)
Ministry of Education, Culture and Science (Monbu Sho)	138,090	Agency for Cultural Affairs (Bunka Cho)
Ministry of Health and Welfare (Kosei Sho)	75,963	Social Insurance Agency (Shakai Hoken Cho)

Ministry of Agriculture, Forestry and Fisheries (Norin Suisan Sho)	37,295	Food Agency (Shokuryo Cho) Forestry Agency (Rinno Cho) Fisheries Agency (Suisan Cho)
Ministry of International Trade and Industry (Tsusho Sangyo Sho)	12,406	Agency of National Resources and Energy (Shigen Enerugi Cho) Patent Office (Tokkyo Cho) Small and Medium Enterprises Agency (Chusho Kigyo Cho)
Ministry of Transport (Unyu Sho)	37,711	Maritime Safety Agency (Kaijo Hoan Cho) High Marine Accidents Inquiry Agency (Kainan Shimpan Cho) Meteorological Agency (Kisho Cho)
Ministry of Posts and Telecommunications (Yusei Sho)	307,729	
Ministry of Labor (Rodo Sho)	24,935	
Ministry of Construction (Kensetsu Sho)	24,017	
Ministry of Home Affairs (Jichi Sho)	583	Fire-Defense Agency (Shobo Cho)
Board of Audit (Kaikei Kensain)		

Source: Who's Who in Japanese Government (1988, 287–88); Gyosei Kanri Kenyu Center (1996, 44).

Until the administrative reform effective January 2001 there were twelve ministries and some thirty-one agencies (table 1.1).[6] Roughly speaking, public employees (*kokka komuin*) serving the central bureaucracy are classified as *ippanshoku* (general category) or *tokubetsushoku* (special category).[7] The type of examination (types I, II, and III) further divides personnel in the general category. Those entering the administrative service of the central bureaucracy with type I constitute the elite class of the bureaucracy. Annually, there are approximately 1,700–1,800 who pass the type I examination. However, only approximately 600–650 of them are hired by the central bureaucracy. For example, in 1995, the Ministry of Finance (MOF) hired twenty-one, Ministry of International Trade and Industry (MITI) thirty-three, Ministry of Construction sixty-four, Ministry of Education twenty-seven, and Ministry of Posts and Telecommunications twenty-four. In 1998, the total number of these elite bureaucrats was 11,229 and constituted 4.8 percent of the total administrative servants.

The population of *amakudari* is small. Annually, there are approximately 3,000 in the administrative service who have reached the rank of section chief or above but who leave the ministries and agencies at relatively young age (in their fifties) (National Personnel Authority [NPA] 1998).[8] Of the 3,000 bureaucrats leaving the ministries and agencies each year, approximately 1,300 take positions at research institutions and public universities. The remaining population, approximately 1,700, move to private firms, public or semipublic corporations, local political offices (are elected or appointed by governors or work at a local political office), or industrial associations or run for national political office.

As uniform and systematic as bureaucratic promotion appears, not all paths of *amakudari* are the same. The most prominent include movements to political office and the boards of directors of private and public corporations. *Amakudari* can also involve a multistep movement of retired civil servants. This indirect variant of the *amakudari* process is not distinguished by destination but by the seriality of the reemployment, for example, the movement from the bureaucracy to a public corporation and then to another public corporation or private corporation. Japan's elite bureaucrats have been noted as saying that their careers promise them at least three professional lives—the first life is their career within the ministry as civil servants, the second life is the first *amakudari* they take after they leave their ministry, and the third life is after the requirements of Japan's two-year *amakudari* law have been met and they can freely work for the firms they regulated as public officials.

In its broad sense, *amakudari* involves four distinctive forms of movement:

1. Bureaucrats move into profit-making enterprises. The movement from ministry or agency to a private business is a strict *amakudari* (descent from heaven) and is subject to legal restrictions.
2. Bureaucrats move into public corporations or special legal entities. These public corporations are established by law and financed, in whole or in part, by public funds. Reemployment in such an organization is called *yokosuberi* (sideslip) and is not subject to legal restrictions.
3. Bureaucrats have serial retirements in the public and/or private sector. This multistep retirement is called *wataridori* (migratory bird). *Wataridori* among special legal entities is prohibited by the Diet, yet it is a prevalent institutionalized pattern of reemployment among ex-civil servants.
4. Bureaucrats move into the political world, chiefly by becoming candidates for election to the Diet, most commonly as members of the Lower House. This postretirement career is called *seikai tensin* (movement to political office). This path is usually open only to bureaucrats who served in choice national or regional posts suitable for building general political support.

Figure 1.1 illustrates the conceptual space of *amakudari* and its four paths. The examination of any one path minimizes the interdependence among the paths and obscures the overall structure of *amakudari* movements. All four paths must be examined to provide a more holistic view of *amakudari* as an institutionalized network cutting across a matrix of formal and distinct institutional spheres. By examining these diverse paths of *amakudari*, we reveal a resilient institution that surrounds and permeates the various sectors of society. In this book, we examine the institutionalized networks created by *amakudari* systematically and over time. We assess the extent to which *amakudari* constitutes an institutionalized power structure with stratified properties across ministries with distinct patterns of change over the last several decades.

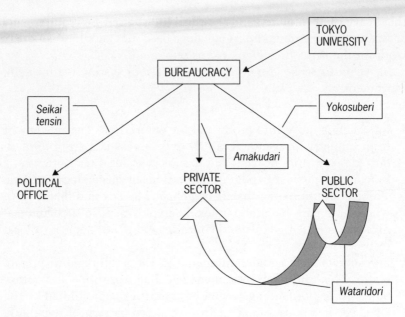

Figure 1.1 *Amakudari*

The Japanese Political Economy and *Amakudari*

The early literature on Japan was animated by questions of whether its postwar development was the result of the efficient market operations based on a configuration of institutions similar to the West (Patrick-Rosovsky 1976; Saxonhouse 1982) or of an alternative government-market configuration fundamentally different from the advanced economies of the West (Lockwood 1965; Abegglen 1970; Johnson 1982). During much of the 1970s and 1980s, debates on whether free market operations or bureaucratic guidance facilitated economic growth persisted. By the 1990s the literature had refocused on subtle relations among these formal institutional spheres as being responsible for both Japan's economic success and its inability to extricate itself from a decade-long recession.

In the 1960s and 1970s, scholars of Japan emphasized the importance of the bureaucracy in the guidance of the economy and a web of formal and informal ties referred to as Japan, Inc. (Lockwood 1965; Abegglen 1970). In the 1980s, *amakudari* was identified as key to the policymaking of a rational bureaucracy and as a critical personnel apparatus linking a dominant bureaucracy and other sectors of Japanese society (Johnson 1982) in the iron triangle of bureaucrats, politicians, and businesspersons.

By the late 1980s, challenges arose to the notion of bureaucratic dominance and questioned the nature of cohesion and cooperation among Japanese elites. These authors shared the view that the dominance of the Japanese bureaucracy in the political process had been exaggerated—policymaking processes in Japan were far more complicated than the image offered by Japan, Inc. The Diet, the courts, local governments, and the LDP had gained influence in policymaking since the 1970s at the expense of the national bureaucracy. The centripetal politics of Japan, Inc. had been superseded by a centrifugal politics of numerous pockets of pluralist power (Pempel 1987). The iron-triangle model had obfuscated the realities of governance in Japan (cf. Haley 1987, 1991). No single ministry dominated the economy—ministries and the private sector engaged in reciprocal consent among equals in which private firms gave the state jurisdiction over markets in return for their continued control of these markets (Samuels 1987). Rather than the bureaucratic domination of institutional spheres, scholars were inclined to the idea of a cooperative alliance of institutional elites. Bureaucratic dominance was rejected, but an alliance was recognized in Japan's elite power structure.

Further work on the concept of reciprocal consent focused on the overall pattern of relations among the MITI (long considered the most powerful ministry), the LDP, and the private sector. "The fusion of what tends to be regarded as mutually exclusive opposites—organization and markets, public and private, and formal and informal—stands out as a notable characteristic of government-business relations in Japan" (Okimoto 1989: 157). A network of ties between the state and the private sector provided a basis for a subtly conditioned cooperation in which terms of force and domination were too clumsy. *Amakudari* provided an important link in this network of cooperation.

Networks, the "maze of connections that link the public and private sectors together," are a major element of a cohesive and cooperative power structure. Among the "ad hoc, informal ties ... that give industrial policy and government-business interaction the resilience and adaptability for which Japan is renowned"[9] (Okimoto 1989: 152), there are two types of policy networks of intermediate organization: formal and informal. Formal networks include quasi-governmental organizations (e.g., Nippon Telegraph and Telephone and Japanese National Railways) and public enterprises (e.g., Japan Housing Corporation). Informal networks grow out of work-related contacts between government and business leaders and are also a product of functional roles and ascriptive affiliations.

Also in the late 1980s, the cohesiveness of bureaucracy-business sectors and the power of the bureaucracy in Japan's iron triangle gained renewed attention. It was argued that the MITI and MOF were first-tier ministries with exceptional influence, most top bureaucrats graduated from the Todai faculty of law, and bureaucrats were imbued with a sense of mission regarding the interests of the nation. As an underlying structural component of elite cohesion and cooperation, *amakudari* thereby reasserts the notion of an iron triangle.

Shift in Framework: Networks

Many authors took up the issues of the nature and structure of the complex apparatuses between the bureaucracy and society as the focus of analysis shifted to networks. They more clearly identified the formal and informal networks operating between the bureaucracy and the private sector, including industry associations; public corporations; and networks based on family, education, regional background, and *amakudari*. Further, some authors began to ferret out the financial and administrative context of the relations between the bureaucracy and the private sector, including *amakudari*; ministry regulation; licensing; administrative guidance; and government loans, grants, and subsidies. *Amakudari* was increasingly defined as an informal personnel network and a ministry-level characteristic intertwined with financial flows and administrative direction. What remained unanswered was the degree to which these personnel networks were distinctly elite, homogeneous, cohesive, and hierarchical and how *amakudari* patterns changed over time. Our analysis speaks directly to this gap in the structural and cultural studies of *amakudari*.

Amakudari *as Elite Networks*
Most texts on Japan take for granted that it is a society ruled by elites. Nonelites (labor, local government, consumers, and members of social movements) are assumed to have little or no systematic influ-

ence on government policy.[10] This is explained by the fact that there are few formal constraints on ministry supervision of the private sector and society (Carlile and Tilton 1998). Japan lacks the basic legal mechanisms for nonelite influence; in contrast, the United States allows class-action lawsuits and has strong judicial-review mechanisms giving unusual strength to consumer interests in the regulation and regulatory reform processes. Nonelites in Japan have few legal tools with which to influence policy decisions. A pervasive cultural image distinguishes elite responsibility and nonelite irresponsibility. Typically, these images take the character of parent-child relations in which elites are the parents who must care for and guide the nonelite children.

Because of the tight connection between Todai and the top positions in the bureaucracy, political offices, and boards of directors of the largest corporations (Funaki 1997; Koh 1989; Schneider 1993), the network of elites is generally recognized as homogeneous. This homogeneity is considered the basis for a "strong *esprit de corps* in the higher ranks of the civil service, and a common social background and university training among leaders in both government and industry" (Lockwood 1965, 493). The taproot of elite homogeneity is the close relationship between a Todai law background and the top positions in the ministries. Since the Meiji period (1868–1912), Japan's bureaucracy has recruited the best and brightest students through the highly competitive educational system and civil service examination. The student body of the University of Tokyo, the pinnacle of academic status and the alma mater of most top bureaucrats, vastly overrepresents the children of people in professional and managerial occupations. In part, this is a result of the expense of preparation for the Todai entrance examination, often requiring attendance at supplementary (*juku*) and preparatory (*yobiko*) schools and hiring private tutors. The fewer universities from which future bureaucrats are recruited, the more like-minded and statist-oriented the graduates are and the more cohesive and homogeneous the bureaucratic elite (Schneider 1993). The shared social background of Todai graduates may explain the value they place on preserving the status quo (Koh 1989, 167–68).

Cohesion, Conflict, and Cleavages
There are differences of opinion on the significance of *amakudari*. Those who characterize the relations among bureaucrats, politicians,

and businesspersons as cohesive consider *amakudari* significant—the "glue" in a cohesive power structure (Prestowitz 1988, 117). At least six arguments have been suggested for *amakudari* as an instrument of cohesion and coordination among bureaucrats, politicians, and businesspersons.

1. *Amakudari* networks are based on the shared socialization of *amakudari* officials.
2. *Amakudari* networks are conduits of information and maintain cohesion by providing reconnaissance between ministries and the private sector.
3. *Amakudari* represents a negotiation channel in which top bureaucrats and business leaders interact closely and continuously to smooth differences.
4. The overall distribution of *amakudari* provides the basis for ministry influence.
5. *Amakudari* networks indicate policy commitments among bureaucrats, politicians, and businesspersons based on policy consensus.
6. The practice of *amakudari* is analogous to hostage-taking on the part of private corporations to guarantee cohesion and cooperation with a ministry.

From hostages to surveillance, *amakudari* is an information circuit and by cooptation provides the basis for cohesion between ministry and private-sector elites (Cho 1995).

On the other hand, those who view relations between and within the bureaucracy, Diet, and private sector as contentious consider *amakudari* less important and less effective. If there is "unruly competition for power and advantage" (Lockwood 1965, 503–4) within and among these three groups, such conflict directly challenges the idea of a cohesive elite power structure.[11] Authors taking this position contend the bureaucracy is divided into ministerial fiefdoms. The once-dominant LDP is considered weakened and factional. Further, the business community is divided by sectoral as well as international interests, with business leadership no longer in control of the rank and file. These cleavages are illustrated with anecdotal cases of competition, policy disagreements, and conflicts (Fukui 1987; Pempel 1987, 1998; Calder 1988, 1993).[12] These authors suggest *amakudari* does not operate to integrate the bureaucracy with the dominant firms in industry, trading, banking, or *keiretsu* firms. Instead, it simply "broadens the access of less economically powerful firms" (Calder 1993, 69). *Amakudari* placements may demonstrate some influence, but the bureaucracy is only capable of placements in second-tier private corporations. Top corporations and banks are separate and impervious to pressures to take *amakudari*.

Those who emphasize the cohesion of the power structure see *amakudari* as the key element or glue in an elite power structure providing a basis for policy coordination. Those who emphasize the cleavages within the power structure argue that the glue of *amakudari* is ineffective. If *amakudari* is the glue of elite alliances, how adhesive is that glue?

Ministry Stratification in Amakudari *Networks*
Beyond the examination of elite cohesion, there is the issue of the stratification of *amakudari* networks. Do ministries participate more or less equally in *amakudari*, or does one ministry dominate (cf. Funaki 1997; Cho 1995; Ishizawa 1995; Kawakita 1989; Ito 1996)? Does the number of *amakudari, yokosuberi, wataridori,* and *seikai tensin* a particular ministry has relative to other ministries reveal the stratification of the *amakudari* network?[13] If there is network stratification, how has it changed by ministry over time for the different paths?

Amakudari paths may involve several forms of stratification. First, a hierarchy exists in any particular *amakudari* path if one or a few ministries have a clear preponderance of placements. Those few ministries can exercise more mechanisms of influence over specific sectors, resulting in greater numbers of *amakudari*. A second form of hierarchy can exist if one or a few ministries dominate all the paths of *amakudari*; that is, one or a few ministries (e.g., MITI and MOF) can exercise a preponderance of placements along all paths of *amakudari*. This constitutes a superministry hierarchy.[14] This more encompassing argument for stratification is based on differences in the regulatory responsibility of ministries. The MOF and MITI are distinguished by their broader responsibilities for regulation and policy, implying broader *amakudari* networks (Cho 1995; Okimoto 1989; Pempel 1998; Prestowitz 1988; van Wolferen 1989).[15] A third form of hierarchy is one in which different ministries or sets of ministries dominate different *amakudari* paths. For example, prewar bureaucrats in the powerful Home Ministry eschewed *amakudari* to the private sector, preferring to join political parties and become *chii riyo* politicians[16] (Kubota 1969). This trend continued through the early postwar period (Garon 1987). We expect different types of ministries to have different rates of placements to different sectors.

Continuity and Change in Amakudari *Networks*

Some authors point to the changing number and distribution of *amakudari* as evidence of change in the cohesion of the alliance among politics, bureaucracy, and business, reflecting a change in the larger political economy. The turning point in the strength of Japan's power elite may have come in the mid-1960s when coopted business groups began to tie the hands of MOF bureaucrats through obligatory increases in budgetary fixed expenses, thus eliminating the MOF's budgetary discretion (van Wolferen 1989). Or the decline in ministerial influence may have paralleled the rise of *zoku* (policy group) politicians in the late 1960s and early 1970s (Mabuchi 1997; Richardson 1997). The LDP's long rule created a stable structural base with specialized groups of career politicians who no longer needed the bureaucrats' expertise. The LDP trained career politicians to tackle the policy issues of specific ministries—the *zoku* politicians. As young LDP politicians mastered policy formulation, which the bureaucrats had monopolized, the MOF increasingly became more like a subcontractor to the LDP (Mabuchi 1997). This independence of the LDP from ministry expertise was expected to decrease the number of *seikai tensin* politicians in the LDP and Diet. It is possible, they reason, that MOF's dominance in *amakudari* networks was being replaced by other ministries without a decline in the overall movement of *amakudari*. Alternatively, there may have been both a decline in the MOF's control over the *amakudari* networks and a decrease in the overall density of *amakudari* networks, suggesting the demise of the elite power structure. In our view, there is a bias toward identifying features of possible or potential change to the neglect of mechanisms of underlying continuity—for some authors, changes have taken place, but the interinstitutional bonds are resilient and maintain their robustness.

To return to the continuing stagnation of the Japanese economy, *amakudari* as an institution provides continuity in the old policy-making structure in the face of apparent change. It resists change by furnishing the webs of mutual support for controlling the succession of diverse institutional elites. "By selection, socialization, controlling conditions of incumbency, and hero worship, succeeding generations of power-holders tend to regenerate the same institutions" (Stinchcombe 1968, 111). The pervasive ties created by *amakudari* are just such an obstacle for reform. According to Jason Hyland, "The *amakudari* system cements institutional commitments to particular industries and firms, making public policy shifts more difficult. In policy terms, the biggest risks of this system probably lie in its inflexibility.... The greater debate is whether to reaffirm or scrap the policy priorities that practices of *amakudari* represent" (1997, 3–4).

Amakudari provides the threads of the fabric of the Japanese power structure. Bureaucratic control of the placement and succession of institutional elites through *amakudari* perpetuates the elite power structure.

The Structure of the Book

The book is organized as follows. Chapter 2 addresses the problem of viewing *amakudari* as a static structural feature of Japan's political economy without history and without culture. We rectify these deficiencies by discussing the historical roots of *amakudari*, discussing the legal and legislative environment that shaped the different types of retirement patterns and emphasizing the history and social mechanisms of reproduction that are shaped by its societal context. This provides the sense of collective understandings held by individuals regarding the orientations of bureaucrats, the timing of retirements, proscribed limits of behavior, and the terms of the *amakudari* movement. Bureaucrats are more than self-interested individuals—they constitute a homogeneous status group, sharing the same culture rooted in their education at the University of Tokyo. *Amakudari* reflects interministerial competition (turf battles) and consciously coordinated personnel movements across diverse sectors of Japanese society.

Chapters 3–6 examine the paths of *amakudari*. *Amakudari* is generally understood as a system of reemployment of elite bureaucrats upon their retirement from the central bureaucracy in positions that promise high income. The passage to this reemployment is variable and we classify *amakudari* into four routes.

Amakudari (descent from heaven) in its narrow sense of elite bureaucrats in the heavenly world moving down to the earthy private corporations upon retirement to take the lucrative board of director
   positions
Yokosuberi (side slip), the movement to the public sector, a lateral
   move to government-related public corporations
Wataridori (migratory bird), two or more moves for reemployment
   within the public sector or a move crossing the public and private
   sectors
Seikai tensin, the movement to national political office by using
   bureaucratic positions and their influence

These four crisscrossing pathways provide a complex and dynamic
picture of *amakudari* (see figure 1.1).

Chapter 3 focuses on *amakudari* to the private sector. We examine
the overall trend in the incidence of *amakudari* for all ministries and
agencies from 1963 to 2000. The number of *amakudari* declined precipitously after 1986 but prevalence of *amakudari* indicate a stable
distribution at 2 percent over time, with 28 percent of the private-
sector firms having at least one *amakudari* on their board of directors. However, the distribution of *amakudari* among the largest one
hundred firms increased over time from 1.3 percent in 1979 to
3.3 percent in 2000. In addition, we show the structure and processes
of *amakudari* with the MOF at the center. There is a concentration
of *amakudari* among three ministries (MOF, MITI, and Construction)
over time in both incidence and prevalence. This chapter
also explores the resource dependence and regulation models of
amakudari.

An alternative location for bureaucratic retirement is to public corporations. Reemployment by such organizations is called *yokosuberi*.
In chapter 4 we discuss the creation and maintenance of public corporations and the different types of public corporations. We delineate
the pattern of *yokosuberi* from the different ministries and agencies
and compare the *yokosuberi* and *amakudari* patterns. *Yokosuberi*
provides another cluster of linkages embedding government ministries and agencies into particular sectors of society. It accounts for
nearly 45 percent of all board positions on *tokushu hojin* (a special
type of public corporation). Three ministries (MOF, MITI, and Agriculture) dominate this path. In addition, *yokosuberi* to *zaidan* and
shadan hojin (another type of public corporation) serves as an alter-

native path when *amakudari* and *yokosuberi* to *tokushu hojin* come under media and political pressure; *yokosuberi* paths have the resilient capacity to shift as changes develop in the relationship between the bureaucracy and society.

The full appreciation of *amakudari* and its implications for understanding Japanese social organization are revealed in *wataridori*, the metaphor of the migratory movements of birds that denotes the movement from one *amakudari* position to another. In chapter 5 we present a description of the structure and process of this serial reemployment of high-ranking bureaucrats. *Wataridori* accounts for a significant proportion of *amakudari* positions (almost one in three positions) in the private sector. Whereas *amakudari* and *yokosuberi* reveal the relational aspects of embeddedness of the bureaucracy in the private and public sectors, *wataridori* provides the larger structural picture. The three ministries (MOF, MITI, and Construction) that dominate the *amakudari* also dominate *wataridori* paths. Conscious and calculated operations of ministry coordination are required for the *wataridori* scheduled sequence of postretirement positions.

Chapter 6 addresses historical changes in the integration of the bureaucracy and parliament by examining changes in *seikai tensin* in the positions of prime minister, cabinet membership, and Diet membership. *Seikai tensin* among prime ministers and cabinet members has declined since the 1980s, but has remained stable in Lower House LDP membership. The coherence between the bureaucracy and political office, as represented by *seikai tensin*, appears to be frayed at the top, but stable at the levels of cabinet and LDP membership. Three ministries (MOF, MITI, and Agriculture; and possibly also Construction) dominate this path. In addition, the percentage of politicians graduating from Todai has declined among prime ministers and cabinet members since the 1970s, but is stable in the Lower House. There is, however, a significant rise in the percentage of hereditary politicians at all levels of political office. Our analysis suggests that the relations among Todai, the bureaucracy, and politicians are too decentralized for the strong models of the iron triangle; yet they are also too structured, continuous, and stable to support those who argue that the iron triangle never existed or has long since met its demise.

Chapter 7 brings us back to the resilience of Japan's institutions in the face of overwhelming and protracted pressures for change. We contend that *amakudari* networks are institutions representing an elite power structure that provides a bulwark against change to markets and society. *Amakudari* is one of the defining institutions of the Japanese political economy, oriented to the coordination and stability of the economy and society, in which effectiveness and survival are the objectives of corporate operations. This contrasts with the orientation toward quick change and corporate efficiency that is presumed by many critics.

Data Sources

In this book we use seven sources of data that are published in Japanese. As Cho (1995) illustrates well, no single data source captures the entire scope of *amakudari*; each source captures only a piece of the overall picture. Systematic studies of *amakudari* are difficult because of the many paths that exist and the lack of data readily available to English-speaking researchers. Few researchers have used data on *amakudari* and even fewer have used systematic data for all ministries over time.

National Personnel Authority
Publications on *amakudari* to private-sector jobs include the annual report published by the NPA. This source gives the incidence of *amakudari* to the private sector for each year since 1963. NPA began its publication after the Diet amended Article 103 of the Government Employee Act (Kokka Komuin Ho 103) and mandated the public disclosure of *amakudari* in 1962. The Civil Service Law 103, section 2, states that bureaucrats are prohibited from taking jobs for two years after their retirement in the sector they regulated in the five years before their retirement. When the director general of an agency requests permission for such employment and that request is approved by NPA, this prohibition is relaxed. Each annual publication contains information on ministry positions of each bureaucrat in his or her last five years of service (position) and descriptions of new positions in the private sector when NPA granted an exception to the act and allowed *amakudari* for that year.

The major limitations of NPA data are threefold. First, the NPA data do not capture *amakudari* among high-ranking bureaucrats because they seldom descend from heaven through direct reemployment in the private sector. Second, NPA review is limited to those civil servants at the level of section chief (*ka-cho*) or salary rank 10 and above who take private-sector jobs. Civil servants whose ranks are below the section-chief level or salary rank 10 are not subject to NPA review unless they take a board-of-director position in a private corporation. In addition, the *amakudari* of civil servants from the Defense Agency is not subject to NPA review but instead is made separately by the director-general of the Defense Agency. NPA inspection applies only to civil servants from the central government and does not extend to those employed by local governments. Third, the NPA has limited personnel resources and does not provide an exhaustive review and evaluation of private-sector *amakudari*. Each year there are approximately 3,000 people who leave their ministries and agencies at the rank of section chief or above. Of these 3,000 bureaucrats, approximately 1,300 take new positions at research institutions and universities; most of these research and teaching positions are in public entities and therefore are not usually subjected to NPA review. NPA review efforts are directed to the remaining 1,700 or so public employees. Yet each year only approximately 200–250 cases are traced, documented, and approved by the NPA. Thus, questions must be raised about the movement of the remaining 1,500 or so retirees. If retiring bureaucrats take positions in private enterprises not regulated by their ministries/agencies, then these positions are not subjected to NPA review.[17] If retiring bureaucrats take positions in public corporations, including *tokushu hojin* (a special type of public corporation) and *koeki hojin* (a general type of public corporation), they are not subject to NPA inspection. After waiting for the two-year clearance period, these bureaucrats may move into private sector jobs. In short, the NPA data show only a fraction of total retirements (200–250 cases out of 1,700 annually).

Also, the status and nature of the 200–250 approvals must be considered carefully. In 1981, for example, there were 249 cases of *amakudari* in the NPA report. Of those 249 cases, only six were bureaucrats at the rank of bureau chief or above, and only forty-nine (19.6 percent) were at the level of section chief or above (Cho 1995, 32). In all, NPA reports include only 20–30 percent of high-ranking bureaucrats. In tracking the whereabouts of high-ranking bureaucrats, this source needs to be used with great caution.[18]

Kigyo Keiretsu Soran

Kigyo keiretsu soran, published annually by Toyo Keizai Shinposha, contains a triangle research that summarizes prevalence data on *amakudari* by public employees who are currently on the boards of directors of listed private-sector firms (*jojo-kaisha*). Listed firms are those companies whose stocks are publicly traded (Dodwell Marketing Consultants 1990). Unfortunately, Toyo Keizai Shinposha stopped publishing its triangle research in 2001, and the latest triangle research published is for 1998 (published in 2000). We therefore used this source to assemble data on *amakudari* from 1982 to 1998. The number of listed firms included in these volumes varies from 1,773 in 1982 to 2,432 in 1998. The limitations of this data source are, first, that listed firms represent only approximately one-third of large corporations and do not include many of the large *keiretsu*-affiliated firms in Japan (Dodwell Marketing Consultants 1990). Second, the data are limited to board-of-director positions; they do not include *amakudari* in management positions or advisors, consultants, and councilors to the board of directors.

Seikai Kancho Jinjiroku

Seikai kancho jinjiroku (Toyo Keizai Shinposha 1995) provides another type of prevalence data on *amakudari* in 2,220 firms (2,168 listed firms and 52 nonlisted financial firms and major commerce associations) for 1994. It lists the names of people on boards of directors, their originating ministries and agencies, and their current positions in the private sector. The data are arranged by the originating central ministry (or agency), *tokushu hojin*, or other quasigovernmental organization. For example, if someone currently on the board of directors of a private manufacturing firm started his career with the MOF, he is listed under the MOF. The data set lists the name of the private company with which he is currently employed and the name of the company he worked for just before joining the current private firms, if different from the original ministry. This data structure allows the discrimination of *amakudari* from *wataridori*. For example, if a person started his career at the MOF, moved to a *tokushu hojin*, and then went to a private firm (as a member of the board of directors), his name is listed under the MOF, along with his current private-sector position and his path through the *tokushu hojin*. To our knowledge, this is the only source of data that readily provides the prevalence of *wataridori* in the private-sector. As in the previous data source, however, the data contained in *Seikai kancho jinjiroku* are limited to positions on boards of directors.

Kaisha Nenkan
We also used the *Kaisha nenkan* (corporation reports) published annually by Nihon Keizai Shinbunsha. This source provides company information for listed firms (e.g., 2,852 firms in 2000), including the address; type of business; brief company history; and names of the members of the board of directors, their career history, universities graduated, and year they entered the company. Company information is arranged by industry (e.g., machinery, paper, steel, food, transport, and utilities). For example, if someone from the MITI is on the board of directors at Toyota Motor Corporation, he is listed as on the Toyota board along with his or her former ministry, his position at the MITI, and his education. At the end of each annual volume, company ranking is listed based on sales. From this list, we selected one hundred top corporations, examined the composition of board members for each of the one hundred firms, and assembled a data set on *amakudari*. Ulrike Schaede (1995) uses this data source in her analysis of *amakudari* for 1979–91. We have extended the time span by adding data for 1997 and 2000. The major limitation of this data source is that data are not organized according to the original ministry/agency.

Data on Public Corporations
Data on *yokosuberi* (post retirement career movement of ex-civil servants to public corporations) are least accessible to researchers because there is no central organization responsible for data collection and publication on such employment and there is no law mandating the disclosure of a systematic enumeration, except for *tokushu hojin*. There are three major types of public corporations: special legal entities (such as *tokushu hojin*), *zaidan* and *shadan hojiin*, and other types of public organizations serving social welfare, educational, religious, and medical needs.[19]

We obtained data on *yokosuberi* to *tokushu hojin* from the annual report published by the Government-related Organization of Labor Unions (Seifu Kankei Hojin Rodo Kumiai Rengo, or Seiroren) for 1974–94. Seiroren began publishing its survey results in its white paper on *amakudari* (*Seiroren amakudari hakusho*) in 1972 as part of its campaign against *amakudari* to *tokushu join*. The number of entities participating in Seiroren's survey range from 32 (in 1969) to 109 (in 1981). This source provides the names of the members of the board of directors and their age, length of appointment at the *tokushu hojin*, original ministry, and salary. Despite the fact that Seiroren began publishing its survey results in 1972, Inoki (1995) is the first researcher who made the full use of the data. Unfortunately, Seiroren stopped publishing its reports in 1995 and there is no other source that provides comparable data on *tokushu hojin*. Seiroren's *amakudari* reports fueled controversy and criticisms of *amakudari* by the media in the late 1980s and 1990s, and Seiroren was shocked by the sudden surge of media interest in criticisms of *amakudari*. The Seiroren staff had mixed reactions and this led to the suspension of its *amakudari* report starting in 1995. We obtained the internal data on *yokosuberi* to *tokushu hojin* for 1998 directly from Seiroren.

Like the NPA data and other sources of *amakudari* data, Seiroren's data have limitations. First, not all *tokushu hojin* are included consistently over time; until 1981, Seiroren surveyed a limited number of *tokushu hojin*. Unfortunately, no studies have assessed how such a change may have affected the nature of its analysis (Cho 1995, 35).

We also used *Tokushu hojin soran*, published annually by the Management and Coordination Agency to supplement Seiroren's data. This source provides data for each *tokushu hojin*, including a brief organization history, ministries that supervise *tokushu hojin*, the major functions of the organization, the size of capital, the budget sources, and the names of the members of the board of directors.

Tokushu hojin, however, represent only 87 of some 27,000 public corporations that are known to exist. The public disclosure of the vast entities was only beginning as Hayashi and Iriyama (1997) undertook their large survey of *zaidan* and *shadan*. In response to media criticisms, the Prime Minister's Office (PMO) published a long-awaited report on *zaidan* and *shadan hojin* in 1998. No systematic information on *zaidan* and *shadan hojiin* had existed prior to the publication of these two sources. In this book, we have used both sources to examine *yokosuberi* to *zaidan* and *shadan*. The major limitation of these publications is that they present aggregate data with no information on individual directors (names, age, length of employment, etc.).

Data on National Political Office
There is no single publication that summarizes the career movement of ex-bureaucrats to national political office (*seikai tensin*). The most complete data source is *Kokkai benran*, which is published annually by Nihon Seikei Shinbunsha. It provides a list of cabinet members and members of the Diet with their personal background information (party affiliation, number of elections won, place of birth, brief political career history, education, etc.). We also used other sources to piece together the pattern of *seikai tensin* since World War II, including *Saishin rekidai naikaku soran* (J. P. Tsushinsha 1996), *Japanese Statesmen* (Nichigai Associates 1990), *Modern Japanese Statesmen* (Nichigai Associates 1999), *Gendai Nihon no seito to seiji* (Scalapino and Masumi 1962), *Gendai Nihon no hoshu seiji* (Uchida 1989), and data published in the *Asahi Shinbun*.

Surveys and Interviews
We used survey questionnaires and in-depth interviews with *amakudari* officials and key informants, including journalists and associates of *amakudari* officials. Our survey questionnaire used a snowball sampling technique. Initially we contacted several ministry officials, retired officials, and journalists we already knew; other names were added through those we were introduced to. We constructed a brief list of questions, mailed it to forty-five individuals, received responses from thirty, and then conducted in-depth interviews with eighteen of these individuals. Our interviews were with current and former officials of the Ministry of Construction, MITI, MOF, and Ministry of Labor; associates of *amakudari* officials; and journalists. The cover letter and questions we sent out in 1998 appear in the appendix. The data we gathered from the survey and interviews helped redirect our data search, validate information, and identify processes involved in *amakudari*. We also used biographies and ethnographies of *amakudari* people and processes to supplement the descriptive material.

In this chapter we have identified several features and structures of policy networks for the study of *amakudari*. First, *amakudari* creates elite personnel networks of senior bureaucrats, top business leaders, and politicians. Second, the members of these networks have a homogeneous outlook based on their education at the University of Tokyo. Third, there is stratification or hierarchy in the networks based on the ministries' participation in these *amakudari* networks. Network relations are negotiated, mutual, and reciprocal relations between the government and various segments of society. The questions that persist include the breadth, extent, and structure of *amakudari* networks and how they change over time.

This study of *amakudari* as networks of elites distributed throughout the sectors of Japanese society is not a study of bureaucratic domination of politicians or big business. Rather, it is the study of an institutionalized element of an elite power structure whose influence is not over other elites but over Japanese society as a whole. A complex network of social relations maintains elites in their top positions in the key institutions of society (Mills 1956). The domination component of the elite policy networks is the subordination of electoral politics and subgroups (the masses) to the cohesive alliance of the various institutional elites (Alford and Friedland 1985, 199). A power structure has been defined as a network of roles and organizations within a society that is responsible for maintaining the general social structure and shaping new policy initiatives. *Amakudari* represents positions at the top of Japan's public and private sectors as well as political offices. A power elite is the set of ex-bureaucrats who are the individual actors within the power structure.[20]

In early studies of *amakudari*, the elites were found to rule not as much through domination as through cohesiveness based on loosely united networks, shared educational backgrounds, and a consensus on national goals. This notion of cohesive homogeneity is still popular, yet it fails to address institutional continuity and change.

2 *Amakudari* as an Institution

Amakudari is a unique institution with history and social mechanisms of reproduction that are shaped by its societal context. Whereas some authors view *amakudari* as the ad hoc and informal movement of individuals resulting from individual motives, preferences, and choices, others see *amakudari* as an interorganizational linkage that structurally embeds the bureaucracy in Japanese society. We define *amakudari* as personnel retirement paths linking the central bureaucracy to its wider environment, identifying the domain of operation for the ministry of origin, establishing the boundaries of its territory, and attempting to secure its own legitimacy (see Scott 1992, 99). And although *amakudari* has cultural mechanisms that motivate individual effort to reproduce the institution, it also manifests structural patterns among a matrix of organizations and formal institutions. We take this recognition one step further to capture the institutional features combining culture and structure to explain the resilience of *amakudari* in the face of changing circumstances. After briefly reviewing the origin of *amakudari* and discussing how common socialization, experience, and identity lead to a homogeneous outlook among *amakudari* personnel, we discuss the causes of *amakudari* and review legislation influencing the practice. We then discuss how *amakudari* reflects interministerial competition (turf battles) and consciously coordinated personnel movements across diverse sectors of Japanese society.

The Origin of *Amakudari*

Amakudari is the reemployment of high-ranking civil servants in key positions in diverse sectors of Japanese society upon their retirement from the central bureaucracy. It includes moves to the private sector (*amakudari*), public corporations (*yokosuberi*), and the political world (*seikai tensin*). The literal translation, "descent from heaven," invokes the cultural symbolism of the life of the sacred and profane. Before World War II civil servants worked directly for the emperor, who was considered sacred, a god, and the embodiment of the Japanese nation. Bureaucrats were seen as being in heaven by their noble and sacred work for the god and the nation, but descended in status upon retirement and reemployment in the profane world of material self-interest (Colignon 2002).

Because of the different interpretations of what constitutes *amakudari*, its historical origin is not apparent in the literature. *Amakudari* has no clear beginning as a single event. Rather, what appears to have begun as the diffuse movement of individuals from the central ministries to private firms and public offices has over time become institutionalized within the administrative apparatus of the central ministries.

References to the retirement pattern of top-level bureaucrats into the business sector are found as early as the Meiji period (1868–1912). According to Inoki (1995), a popular novelist and social critic, Roan Uchida (1868–1929), used the term *amakudaru* (whose noun form is *amakudari*) in his social criticism, entitled *Shakai hyakumenso* (Society of kaleidoscope) published in 1902. In the interwar years, *amakudari* to the private sector or political office appears to have occurred on an individual basis. At this time, two distinct paths (*amakudari* and *seikai tensin*) emerged, roughly corresponding to transfers from the economic and social ministries. After World War I, bureaucrats retiring from the economic ministries (e.g., Finance; Agriculture and Commerce, which was later reorganized into Agriculture and MITI) drew on "contacts with business clientele" to take top positions in private corporations (Garon 1987, 80). Retiring bureaucrats from the social ministries (e.g., the Home Ministry, which was later reorganized into the Ministry of Home Affairs and the newly created ministries such as the Ministries of Labor, of Health and Welfare, and of Construction[1]) took high political posts or joined political parties, often with cabinet appointments (*seikai tensin*). High-ranking bureaucrats enjoyed social and political prestige and found positions outside the bureaucracy with relative ease (Kubota 1969). However, the number of retirements was small and *amakudari* was not systematically incorporated into a system of personnel management before World War II (Inoki 1995).

Amakudari became routine and institutionalized after World War II, from the individually negotiated retirements of the prewar years to each ministry's delegation to a specific office of the task of systematically finding employment for retiring personnel. Revisions to the National Mobilization Order in 1941 provided an important impetus to the institutionalization of *amakudari* (Johnson 1974, 958; Calder 1989). For top *amakudari* positions, the chief of the secretariat and the political and administrative vice ministers were involved (Johnson 1974, 960). A secretariat office belonging to a minister devoted itself to finding and arranging *amakudari* for bureaucrats forced to step down (retire) by their early fifties. This office kept these bureaucrats employed until they reached age sixty-five. Caught between the systems of lifetime employment and rules of seniority, ministries used *amakudari* as a solution. As ministries institutionalized the placement of retirees, they set in motion mechanisms for ministry control of the incumbency of elite positions in the public and private sectors as well as political office.

In his empirical analysis of *amakudari* for the period 1949–59, Kubota (1969) distinguishes several paths of *amakudari*. Some economic ministries (e.g., MITI, Transport, and Agriculture) placed a higher proportion of their ex-officials in the business sector (*amakudari*), particularly in firms affiliated with industrial groupings. However, other economic ministries (e.g., Finance, Construction, and Posts and Telecommunications) had more placements to public corporations (*yokosuberi*), which was a new pathway that opened up with the proliferation of public corporations after World War II. These two paths (*amakudari* and *yokosuberi*) accounted for over 60 percent of postretirement jobs between 1949 and 1959; the share of *seikai tensin* during this period was 12–15 percent. Thus, the three major paths of *amakudari* accounted for up to 75 percent of postbureaucratic mobility (Kubota 1969, 155, table 4).[2] Although the tendencies for economic ministries to use *amakudari* and social ministries to use *seikai tensin* stood well into the 1960s, both types of ministries increased the use of *yokosuberi* in the postwar years, suggesting differentiated relations between the central ministries and various sectors of society.

Elites and Homogeneity of Outlook

Bureaucrats have long been recognized to hold a common orientation to the national interests based on a common socialization in educa-

tion and training coming from the same universities and career experience (Lockwood 1965, 593; Abegglen 1970, 35; Koh 1989, 148, 191).
Others refer to bureaucrats' orientation to "broad custodial responsibilities" for the nation (Fukui 1987, 163) and as "managers of
economic life" (Haley 1987, 191). Top-level bureaucrats (those taking
amakudari) have a similarity of socialization and experience that
produces a common culture of cognitive and normative categories.
They share a sense of what is right and wrong and what is real. Thus,
they also share a similar orientation to government politics and
policy.

The fusion of the University of Tokyo, top ministry positions, and
top *amakudari* placements is not only a structural pattern but also
a cultural milieu. Intense competition shapes the orientation of civil
servants because elite bureaucrats come from families of elite backgrounds and are recruited from only a handful of universities,[3] producing more "like-minded and statist oriented" graduates (Schneider
1993, 334). High levels of competition to enter top universities and
then the ministries contribute to the public's perception of them as
a legitimate elite based on merit.

Early Socialization and Gakubatsu
Elite orientation refers to a shared orientation to rules, relationships,
commitments to the good of the nation, and a conception that
common people are incapable of determining what is good for the
country. Only certain people have the capacity and commitment to
decide and implement policies in the best interests of Japan.[4]

The fusion of Todai, the ministries, and *amakudari* begins with
the high schools that provide the main pathways to the University
of Tokyo. Todai is the most prestigious university and has provided
the training ground for most elites. One pathway is well illustrated
by the experience of an interviewee who attended the prewar Ichiko,[5]
an elite higher school located on the current site of the Komaba
campus of Todai. There were thirty-three higher schools (military
education had a parallel system) before the war and only a small
fraction of the population (less than 10 percent) went to higher school
in those days. Those entering Ichiko were considered the country's
future leaders.[6]

Ichiko was the main feeder higher school to the University of
Tokyo before World War II and provided a common school experience
and training for many top-level bureaucrats after the war. All the

students were male, wore uniforms, and lived in the dormitory, which was the basic governmental unit of the higher school. The dormitory was organized into ninety rooms, with ten to twelve students in each room. Students were distributed to these rooms based on club interests (e.g., archery, mountain climbing, or Marxism). One person from each room participated in a school parliament of ninety students. This ninety-person assembly had discretion in fundamental school decisions. Students were taught to think of themselves as having a special responsibility to guide the nation because common citizens were too lazy or ignorant to take that responsibility.

Several symbols and rituals shaped the students' identity, cognition, and orientation toward the nation: uniforms, insignia, gates, and a school flag called the "flag to protect the nation." Although there was no official school song, one song, "Cherry Blossoms Received in the Jade Sake Cup," was taught to every student and was sung at student gatherings. Composed in 1903, it was sung as late as the 1970s by students at newer schools in the same district of Tokyo (Azabu). The lyrics convey the importance of responsibility:

> Common people lead the lazy life, but we despise such attitude
> The people are drowning in a sea of international struggles, but we
>   have to save them and steer the ship
> Draw the sword at the top of the ship, the devils now hide, seas are
>   calm.

One of our interviewees gave examples of how the common experience at the school and ritual ceremonies served to maintain an elite identity, culture, and networks. Twice a year—spring and fall—alumni return to Ichiko for festivals. Alumni groups also gather away from Ichiko. These groups are organized on diverse bases including industry of employment, sports interests, and cultural groups. Each group gets together at least once a year. One individual may participate in several groups, which has the effect of reproducing and reinforcing the cultural orientation and personal networks.

Gakubatsu (school-based cliques) have a strong influence over other competing group identities, cutting across formal institutional boundaries.[7] In the United States, the public and private sectors are viewed as distinct and opposed to one another. In Japan, shared *gakubatsu* identity blurs sector distinctions. One interviewee said the common experience gained at Ichiko is so strong a bond that graduates do not perceive classmates working in different sectors as outsiders. Receiving an *amakudari* person is simply a matter of people in the private sector saying "come and work with us" (we just happen to be in a different sector). Thus *gakubatsu* ties override the distinction between public and private sectors. They do not just exist as natural and immutable but are socially created through school and work experience and are reproduced over time.

Todai has a mystique as an insulating and homogenizing institution. Because Japanese education is centrally controlled and hierarchically structured, the stratifying influence of education, especially of Todai, is considerable. Todai has produced a variety of elites both before and after World War II. Its graduates represent a subculture of the top leaders in modern Japan (Kubota 1969). According to Robert Cutts, "education could in a sense be called Japan's national religion. Like any established religion it is intended to instill in people beliefs, values, and character, including national character" (1997, 3). Todai and its link to the bureaucracy set the stage for understanding the orientations of top-level bureaucrats taking *amakudari*. This institutional fusion of education and bureaucracy is critical for understanding the cultural homogeneity of *amakudari* because top-level bureaucrats are a category of personnel with a shared culture and mindset that operate across a matrix of organizations within the government and the private and public sectors. The link between Todai and the central ministries is the first step in the establishment of *amakudari* as both a cultural and structurally cross-cutting institution.

Recruitment into the Bureaucracy

Recruitment into a ministry, although ostensibly open, is strongly biased toward Todai graduates. Article 15 of the 1946 constitution requires public service to be open to all; there must be equal opportunity to compete for civil service positions. Merit is the guiding criterion for selection, and merit is measured through competitive examinations. Reliance on both competitive examination and evaluation (*senko*) represents an important continuity between the prewar and postwar eras (Koh 1989, 69–72; Kerbo 2000; Muramatsu 1997).

The examinations have three levels: *isshu*, college graduates (type I); *nishu*, junior college graduates (type II); and *sanshu*, high school graduates (type III).[8] Applicants are required to pick a field of specialization from twenty-eight possible fields. The hiring is decentralized—NPA publishes the names of successful candidates by specialization, in order of examination score, and forwards the list to the ministries. Regular public employees subject to the regular compensation law are subdivided into seventeen categories; each category carries its own salary schedule.

Elite-track bureaucrats are divided into an administrative group (*jimukei*) and a technical group (*gijutsukei*). Administrative-track personnel have a wider set of career options as well as the prospect of rapid advancement in the civil service.[9] Both groups must pass the type I examination.

Between 1949 and 1994 more than 95 percent of those who took the type I exam failed (Koh 1989, 80; Gyosei Kanri Kenkyu Center, 1996, 49); between 1989 and 1992, 93 percent failed; and in 1995 96 percent failed (Pempel and Muramatsu 1995, 45–46; Funaki 1997, 190). The passing rates remained below 10 percent for any one year.

Passing the examination creates the opportunity for entry into the bureaucracy, but only approximately one-half of those who pass the examination in any year are hired, and the hiring process favors Todai graduates. The difference between the percentage of those passing the civil service exam and the percentage hired by the central ministries is indicative of institutional fusion between Todai and the ministries. Todai graduates made up 24 percent of those who passed the type I examination in 1992, 27 percent in 1993, and 25 percent in 1994 (Funaki 1997, 195), yet more than 70 percent of those hired between 1965 and 1985 by the MOF and Ministry of Home Affairs were from Todai (Koh 1989, 91–92).

Promotion within the Bureaucracy
Promotion is another selection feature that continues to shape and reproduce the elite orientations and consciousness fusing the University of Tokyo and the top levels of the ministries. The promotion system facilitates a more homogenous and statist view of issues among bureaucrats while at the same time shaping particular ministry identities. Upon entering the ministries, bureaucrats are socialized to internalize their ministry's goals, values, and norms through on-the-job and off-the-job training. First-year career bureaucrats are paired with someone who is one year senior to them. The *senpai* (senior) becomes the novice's guide, teacher, and companion. Entrants are placed in a variety of positions ("go around the track")

to gain an overall familiarity with ministry operations and interests. Off-the-job training includes gaining an understanding of cultures abroad through such means as earning a master's degree from a foreign university.

The basic pattern of promotion for those on the administrative track is slow but uniform for the first ten years or until the bureaucrat reaches the level of assistant section chief. Only those who demonstrate competence in research, negotiation, and drafting bills and policy proposals are recruited to these assistant-section-chief positions. Promotion to section chief requires leadership, coordination, and the capacity to deal with personnel matters (Koh 1989, 132–33). Job rotation throughout the ministry promotes an understanding of the ministry's interests and a kind of collective conscious shared by ministry officials. Further, it facilitates closer ties to the ministry's clientele groups (Schneider 1993).

The promotion system provides the motivation for individual competition in a context of loyalty to the ministry. The highly competitive systems of education and examination instill norms of disciplined hard work, dedication, and competition. These norms are amplified by a promotional system that rewards effort toward ministry goals, with *amakudari* placement as the ultimate reward. Yet, despite all the hard work required, the system of promotions demonstrates the importance of a Todai background in the bureaucracy. The numerical preponderance of Todai graduates increases in the higher echelons of the bureaucracy. In 1986, close to one-half of all senior bureaucrats and more than 86 percent of vice ministers were graduates of the Todai Faculty of Law (Koh 1989, 159). This is similar to Kubota's figures of 69 percent of senior bureaucrats and 80 percent of vice ministers being from Todai between 1949 and 1959.

Promotions are regular and somewhat standardized, and salary is tied to seniority. Yet, the best positions go to those who were deemed high performers in their early positions. These best positions offer training, experience, and exposure, and they are the keys to future promotions. The closed nature of recruitment and the continuous distribution of personnel to the best positions at each promotion level make personnel competition a career-long process.

Retirement from the Bureaucracy and Amakudari
Amakudari provides a postretirement carrot, a form of deferred compensation facilitating intense intraagency competition that con-

tributes to overall bureaucratic efficiency (Inoki 1995). As a long-term promotional incentive, *amakudari* depends on how individuals' superiors perceive their ability and loyalty to the ministry. *Amakudari* placements may be prestigious and even lucrative. Personal self-interest drives the bureaucrats' continuous hard work and dedication to the ministry for their entire careers in order to secure the best possible pension and *amakudari* position. A "major consequence of this system is to link individual career fortunes to hard work, approval of superiors, competition with one another, and a long-standing dedication to one's agency" (Pempel and Muramatsu 1995, 52).

The educational and career experiences of top bureaucrats provide them with *amakudari* positions within the larger *amakudari* network. However, this network is not only the movement of ex-bureaucrats to different sectors; it is also a cultural network. The same socialization and experience that got them to the top of the bureaucracy also produce a cultural-cognitive orientation to act. *Amakudari* networks are culturally embedded in the sense that they are collective understandings on the part of individuals and organizations about the orientation of bureaucrats, timing of retirements, proscribed limits of behavior, and terms of *amakudari* movement. *Amakudari* is culturally embedded in the form of beliefs and ideologies, taken-for-granted assumptions, events, and formal rule systems; it prescribes strategies of self-interested action on the part of bureaucrats, defining or circumscribing who may legitimately engage in *amakudari* and their appropriate placements. Norms and constitutive understandings regulate the process of *amakudari*, causing behavior within culturally specific definitions of integrity, even in the face of opportunity. Institutionalized norms and culturally defined sanctions are used to discipline those who cheat. Thus, culture has a dual effect on *amakudari*. It constitutes the structure in which bureaucrats may express self-interest, and it constrains the free play of self-seeking behavior (Zukin and DiMaggio 1990).

Socialization and experiences create and reproduce cognitive categories and typifications of how a ministry relates to the rest of Japanese society. They infuse beliefs and ideologies of national purpose and constraints. The experience of moving through the elite educational system and the ministries of the central bureaucracy provides not only a sense of should be but also a sense of what is. The link between the educational system and the bureaucracy provides a building block for the social construction of common orientations and the collective consciousness of *amakudari* personnel.

Causes of *Amakudari*

The causes of *amakudari* are complex, but they can be divided into distant, intermediate, and immediate causes. This sense of layered causality more accurately captures the conditional sense of cultural and structural forces facilitating and obstructing the development of *amakudari* networks.

The distant causes of *amakudari* are the larger social forces that emerged after World War II, including expectations of early retirement and the increasing strength of the seniority system combined with the salience of *gakubatsu* in employment matters. "The prewar civilian bureaucracy did not retire as early as contemporary officials do, was better paid, was not so large in numbers, and its most senior members (vice-ministers, directors general, and bureau chiefs) commonly received Imperial nominations to the old House of Peers upon retirement. Perhaps most important, prewar officials regarded it as an affront to their pride and contrary to their responsibilities as officials of the Emperor . . . to join a civilian, profit-making enterprise" (Johnson 1974, 958). Furthermore:

> early retirement results from the workings of two basic norms in the context of the overall forces of supply and demand for labor and the general expansion of the bureaucracy that occurred during and after World War II. These two practices are the *nenko* system, or rewards and ranking on the basis of strict seniority, and the influence of so-called "academic cliques" (*gakubatsu*), which refers to the fact that over 70% of all senior officials in 1965 were graduates of Tokyo University and their internal rivalries establish the rules for the bureaucracy as a whole. (959)

Thus, the Japanese bureaucracy produced two contextual forces that drove and shaped *amakudari* after World War II: (1) new administrative norms and practices for the hiring of new recruits, promotion based on seniority, and the earlier timing of retirement and (2) the increased salience of *gakubatsu* in the bureaucracy.

The intermediate causes of *amakudari* involve postwar pressures on the central bureaucracy's size and interministry competition. The lack of administrative resources drove network-based activities. Ministries developed personnel networks to compensate for the shortage of administrative resources after World War II. The formation of these ministry-based networks gave rise to a resource-maximizing mentality and sectionalism. Competition among ministry-based networks worked to maximize resources within a particular ministry while pushing policy formulation. Of course, desires for more authority, power, and benefits (such as *amakudari*) worked as incentives for competition (Muramatsu 1994, 26).

The Japanese bureaucracy operates with significantly fewer public employees than do other OECD countries. There is a history of the active use of local governments by the central government to keep the central bureaucracy small. The central bureaucracy outsources many government projects to local government but monitors their operations. This monitoring of the local governments by ministries contributes to sectionalism among the central ministries. The central bureaucracy also emphasizes the use of industry associations and public corporations for specific projects instead of expanding existing ministries (Muramatsu 1994, 29–30). The extended use of local governments, industry associations, and public corporations has provided the central ministries with its "arms and legs," and *amakudari* to these entities provides the central ministries with a mechanism of control. *Amakudari* and other personnel networks emerged as the compensating tool for mobilizing resources when the bureaucracy faced a shortage of resources. These networks in turn gave rise to a turf-maximizing group mentality and sectionalism. Thus, sectionalism and personnel networks such as *amakudari* resulted from the constraints on administrative resources. Competition between ministry-based networks worked to maximize resources within a particular ministry, and interministry competition led to bigger local governments, more industry associations and public corporations, and wider personnel networks between the central bureaucracy and society.

The immediate causes of *amakudari* take three forms: push arguments emphasizing ministry motives, pull arguments emphasizing private corporate interests, and consensus arguments focussing on the mutual benefits of the two.

Push Arguments
Resource Compensation
Some authors explain *amakudari* as ministries' efforts to make up for the loss of other resources. For example, by 1960 the MITI had lost several key administrative powers including control over foreign

currency reserves and the regulation of the building of new industrial plants. Beginning in 1970, the MITI sought to maintain its influence through the provision of information and administrative guidance and later through the mutual penetration of networks animated by administrative guidance, *shingikai* (policy deliberation councils), industry associations, and *amakudari* (Cho 1995, 15; Johnson, 1982, 266).

Deferred Compensation

The explanation of *amakudari* as deferred compensation presents a personnel management and promotion system involving intense competition and early promotion that pushes bureaucrats out by their mid-fifties (Kubota 1969; Inoki 1995; Mabuchi 1997). *Amakudari* provides the end point of the competitive forces built into the civil service system. Attracting the best, most talented personnel drives high levels of internal and external competition. The recruitment of the top performers on a national civil service examination selects highly competitive civil servants. They then receive extensive training and work long hours at demanding tasks to compete for promotion and ever more responsibility. The promotion system requires early retirement and *amakudari* represents the final element in this internal competition. The early retirement system helps keep the bureaucracy young, and *amakudari* compensates these civil servants at a later career stage for their modest bureaucrat salaries.

Surveillance

Amakudari also provides windows into the operations of private corporations and an avenue for monitoring changes in their planning and operations.

High officials in the ministries take much time in placing their former colleagues in good positions. They are sprinkled throughout the large companies and banks. Trade and industry associations are another favorite destination for out-placements, particularly because most such organizations must be chartered by one of the ministries. Sometimes former ministry officials are even placed on the boards of the Japanese subsidiaries of foreign companies, which may think they are obtaining a window on the ministry. While they may be, what is certain is that the ministry is obtaining a window on them. This network is one of the key ingredients in the glue of Japan, Inc., and one of the subtle levers of the power of the ministries. (Prestowitz 1988, 117)

Pull Arguments

Resource Dependency

The resource dependence model focuses exclusively on market and technical dependency as giving rise to political solutions (Scott 1992; Hall 1991). Individual organizations act to improve their chances of survival through their adaptation to changing environmental circumstances. *Amakudari* is driven by the resource dependency of private companies that act to equalize their access to information and political influence in the market—organizations need *amakudari* to stay competitive in the market. The interdependence between private corporations and government ministries generates the need of private organizations to influence government to reduce the uncertainty of state regulatory policy and to increase the chance of receiving government contracts and strategic information (Calder 1989, 379–80). Organizations less capable of gaining influence and information through the market are more likely to receive *amakudari* and gain the required resources, thus equalizing competition with their more powerful (less dependent) competitors. *Amakudari* provides connections between the government's technical resources (money and information) and the needs of private organizations to garner and mobilize these resources in market competition. Placements through *amakudari* are links between the government and private firms, representing a way of managing and indexing resource dependencies. Accordingly, organizations that are powerful and not capital or information dependent are less likely to receive *amakudari*.

Transaction Costs and Contingency Theories

According to transaction cost economic theory, hierarchical organizations emerge in the process of minimizing risk and maximizing predictability. Linkages between the central bureaucracy and private-sector firms, created by *amakudari*, give rise to a new organizational structure and culture. Similar to invasive shrubs, once transplanted they continue to grow and spread in new spaces. Retired bureaucrats maintain informal ties with the central ministries, even though their formal ties are severed. These informal ties reduce the risks and maximize the predictability of dealing with the government by a private firm. A bureaucrat, once a part of a ministry, becomes part of networks connecting the bureaucracy and the private-sector economy, which effects an alignment between the structures and processes of the company and those of the ministry.

In the transaction cost and contingency perspective, *amakudari* carries the embodiment of the originating ministry into the private firm. The receiving firm, in turn, incorporates a part of the government ministry into its organizational structure. Thus, the organization incorporates the complexity of the environment into its own structure, thereby satisfying its intrinsic needs for surveillance of the environment and reducing uncertainty. In the Japanese context, the government is not only a large source of uncertainty, but it also is a crucial provider of resources controlling 30–40 percent of gross domestic product (GDP) (Cho 1995, 60). Private firms obtain *amakudari* due to their desire to form and maintain osmotic networks for mobilizing resources from the central government (Tsujinaka 1990). In this way, *amakudari* bureaucrats function according to special needs and profit motives of those companies to which they took *amakudari* positions.

Hostages and Cooptation

Using marriage and hostage-taking as analogies, Cho (1995) indicates how *amakudari* works for the private firm. In the feudal era, political alliances were formed through marriage. The spouses were not only influential at court, they were hostages underwriting the trust between political allies. *Amakudari* personnel, like marriage partners, provide the basis for a relationship of mutual influence and trust. For example, when a bank joins a convoy system led by the MOF, it receives an *amakudari* bureaucrat from the MOF. This provides a basis for understanding *amakudari* as a managed alliance. From the receiving company's point of view, *amakudari* personnel may be thought of as hostages for protection from government sanctions. By taking a hostage, a receiving company may not have to rely on other means of resource mobilization, namely, cultivating ties with politicians or resorting to other legal means, reducing the uncertainties and risks involved in negotiations with the ministries. For the private corporation, lobbying efforts are directed at the ministries as well as key actors in the LDP who can influence the ministries. Rather than employing lobbyists for this task, companies take *amakudari* officials into their organizations. This allows the corporation "to keep abreast of what the ministries are doing because laws, their implementing ordinances, and other policy initiatives originate in the ministries" (Prestowitz 1988, 117).

Consensus Arguments

In contrast to the push and pull arguments of the immediate causes of *amakudari*, consensus arguments focuses on mutual negotiations between ministries and the private sector. The networks that bind the government and the private sector are not formal or legal ties. Instead, they are informal, based on mutual consensus. They are maintained through *nemawashi*, an informal Japanese convention of negotiation and renegotiation. Consensus is only achieved through repeated discussions of definitions and appropriate rights and obligations. The *nemawashi* explanation combines the self-interests of the ministry and private firm with a cultural context. Thus, out of repeated *nemawashi* a reciprocal consent emerges based on the understanding of mutual cooptation of ministry and company, which is ritualized, repeated, and reaffirmed in continuous discussions.

Amakudari has multiple and overlapping causes and functions that are difficult to tease apart. This complexity is inherent in describing an institution involving individual motives as well as institutional functions. Adding to these complexities, the character of these motives and functions are both economically and politically rational with an overlay of cultural reproduction. Yet essentially, *amakudari* is supported and maintained because of the mutual benefit derived by the bureaucracy and private and public organizations.

Legislative Constraints on *Amakudari*

Postwar legislative constraints provide another set of intermediate causal forces shaping *amakudari* paths. The various *amakudari* paths out of the different ministries reflect legislative rules and structures in the form of constitutional, statutory, and regulatory laws. "The legal framework along with the mechanisms for law-making and change are critical to any understanding of the performance and role of Japanese civil service and the factors that foster or inhibit its performance. I argue here that the legal structure within which Japan's civil service operates has been instrumental in defining its role in the economy and channeling its behavior. Like the banks of a fast-flowing stream, the legal institutions of postwar Japan have determined the direction and often the intensity of bureaucratic activity" (Haley 1995, 78).

We agree that legal and administrative structures shape behavior, but they do not determine the flow and pattern of *amakudari*. Instead, legislative constraints direct *amakudari* behavior only loosely. If we remember that bureaucrats are the targets of legislation as well as the implementers and monitors of that legislation, this begins to explain the continuity and resilience of the institution of *amakudari*. As an institution, *amakudari* has been sensitive to changes in rules and legislative structures since World War II. After *amakudari* became institutionalized in ministry operations, the flow and patterns continued in a more path-dependent fashion, less sensitive to the changing legal and structural context. Although *amakudari* (as part of the civil service) may be analogous to a stream bank, such banks are neither immutable nor deterministic. To provide a better understanding of the relationship between *amakudari* paths and the wider legal environment, we review here the legal reforms that have affected *amakudari* networks.

There were no restrictions on *amakudari* prior to World War II (Kubota 1969; Cho 1995). In 1947, however, a government labor union (*zenkan koro*) submitted a proposal to ban the *amakudari* of civil servants to private-sector jobs. In that year, an investigation by the General Headquarters of the Allied occupation (headed by Blaine Hoover) reported potentially negative consequences of *amakudari*: "if civil servants are asked to retire in their 40s and 50s, it is possible that civil servants would be insecure about their post-retirement life and would be likely to compromise their duties. It is a problem created by the organizational structures, not by individual civil servants" (Cho 1995, 29 citing Kawamura 1994, 73–74). The Hoover commission advocated legislation to limit the potential compromise posed by *amakudari*. The original civil service legislation, adopted in October 1947, prohibited civil servants from taking jobs for two years after retirement in a private sector they had regulated in the two years prior to retirement. In 1948, the Hoover commission changed the stipulation to five years before retirement.

The 1947 civil service legislation created the National Personnel Authority (NPA) with the authority to approve the employment of former bureaucrats following the stipulations of Civil Servants Law 103, Section 2, and NPA rule 14-4. Section 2 states that this prohibition is lifted when the director general of each agency requests permission for such employment and it is approved by the NPA. Those ostensibly prohibited from taking *amakudari* positions can take such positions if approved by the NPA. The requirement of NPA approval is imposed on high-ranking civil servants whose salary scale is 1 or 2 (typically section chief or above) (Cho 1995, 30).[10]

In 1949 the first set of administrative reforms took place that addressed Japan's postwar inflation. Named after Joseph P. Dodge, the U.S. banker sent by the Harry Truman administration, the Dodge Line reforms cut government expenditures by reducing the number of bureaucrats in each ministry and agency by 30 percent and dismissed personnel in 1951 and 1954.

> Immediately after the war, the Japanese government had recruited veterans and civilians who had been demobilized or returned to Japan from abroad, and had increased the number of administrative personnel to carry out economic control. However, under a restrictive fiscal policy adopted in 1949 by the Yoshida Administration, the number of administrative personnel was reduced from 1,600,000 to 1,400,000. GHQ's Hoover investigation team of 1947 had already pointed to the need for reform in the bureaucracy, noting it was too large and bureaucrats lacked discipline. (Muramatsu 1994, 39)

The Dodge Line personnel reductions increased pressure on the ministries to find retirement positions.

Following the Korean War, tax revenues began to rise in the mid-1950s. The size of the government also began to grow through the addition of new ministries and agencies to help Japan recover and catch up with western countries. In the 1950s, old ministries were dismantled (e.g., the Ministry of Railways and Home Ministry) and new agencies and ministries were created (e.g., the Economic Planning Agency 1955; Science and Technology Agency 1956; and the Ministry of Home Affairs 1960). Many new public corporations as auxiliaries to the central government ministries were created at this time. These new public corporations provided additional positions for retired ministry officials (*yokosuberi*).

An amendment to the Election Law in 1962 prohibited certain high-level bureaucrats from entering the first election to the House of Councillors (the Upper House) after retirement (*seikai tensin*) (Johnson 1978, 104). The movement to the Upper House had been in place for decades and this amendment was designed to inhibit the flow of ex-bureaucrats to public office. Also in 1962, the Diet amended the Government Employee Act, Article 103 (Kokka Komuin Ho 103) mandating the public disclosure of *amakudari* reports in 1962 and the annual publication by the NPA, which started in 1963. This amendment was aimed at making *amakudari* to the private sector more transparent.

Following the public disclosure of *amakudari* by NPA came a 1965 cabinet decision that *amakudari* to the same post at a public corporation (*yokosuberi*) should not exceed eight years. This regulation came in response to criticisms that *yokosuberi* at public corporations were excessive in duration. However, this cabinet decision did not stop *amakudari* but instead created the *wataridori* syndrome, the serial retirement movement from the central ministry to a public corporation, followed by movement to a different public corporation or to a private enterprise.

Additional efforts were made in 1968 to control the size of the central government. A law was passed calling for the abolition of one bureau in each ministry under the order of Prime Minister Eisaku Sato. Eighteen of the 120 bureaus of the central ministries were abolished. The policy of "scrap and build" became entrenched, and no new bureau could be established in response to socioeconomic changes unless a comparable bureau of declining need was abolished (Ito 1995, 241). Quickly, the Diet passed a law limiting the number of central public employees in May 1969 to keep the size of the central bureaucracy under control. This led to the delegation of functions to public corporations and local governments. No law, however, restricted employment by local governments. The legal restrictions imposed on the size of the central bureaucracy led to the creation of more public corporations to allow the government to outsource its work as well as to provide new landing spots (*yokosuberi*) for ex-officials. Thus, the active use of local governments (which expanded in size) and public corporations by the ministries made it possible to keep the bureaucracy small and to comply with the law (Muramatsu 1994, 24).

In response to the consequences of this 1969 law, the Diet passed a regulation in 1979 limiting boards of directors of *tokushu hojin* (a special type of public corporation) to 50 percent *yokosuberi* (Seifu Kankei Hojin Rodo Kumiai Rengo [Seiroren] 1992). Since that time, criticisms of *yokosuberi* to *tokushu hojin* have intensified, including calls for the total dismantling and privatization of *tokushu hojin* such as Nippon Telegraph and Telephone (NTT)

and Japanese National Railways (JNR). The cabinet also passed
in 1979 a resolution prohibiting multistep transfers of retired
officials among public corporations (*wataridori*) with a one-time
exception only when it is definitely necessary. This cabinet decision,
however, had little binding force and brought little change in the
sequential pattern of reemployment it attempted to control (Inoki
1995, 223).

In 1981 Japan initiated a series of hearings aimed at government
structural reform (or administrative reform; *gyosei zaisei kaikaku*)
in response to the huge government deficits carried over from the
1970s. JNR, a government-owned corporation with a large number
of employees and a large debt, was privatized and broken up into
six regional JR entities in 1987. This move was possible because of
the historical separation of the Ministry of Transport and JNR. In
1985 NTT was privatized and so was the Japan Tobacco Public
Corporation (into Japan Tobacco, Inc. in 1985). Similar to the JNR
case, the Ministry of Posts and Telecommunications did not try to
stop the privatization process. It is important to keep in mind,
however, that the term "privatized" does not mean what we expect—
rather, these corporations were transformed into a special type of
public corporation, *tokushu hojin*, and not fully privatized in a
substantive sense. Their component entities still provided landing
spots for *yokosuberi*.

In 1985, the salary classifications of civil servants were changed
and the range of NPA inspection was narrowed (Cho 1995, 30). Until
1985, salary classification had had eight ranks (with rank 1 as the top)
and *amakudari* among those in rank 2 and above was subject to NPA
inspection. In the new classification, there were eleven ranks (with
rank 11 as the top). Those at the rank of 10 or 11 (roughly section
chief and above) plus those with rank 9 and below who take board-
of-director positions in the private sector are subject to NPA inspection. The NPA inspection does not apply to postretirement jobs in
nonprivate sectors.

Some authors argue that the reforms of the mid-1980s strengthened links between bureaucrats, politicians, and business interests.
The administrative reforms of the 1980s took place in the context
of a rising fiscal deficit and a political unwillingness to raise taxes.
This led to *minkatsu* (private-sector vitality) projects such as the
multibillion-dollar third-sector megaprojects of the New Kansai
International Airport and the Trans-Tokyo Bay Bridge. *Minkatsu*

projects were popular among the LDP construction *zoku* as well as ministry officials. According to Lonny Carlile,

> *Minkatsu* in practice had the effect of expanding bureaucratic influence. Rather than creating new "spaces" in which the private sector could give free rein to its vitality, *minkatsu* projects frequently served as cost-effective mechanisms for expanding the scope of both formal and informal regulation. Executive positions in the newly formed third-sector firms tended to be monopolized by ex-bureaucrats [*yokosuberi*]. Ministries and agencies used third-sector projects as opportunities to draft new regulation governing procedures for selecting participating firms, to impose new licensing and reporting requirements, and to promulgate ordinances that granted them supervisory oversight over what were de facto "state" projects. (1998, 87)

Likewise, the privatization of NTT and JNR actually strengthened the regulatory authority of the supervising ministries by eliminating the organizational autonomy of these formal public-sector corporations (Carlile 1998).

Throughout the 1990s the bureaucracy became the target of criticism involving revelations of serious corruption, the inability to solve economic problems, and the charge that the bureaucracy was responsible for the bubble economy and its disastrous aftermath. Public dissatisfaction with the bureaucracy peaked in 1996 with the tainted blood (tainted with the human immunodeficiency virus, HIV) scandal. Public outrage emboldened politicians to call for sweeping administrative reforms. Riding on the momentum for change, the cabinet of Prime Minister Ryutaro Hashimoto introduced major reforms of government agencies and gave greater authority to the prime minister and the cabinet, ensuring the transparency of administrative rules and practices. The reform called for decentralized and efficient administrative processes to meet the challenges of the twenty-first century. The most critical changes were the reorganization of the twelve ministries and some twenty-five agencies into ten new ministries and ten agencies (which took effect in 2001) and the restriction of *amakudari*.[11] The new legislation (adopted on 10 September 1999) removed the power of each ministry to make *amakudari* arrangements by creating a human resource bank to handle postretirement arrangements and assure the employment of bureaucrats until age 65.

In our view the new legislation and the establishment of a human resource bank will not affect current *amakudari* practices. First, the restriction applies only to private-sector *amakudari* and most high-ranking officials do not descend through this route. As we show in subsequent chapters, the ministries have devised less transparent paths, such as *yokosuberi* and *wataridori*, which are not subject to legal restrictions or public disclosure. It is more likely that the new legislation will affect *amakudari* among lower-ranking bureaucrats who are more apt to move directly to private firms. Second, the NPA was created in 1947 as an independent monitoring authority over the personnel matters of the central ministries. In reality, however, the agency was never staffed to carry out such legal mandates. As a result, the NPA has regularly relied on personnel on temporary loan (*shukko*) from other ministries in reviewing and deciding the personnel matters of those ministries. It is highly unlikely that the new human resource bank will receive the necessary manpower to arrange, monitor, and maintain postretirement jobs for the entire bureaucracy. As in other sweeping economic reforms of the 1990s, the exclusive focus on formal changes in structure often misses the continuities in functions and may altogether mislead.

Our review of legal reforms affecting *amakudari* indicates a non-static nature to the institutionalization of *amakudari*. The bureaucracy managed various legislative constraints by developing networks with local governments, industry associations, and public corporations. The legislative constraints placed on the bureaucracy created the impetus for the creation of additional *tokushu hojin* and other forms of public corporations, diversifying *amakudari* placements. *Amakudari* cannot just be turned on or off in a mechanical or deterministic fashion. Instead, legislative history suggests *amakudari* paths have been continuously created, redirected, reproduced, and transformed since World War II.

Organization and Coordination of *Amakudari*

The view of *amakudari* as ad hoc and informal misses the routine, institutionalized, and consciously coordinated nature of *amakudari* practices. The institutional nature of *amakudari* is not exactly preconscious or taken for granted, a fully routine process to which no one gives a conscious thought. In a sense, *amakudari* is a set of practices that are understood as the way things are done and entails a certain taken-for-grantedness. Just as ministries develop a hierarchy of authority and periodic review procedures, so too do *amakudari* practices represent the taken-for-granted timing of personnel movements, definitions of appropriate placements, and ministry positions responsible for placements; in this sense, these categories and practices represent the institutionalization of *amakudari* into the ministries. Yet *amakudari* placements are not preconscious, ad hoc, or informal—rather, the timing, exact placement, and replacement of retiring bureaucrats is conscious, calculated, and routine in ministerial practices.

Ministries operate in a competitive interministry field, yet they monopolize the sectors over which they have regulatory responsibility. *Amakudari* is both the mechanism of monopoly control and communication and the instrument of interministry competition. It is a mechanism of appropriation by claiming territory for the ministry, and not all central ministries are equal in this competitive and monopoly power. There is a relatively stable hierarchy among the ministries based on their number of *amakudari*. Interministry competition for *amakudari* placements is a special type of appropriation that gives a ministry rights to the benefits that result from *amakudari* placements. This flow of benefits, monopolized by ministries, maintains a ministry's rank within the system (Stinchcombe 1998, 269).[12] Ministries with initial advantages in placing *amakudari* use these advantages to reproduce their position in the hierarchy of ministries.

Amakudari placements are conscious, self-interested efforts on the part of bureaucrats and the administrative units of each ministry to gain deferred compensation for individual bureaucrats and to claim sectoral turf for the ministry. The placements of ex-officials create and maintain representatives who define and monitor the boundaries of the ministry's sectors, cultivate policy networks, and represent ministry interests. The combination of the rational self-interests of individuals with administrative rationality explains the drive behind *amakudari* placements (Pempel and Muramatsu 1995; Cho 1995; Muramatsu 1994). These processes are institutionalized in the sense that they are conscious and calculated strategies coordinating the logistics of *amakudari*, *yokosuberi*, and *wataridori*.

As early as 1974, Chalmers Johnson established the key discussion points by stating that a recently promoted vice minister is under "compelling obligation to find suitable positions" for those retiring from his ministry (Johnson 1974, 960). He goes on to say the key man in each ministry responsible for orchestrating *amakudari* placements is the chief of the secretariat (*kanbocho*), a position equivalent in rank to the most senior bureau chief. This position, a stepping stone to the vice ministership, involves the institutionalized and formal responsibility for the placement of ex-officials. Johnson views *amakudari* decisions as emanating from each ministry with a high-ranking bureaucrat specifically responsible for creating and orchestrating these decisions.

Our interviews indicate that each ministry personnel office has a list of companies and positions that it has accumulated over time. This represents a codified description of its territory or turf. The personnel office maintains contacts with these companies to make *amakudari* arrangements for its soon-to-be-retiring bureaucrats. Sometimes companies initiate contact with ministries to request *amakudari* placements. According to Yoshimitsu Kuribayashi (1990), there are approximately 19,000 *yokosuberi* destinations for MOF bureaucrats in many kinds of organizations. These public-sector destination entities receive subsidies or investment funds from either the MOF or the National Tax Agency. Private-sector companies participate in *amakudari* in the hopes of obtaining information or establishing friendly ties with the MOF, but they do so at a price. Once a private company receives an *amakudari* person, it is difficult to terminate the position. Sometimes the company increases the number of *amakudari* positions, but the number never goes down (Ishizawa 1995, 90). *Amakudari* placements represent a kind of colonization of the public and private sectors by the ministries.

A clearer image of *amakudari* is gained by the metaphors used by one of our interviewees. An *amakudari* official from the MOF indicated that available *amakudari* positions are like stock certificates that the MOF holds. These positions might be thought of as a number of "stocks" or, better, a "portfolio of stocks." He then shifted his metaphor to explain the coordination process of the movement of ex-MOF officials across positions and their orchestration by the ministry officials. All MOF *amakudari* must move at a set time like "a tree with limbs moving out from the trunk," with the *kanbocho*, secretary, and vice minister coordinating this movement. Continuing the metaphor, he indicated that *amakudari* tend to be cumbersome at ages 65–70. At this point, the orchestration of future jobs is no longer the responsibility of the MOF. The ex-officials are on their own. The ties between ex-officials and the ministry weaken with time, and these weaker ties are reflected in the decline in the rank of their subsequent positions.

Extending the metaphor of positions as stocks, we might ask: How do the portfolios of positions change? The MOF's control over a bank typically increases when the bank experiences some crisis or trouble (e.g., an unrecoverable loan). Retiring bureaucrats are sent by the MOF with a restructuring or rescue plan devised by the MOF. Once established, the positions tend to become permanent *amakudari* positions for the MOF. This suggests that the MOF should be increasing the number of potential *amakudari* locations throughout the banking crisis and thus increasing its portfolio (Ishizawa 1995, 130).

A more nuanced approach to this conscious placement process recognizes the variation in who handles *amakudari*, *yokosuberi*, and *wataridori* by ministry and by the rank of the retiring official. High-level administrators handle the retirements of top officials at the high-profile ministries. For example, the MOF places approximately twenty top career bureaucrats through *amakudari* every year (Ishizawa 1995, 94). Every July, the MOF has a meeting (*tanabata kai*) at the finance minister's residence that includes career bureaucrats of the most powerful bureaus and *amakudari* ex-officials already in the public and private sectors—this is where *amakudari* arrangements are discussed. In the 1990s, there was a group of three men (called "NTT") believed to perform most of the planning functions for this group: Minoru Nagaoka (N), Michio Takeuchi (T), and Hiroshi Tanimura (T). All three had been vice ministers of the MOF and all three took *amakudari* to the Tokyo Stock Exchange. This "NTT" group made careful plans for the *amakudari* locations of top career bureaucrats in the early 1990s. In addition to these high-ranking career bureaucrats, the MOF places lower-ranking career and noncareer (technical track) bureaucrats; however, lower-level bureaucrats handle these placements. Cho's (1995) survey of 331 ex-officials from diverse ministries in 1994 generally supports the notion that those finding high-ranking positions on boards of directors attributed their placement to the *kanbocho*.

Our interviews with *amakudari* and *wataridori* officials also support this contention that high-level ministry officials handle the reemployment arrangements for top-ranking bureaucrats. For example, a high-ranking MITI civil servant, reemployed at one of the highest positions in a major corporation, corroborated the notion that ministry rank distinguished the ministry unit making the reemployment arrangement. At the MITI, high-ranking *amakudari* and *wataridori* placements are handled by the *kanbocho*. This is the primary job of the *kanbocho*, and the interviewee implied that the vice minister directly oversees this work. This interviewee tied the "compelling obligation" of the vice minister to the *kanbocho*'s operational responsibilities, as stated by Johnson (1974).

This former MITI official described the job of placing high-ranking MITI officials as subtly mechanical, and he used the metaphor of an army to express the precise and systematic nature of the placements. They are mechanical in two respects. First, the position of *kanbocho* rotates in the MITI every one to two years, so each *kanbocho* executes the decisions of his predecessors both for *amakudari* and *wataridori* movements. Second, appropriating new *amakudari* positions or moving retired MITI personnel to their new reemployment positions is a straightforward process. A telephone call is typically the way that arrangements are made by the *kanbocho* for the placement of a retiree. The *kanbocho* merely expresses to the personnel officer of a private corporation "a suggestion that a placement could be made." This, the interviewee assured us, provides a sufficient "implied threat." All arrangements are very discreet and subtle, yet there are certain pressures involved. Pressure on the *kanbocho* is great because he must find appropriate positions for retiring (*amakudari*) and retired (*wataridori*) high-ranking MITI officials until they reach ages 68–70—each position must correspond to the prestige and rank of the MITI retiree.

Ministries vary in how *amakudari* is arranged and coordinated. *Amakudari* arrangements in the MOF, MITI, and Posts and Telecommunications are made at a high level in the minister's secretarial office. In contrast, *amakudari* arrangements at the Ministries of Construction, Transport, and Agriculture tend to be made lower in the hierarchy, by bureau and section chiefs and by individual negotiation. Thus, the placement of *amakudari* is a more centralized process in the MOF, MITI, and Posts and Telecommunications, whereas Construction, Transport, and Agriculture use more decentralized mechanisms. The variation between centralized and decentralized mechanisms of *amakudari* placement may be related to how the ministries are embedded in different sectors, their clients, ministry organization, or value of *amakudari* personnel to the private sector. *Amakudari* that are used to bring government grants to private firms (e.g., construction contracts) are more likely to be the result of a decentralized process, as in Construction (Cho 1995).

The ministries with the lowest percentages of placement directly into the private sector upon retirement are the MOF at 32.7 percent and MITI at 35.7 percent. Yet within five years of retirement these percentages go up to 73 and 88.1 percent, respectively (Cho 1995, 95, table 3-19). The centralized mechanisms of the MITI and MOF correspond to ministries with large numbers of reemployment positions in the public sector (*yokosuberi*). Cho's data suggest, however, that the centralized mechanisms of reemployment are associated with ministries that take longer to get their people to private-sector positions, thus involving more indirect coordination and organization of *wataridori* placements.

Four key features help compose or combine the different conceptions of *amakudari*. First, *amakudari* positions define a formal and codified territory of positions for the ministry; once new positions are filled, these become the additional territory of the ministry. Second, the responsibility for the placement of and the coordination of the placement of ex-officials is a more or less formally centralized responsibility of a specific office of the ministry. Third, there are certain cultural norms and expectations that surround *amakudari* movements involving appropriate placement and procedures for placements. Fourth, these *amakudari* personnel provide tangible benefits to private organizations' abilities to compete in a regulated economy substantially driven by government grants and contracts.

Amakudari is a personnel system that is shaped by and part of the dynamics of politics among the ministries and the public and private sectors. Bureaucrats are more than self-interested individuals—they constitute a status group. *Amakudari*, the end point of a bureaucrat's career, is institutionalized—it connects a matrix of organizations across a number of institutional spheres. These connections involve practices that are the conscious and the agreed-on yet taken-for-granted modes of relationships among the ministries and those organizations receiving ex-bureaucrats.

Amakudari is also the product of competition among ministries that exemplifies Japan's penchant for vertical administration and the development of sectoralism. Ministries and agencies responded to the shortage of administrative resources and to a series of administrative reforms by extending their administrative and regulatory control and creating new networks of *amakudari*. The formation of ministry-based personnel networks has given rise to a turf-maximizing group mentality and sectionalism, and the lack of administrative resources has caused network-based activities. Competition between ministry-based networks have worked to maximize the resources within a particular ministry, and interministry competition has pushed aggressive policy implementation. Bureaucrats created industry associations and public corporations and widened their networks. They created "legs and arms" through which they can exercise their influence rather than creating new intraministry organizations or adding personnel. Sectionalism intensified as each ministry adopted these strategies. The constraints on the size and resources of the central ministries, and the consequent development of *amakudari* networks linking sectors and institutions, represented a different type of bureaucratic imperialism. Of course, the desire for more authority, power, and benefits (such as *amakudari*) worked as incentives for competition. It is popular to suggest such resource-maximizing networks become obsolete when faced with new challenges; we believe that the intra- and interministry competition resulting from administrative constraints and public criticisms has also led to inventiveness, adjustment, and continuity.

Amakudari continues because it addresses the interests of both private corporations and government ministries. In this way, *amakudari* networks connect a matrix of organizations across formally differentiated sectors of Japanese society, based on mutual interdependence between the government and the private sector. First, *amakudari* continues because Japan is a regulatory society. The economy is regulated by approvals, guidance and permits issued by the regulating ministry or ministries. Similarly, nonprofit areas of Japanese society (labor, welfare, education) are regulated by corresponding ministries. Conversely, these private and public corporations use *amakudari* to improve their ability to survive by gaining access to the ministry and interpretations of these regulations. Second, *amakudari* continues because Japan is a public works driven economy. Private corporations, as well as public corporations, use *amakudari* personnel to increase their information and gain grants and contracts dispersed by the government. Third, *amakudari* personnel provide leverage or "hostages" for private and public firms when dealing with government ministries. In extreme cases these hostages may be used to insulate or shield the organization from political or media attack. Finally, *amakudari* provides a basis of information and coordination that reduces the costs that would otherwise be associated with operating in a purely competitive environment.

3 *Amakudari*: Movement to the Private Sector

This chapter examines *amakudari* in its narrow sense of the retirement of top-level bureaucrats to key positions in private corporations. *Amakudari* is part of a labyrinth of informal relations, processes, and decision making that fuses government and business operations. We identify the hierarchy of ministries in the dispersion of *amakudari* to explore this labyrinth. The exploration of *amakudari* by ministry makes specific the discussions of the embeddedness of the state and generalized discussions of the private sector. The NPA provides the most systematic official report on annual *amakudari* to the private sector. Although the NPA data indicate *amakudari* has declined since 1985, prevalence data on *amakudari* serving on the boards of private firms show a stable distribution of *amakudari* that is often overlooked by the NPA data.

In this chapter we use four sources of data.

1. The NPA data provide the annual incidence of petitions and grants of *amakudari* for all ministries and agencies from 1963 to 2000.
2. *Kigyo keiretsu soran* (Toyo Keizai Shinposha 1984–2000) provides prevalence data for *amakudari* on the boards of directors of all listed private firms from 1982 to 1998.
3. *Seikai kancho jinjiroku* (Toyo Keizai Shinposha 1995) provides prevalence data for *amakudari* to the boards of directors of 2,220 private firms (2,168 listed firms, whose stocks are traded, and 52 nonlisted financial firms and major commercial associations) for 1994.
4. *Kaisha nenkan* (Nihon Keizai Shinbunsha 1997, 2000) provides prevalence data for *amakudari* to board-of-director positions among the top one hundred corporations from 1979 to 2000.

Whereas the NPA source captures the number of *amakudari* that took place in a given year, the last three sources identify the number (or accumulation) of *amakudari* on the boards of directors of private firms for a given year. Each of these four data sources has strengths and limitations (see chap. 1) and provides a different part at the same *amakudari* phenomenon. Together they offer a more encompassing empirical analysis of *amakudari*.

We begin this chapter by setting a baseline for contentions on the significance and distribution of *amakudari*. Next, we examine the concentration and dispersion of *amakudari* placement between the ministries and private sector to bring structural specificity to this relationship. Then we examine the resource dependency thesis, which suggests that *amakudari* goes to weak sectors and second-tier corporations, and we evaluate whether there is a systematic relationship between *amakudari* and industrial regulation.

Overall Trend

Most scholars share the view that *amakudari* patterns are changing. Figure 3.1 shows the number of *amakudari* reported by the NPA from 1963 to 2000. The annual incidence of *amakudari* ranges from a low of 40 in 2000 to a high of 320 in 1985, slowly but steadily increasing from 165 in 1963 to 320 in 1985. The magnitude of the increase was almost 100 percent, with an annual average of 196 over the twenty-three-year period. From 1985 to 1994, the number of *amakudari* declined, and the decline was even sharper from 1995 to 2000.

The overall trend shown in figure 3.1 supports the contention that *amakudari* is rapidly on the wane, reportedly because of either administrative reforms and market deregulation or media attacks on *amakudari*. Since 1995, in the context of prolonged recession and scandals involving bureaucrats, the media have run more stories on collusion, bribery, and suspicion of wrongdoing involving *amakudari*. Rising criticisms of *amakudari* in newspaper stories after 1995 are in sharp contrast to earlier media accounts that reported *amakudari* in a neutral fashion.[1] In response to a series of revelations of collusion involving *amakudari*, the central bureaucracy accepted a voluntary restraint on *amakudari* in 1995, leading to a drastic reduction in the number of *amakudari* in the data from official publications.[2]

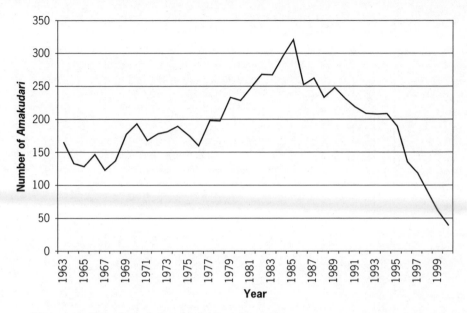

Figure 3.1 Number of *Amakudari*, 1963–2000

Prevalence data suggest a different picture (table 3.1). Between 1982 and 1998 former bureaucrats held 2 percent of all board-of-director positions in listed private firms. Although the NPA data indicate a clear decline in the number of *amakudari* since 1985 and most dramatically after 1995, the prevalence data in table 3.1 suggest a more stable distribution of *amakudari* between 1982 and 1998. Even though the number of *amakudari* from the Ministry of Finance (MOF) decreased after 1994, it was offset by a substantial increase in *amakudari* from the National Tax Agency, which is a semiautonomous external agency of the MOF. There is no dramatic change in the prevalence of *amakudari* from the ministries known for chronic scandals; the Ministries of Construction and Transport, for example, increased their numbers of *amakudari* to boards of directors, probably indicating the strength of public works projects in the postbubble economy.

If we examine a more detailed breakdown of *amakudari* by ministries for 1994, we find a total of 873 *amakudari* in 2,220 firms. As indicated in table 3.2, former bureaucrats held 2.0 percent (873 of 42,625) of all board-of-director positions among 2,220 private firms

Table 3.1 *Amakudari* on Boards of Directors among Private Firms, 1982–1998[a]

Originating Ministry/ Agency or *Tokushu hojin*	Number of *Amakudari*								
	1982	1985	1986	1988	1990	1992	1994	1996	1998
MOF	124	123	119	137	144	119	129	126	111
MOC	98	117	112	117	123	96	151	144	152
TA	76	73	59	49	46	69	71	113	124
MITI	73	70	76	82	96	82	90	92	90
MOT	47	55	46	39	49	38	39	66	69
MOA	35	40	38	48	50	51	51	48	46
National Police Agency	23	23	21	21	18	29	38	44	43
MPT	21	16	20	22	25	22	24	32	25
Defense Agency	na	na	na	13	15	16	18	28	9
Total number of firms	1,773	1,839	1,888	1,985	2,086	2,131	2,232	2,356	2,432
Total number of board positions (a)	30,192	32,123	33,013	36,211	39,482	39,882	42,282	43,825	39,931
Total number of *amakudari*									
From ministries (b)	646	643	587	600	623	846	805	827	797
From public corporations	586	397	384	393	407	265	315	312	264
Percentage *amakudari* (b/a)	2.1	2.0	1.8	1.7	1.6	2.1	1.9	1.9	2.0

Source: Toyo Keizai Shinposha (1984–2000).

[a] MITI, Ministry of International Trade and Industry; MOA, Ministry of Agriculture, Forestry, and Fisheries; MOC, Ministry of Construction; MOF, Ministry of Finance; MOT, Ministry of Transport; MPT, Ministry of Posts and Telecommunications; na, not available; TA, National Tax Agency.

Table 3.2 *Amakudari* on Boards of Listed Private Firms, 1994[a]

Originating Ministry/ Agency	Total Number of *Amakudari*	*Amakudari* by Ministry (%)	*Amakudari* Rank
MOF	213	24.4	1
MOC	180	20.6	2
MITI	115	13.2	3
TA	84	9.6	4
MOT	70	8.0	5
MOA	58	6.6	6
National Police Agency	43	4.9	
Defense Agency	22	2.5	
Defense Facilities Administration Agency	4	0.5	
MPT	28	3.2	
Hokkaido Development Agency	8	0.9	
MOJ	7[b]	0.8	
MHW	6	0.7	
Board of Audit	5	0.6	
National Land Agency	4	0.5	
Maritime Safety Agency	3	0.3	
Labor	3	0.3	
Environment Agency	2	0.2	
MCA	2	0.2	
Food Agency	1	0.1	
Foreign Affairs	1	0.1	
Education	1	0.1	
Home Affairs	1	0.1	
Prime Minister's Office	1	0.11	
Fair Trade Commission	1	0.11	
STA	1	0.1	
Social Insurance Agency	0	0.0	
Economic Planning Agency	0	0.0	
Other[c]	9	1.0	
Total	873 (a)	100	
Total board positions	42,625 (b)	2.0% (a/b)	
Number of firms with at least one *amakudari*	621 (c)		
Total number of private firms	2,220 (d)	28.0% (c/d)	

Source: Toyo Keizai Shinposha (1995).
[a] MCA, Management and Coordination Agency; MHW, Ministry of Health and Welfare; MITI, Ministry of International Trade and Industry; MOA, Ministry of Agriculture, Forestry, and Fisheries; MOC, Ministry of Construction; MOF, Ministry of Finance; MOJ, Ministry of Justice; MOT, Ministry of Transport; MPT, Ministry of Posts and Telecommunications; STA, Science and Technology Agency; TA, National Tax Agency.
[b] The original source reported total *amakudari* for the MOJ as 4, but gives 7 entries under MOJ.
[c] The original source reported total *amakudari* for the Prosecution Review Commission as 8; however, there are 9 entries.

(which is similar to 1.9 percent for 1994 reported in table 3.1). However, 621 of the 2,220 firms (28.0 percent) had at least one *amakudari* bureaucrat on their board, meaning there is a rather broad distribution of *amakudari* in the private sector. The absolute number of *amakudari* is small, but *amakudari* involves the boards of nearly three in ten private firms.

A third data set provides the prevalence of *amakudari* on the boards of the one hundred largest listed private corporations between 1979 and 2000. Table 3.3 shows that 3.3 percent of all director positions were held by *amakudari* and that the number of top one hundred firms with at least one *amakudari* rose from thirty-five to fifty-eight in this period. The total number of *amakudari* more than doubled between 1979 and 2000 from thirty-five to ninety-four or from 1.3 percent of all board positions in 1979 to 3.3 percent in 2000. The comparison of our two prevalence data sets (tables 3.1 and 3.3) suggests two important features. First, the concentration of *amakudari* on the boards of private firms steadily increased in the one hundred largest firms. Second, the concentration of *amakudari* on the boards of the one hundred largest private firms became higher than the overall private firms after 1985 when the incidence of *amakudari* reported by the NPA began to decrease. There is no evi-

Table 3.3 *Amakudari* on the Boards of Directors of the One Hundred Largest Private Firms, 1979–2000[a]

Year	Total Number of Directors (a)	Number of Firms with Amakudari	Number of Amakudari (b)	Amakudari (%) (b/a)
1979	2,715	35	35	1.3
1981	2,727	40	41	1.5
1983	2,965	39	50	1.7
1985	3,122	50	71	2.3
1987	3,217	62	68	2.1
1989	3,423	65	69	2.0
1991	3,605	67	85	2.4
1997	3,434	63	102	3.0
2000	2,852	58	94	3.3

Source: Information for 1979–91 adapted from Schaede (1995, 303, table 1). Information for 1997 and 2000 assembled from Nihon Keizai Shinbunsha (1998, 2001).
[a] The authors calculated percentages from (a) and (b).

dence that large firms were subject to less government intervention and had less need for *amakudari* or that *amakudari* destinations shifted to smaller, weaker, or second-tier corporations.

The discrepancy between the decline in *amakudari* as measured by the NPA incidence data and the stable prevalence of *amakudari* among listed private firms highlights the danger of exclusive reliance on the official disclosure of *amakudari* by the NPA. Ex-bureaucrats were moving to private-sector boards of directors through paths not captured by NPA procedures. Not only is the NPA data limited as to the whereabouts of top-level bureaucrats, reemployment in the private sector is mediated through other routes, such as *yokosuberi* and *wataridori*. The decline in the annual number of *amakudari* reported by the NPA indicates the increasing difficulties in the use of *amakudari* by the central ministries; however, it is not the same as the disappearance of *amakudari*. It may even reflect a tactic on the part of the bureaucracy to create the appearance of change (a media artifact), thus containing the pressures that mounted on the practice of *amakudari* throughout the 1990s.

Trends by Ministry

Overall trends are important to set baseline parameters, but the pattern of distribution of *amakudari* at the ministry level better reveals the structure of relations between ministries and the private sector. Part of the problem with discussions of *amakudari*, as with embeddedness of the state or network ties, is the lack of recognition of the internal distribution of these relationships. For example, Evans (1995, 47–50) views *amakudari* as representing the embedding of the state. "Embeddedness" means connection to. The use of "embeddedness," however, runs the risk that we will view the state abstractly as a homogeneous monolith without a clear specification of ministerial variations. In addition, Okimoto (1989, 163) views *amakudari* as the systematic "structure of ties" between the bureaucracy and the private sector, yet the characteristics of this systemic network need more empirical specification. Centrality and the dispersion of network ties between ministries and the private sector may characterize this internal structure. Centrality identifies specific ministries with the most *amakudari* placements and provides a measure of the hierarchical nature of *amakudari* networks; dispersion identifies the number of ministries that place *amakudari* in the private sector.

Centrality

Some authors contend that *amakudari* placements by ministries are both a measure of their control over the sectors they regulate and their relative power vis-à-vis other ministries.[3] However, these propositions are based on the examination of only one or two ministries and for short periods. The hierarchy or stratification of the *amakudari* path has important implications for the nature of the connections between the bureaucracy and the private sector.

There were twelve main ministries and some twenty-five agencies in the Japanese government prior to reorganization in 2001 (see Table 1.1). Not all ministries and agencies have been equal in importance and power.[4] The MOF and MITI are considered most powerful because of the scope of their responsibilities, but ministries in charge of functionally specific sectors, such as the Ministries of Agriculture, Construction, Transport, Health and Welfare, and Posts and Tele-communications are also powerful vis-à-vis other ministries and agencies.[5] Their regulatory responsibilities are high, and the mutual interdependence of government and business results in the development and maintenance of extensive *amakudari* networks. This raises the question of which ministries participate most in the *amakudari* networks.

Table 3.4 summarizes the ministries that rank in the top five by *amakudari* for selected years between 1965 and 1999 in the NPA data (incidence data) and between 1982 and 1998 for the *Kigyo keiretsu soran* data (prevalence data). The incidence and prevalence data yield similar patterns. In the NPA data, the MOF retained the top rank by placing the largest number of retiring bureaucrats in private corporations. The MITI is less stable than the MOF, but ranked next highest, until it dropped out of the rankings in 1999. After the MITI is the Ministry of Construction, fluctuating between second and fourth places, except in 1970 and 1985. The Ministry of Transport also ranked behind the MOF and MITI, but dropped out of the rankings in 1990 and 1995. Similarly, the Ministry of Agriculture moved up over time, but dropped out in 1980 and 1999; it ranked fifth in 1968, fourth in 1970 and 1975, and third in 1985 and 1995. The Ministry of Posts and Telecommunications (MPT) entered the top five in 1985 and rose to the second highest ranking in 1999. The National Tax

Table 3.4 Ministries Ranked by Number of *Amakudari* and the Share of *Amakudari* in Top-Ranking Ministries[a]

National Personnel Authority Data

Rank	1965	1970	1975	1980	1985	1990	1995	1999
1	MOF (30)	MOF (42)	MOF (47)	MOF (46)	MOF (60)	MOF (64)	MOF (59)	MOF (12)
2	MITI (28)	MITI (30)	MOC (21)	MOC (27)	MITI (36)	MITI (29)	MITI (17)	MPT TA (8)
3	MOT (19)	MOT (21)	MOT (18)	MITI MOT (25)	MOA MOT MPT (29)	MOC (28)	MOA MOC (16)	
4	MOC (14)	MOA (20)	MOA (15)			MOA (23)		MOC (5)
5	MOA (11)	MOC (17)	MITI TA (13)	TA (18)		MPT (18)	MPT (13)	MOT (4)
Top 3[b]	60.1	48.2	48.9	53.9	57.2	52.2	56.8	45.2
Top 5[b]	79.7	67.4	72.2	51.8	57.2	69.8	63.7	59.7

Kigyo Keiretsu Soran Data

Rank	1982	1985	1990	1994	1998
1	MOF (124)	MOF (123)	MOF (144)	MOC (151)	MOC (152)
2	MOC (98)	MOC (117)	MOC (123)	MOF (129)	TA (124)
3	TA (76)	TA (73)	MITI (96)	MITI (90)	MOF (111)
4	MITI (73)	MITI (70)	MOA (50)	TA (71)	MITI (90)
5	MOT (47)	MOT (55)	MOT (49)	MOA (51)	MOT (69)
Top 3[b]	46.1	48.7	58.3	46.0	48.6
Top 5[b]	64.7	68.1	74.2	61.1	68.5

Source: NPA (1982, 1985, 1990, 1994, 1998); Toyo Keizai Shimposha (1984–2000).
[a] MITI, Ministry of International Trade and Industry; MOA, Ministry of Agriculture, Forestry, and Fisheries; MOC, Ministry of Construction; MOF, Ministry of Finance; MOT, Ministry of Transport; MPT, Ministry of Posts and Telecommunications; TA, National Tax Agency.
[b] Percentage of total number of *amakudari* per year.

Agency (an external agency of the MOF) also entered the top five rankings in 1975, dropped out in 1985, 1990, and 1995, but rose to the second rank (tied with the MPT) in 1999.

The relative change in *amakudari* placements by ministry suggests the dominance of the MOF. To the extent that *amakudari* placements are a measure of ministry power, the comparison of the MOF with MITI, in part, substantiates Johnson and Okimoto's contention that the MOF superseded the MITI as the dominant ministry. However, this transition might have occurred considerably earlier than is generally suggested. The MITI was no longer the top ministry by the mid-1960s, although it retained the second or third position subsequently, along with the Ministries of Construction and Transport. By the late 1990s, when the total number of *amakudari* moving through the NPA fell precipitously, so too did the placements of the MOF and MITI. A careful look at these data, however, reveals the relative stability of the ministries in their rankings by *amakudari* for selected years.

The prevalence data shown in the second half of table 3.4 demonstrate patterns of *amakudari* similar to the NPA data. The top five ministries and agencies are the MOF, Construction, the MITI, the National Tax Agency, and the Ministry of Transport. When the figures for the MOF and National Tax Agency are combined, MOF personnel clearly dominate in the placement of *amakudari* on the boards of private firms. The high ranking of the National Tax Agency may suggest the emergence of an increasing finance or accounting logic in the relations between the bureaucracy and the private sector in the postbubble economy in which the urgency of bank clean-ups became more acute. It is also clear that the National Tax Agency has its own substantial and powerful *amakudari* networks, distinct from those of the MOF.

Concentration and Dispersion
Another issue in the structure of relations between the ministries and the private sector is the number of ministries contributing to the relationship. By concentration we mean a high proportion of *amakudari* coming from a few ministries, similar to industry-concentration ratios. Dispersion is the opposite. The NPA data between 1965 and 1999 in table 3.4 indicate that the share of *amakudari* from the top three ministries (MOF including the National Tax Agency, MITI, and Construction) was 60.1 percent in 1965 and decreased to 45.2 percent

in 1999. This pattern suggests an increasing dispersion in the relationship between the central ministries and the private sector. However, the degree of concentration/dispersion in the prevalence of *amakudari*, shown at the bottom of the second half of table 3.4, indicates the top three ministries (MOF including the National Tax Agency, Construction, and MITI) claimed 46–58 percent of *amakudari*. In contrast to the NPA data pattern of increasing dispersion, the prevalence of *amakudari* is stable to slightly increasing (46.1 percent in 1982 to 48.6 percent in 1998).

The NPA data indicate the MOF (including the National Tax Agency), MITI, and Construction are the most stable top-ranking ministries. The prevalence data also indicate the same three ministries as most stable in the top three rankings. In addition, the percentage of *amakudari* concentrated in these ministries is similar in the two data sources; 45–60 percent of *amakudari* are concentrated in the top three ministries in the NPA data compared to 46–58 percent in the prevalence data. The range of *amakudari* concentration for the top five ministries is again similar—50–80 percent in the NPA data and 61–74 percent in the prevalence data. These observations suggest the strong control of *amakudari* by the three ministries over time and demonstrate the power of these three ministries relative to other ministries.

The degree of concentration/dispersion of ministries in the prevalence data for 1994 shows remarkably similar *amakudari* patterns. The third column of table 3.2 indicates that the top three ministries (MOF, Construction, and MITI) accounted for the majority (58.2 percent) of *amakudari*. If we add the National Tax Agency (9.6 percent) and the Ministries of Transport (8 percent) and Agriculture (6.6 percent), we find over 82 percent of all ex-bureaucrats on private-sector boards came from these five ministries and one agency. This suggests a substantial concentration of ministries participating in the *amakudari* network. To the extent that the presence of ex-bureaucrats represents interinstitutional integration between the bureaucracy and private sector, personnel from these three ministries accomplish an important portion of business-bureaucracy integration.

Our analysis of these data sources suggests that the relations between the bureaucracy and the private sector created by *amakudari* are undergoing change, but they also reveal substantial continuity. The incidence data clearly are more sensitive to media criticisms of *amakudari* and the political decisions of the 1990s, as seen in the inverted U-shaped pattern (see figure 3.1) of the rise in *amakudari* until 1985 and the decline thereafter (especially after 1995). Also, the concentration of *amakudari* from the top six ministries declined from 80 to 60 percent, suggesting a decline in both the absolute number of placements by these six ministries and their relative positions in the bureaucracy in *amakudari* placements. However, the incidence and prevalence data reveal the dominance of the *amakudari* network by the same ministries/agency (MOF, Construction, MITI, Transport, Agriculture, and National Tax Agency). This is in light of the fact that the concentration of *amakudari* among a handful of ministries is still high. In short, our analysis suggests that as the aggregate *amakudari* declined, the MOF has maintained a strong centrality and the number of ministries participating increased. This indicates an increasing financial logic in the relations between government and the private sector. The post-bubble economy's emphasis on subsidies and public works projects supported *amakudari* from Construction. *Amakudari* from the National Tax Agency benefited from efforts to clean up the financial sector. Finally, Agriculture benefited from the continued protection of the agriculture sector.

Amakudari and the Resource Dependency Model

Authors emphasizing the self-regulating nature of markets maintain that *amakudari* is directly related to the government's technical resources (money and information) and the need for private firms to garner these resources in market competition. *Amakudari* placements are viewed as links between the government and private firms and as a way of managing and indexing these resource dependencies. Organizations that are powerful, and not capital or information dependent, are less likely to receive *amakudari*.[6] This resource dependency thesis (Calder 1989; Richardson 1997) is built on a series of hypotheses involving the relationship between *amakudari* and private-firm characteristics: firm size, company location, *keiretsu* affiliation, and the industry to which the company belongs.

Company size. According to the resource dependency thesis, firm size is inversely related to the number of *amakudari*. Small- and medium-size organizations are more likely to accept *amakudari* because they try harder than large organizations to influence the process of resource allocation. *Amakudari* is used to make up for market disadvantages. Medium (100–499 employees) and smaller (fewer than one hundred employees) firms are unable to exploit economies of scale and operate at a disadvantage in costs and profitability. Therefore, these firms are more likely to hire retired bureaucrats to acquire government information and contracts and to make up for the disadvantages of size.[7] Conversely, *amakudari* is less important for large corporations because they have their own sources of information, expertise, and financing.

Company location. Non-Tokyo-based firms are more likely than their Tokyo-based counterparts to accept *amakudari*. Location is an important key to accessing political influence, information, and resources. Firms based outside Tokyo are at a disadvantage in their access to established private-sector networks[8] and are expected to compensate for their market disadvantages by recruiting *amakudari*.

Keiretsu affiliation. Keiretsu[9] affiliation is inversely related to *amakudari* placements. Industrial groups represent market pathologies obstructing market forces, and *amakudari* represents a compensatory strategy for nonaffiliated firms. *Keiretsu*-affiliated firms have their own channels for access to capital, information, and other resources[10] and are less likely to need *amakudari*. Therefore, non-*keiretsu*-affiliated firms are more dependent on access to government information, contracts, and resources to stay competitive with *keiretsu* firms in their markets.[11]

Industry. The industries most open to market forces or public scrutiny—those sensitive to international competition and least regulated—are less likely to receive *amakudari* placements. Therefore, expanding industries, deregulated industries, and increasingly international industries should have relatively few *amakudari* placements, whereas declining industries and those designated strategically important to the political economy should receive a disproportionate amount of *amakudari* placements.[12]

Using the NPA data, table 3.5 shows the distribution of *amakudari* placements by company size for five selected years. The distribution of *amakudari* differs by company size, contrary to resource dependency predictions. The share of *amakudari* in 1995 among small firms (fewer than thirty employees) was only 5.2

Table 3.5 *Amakudari* by Company Size

Company Size (Number of Employees)	1963	1972	1982	1992	1995
Fewer than 30[a]	8.5	4.4	2.7	3.8	5.2
30–99[a]	6.7	15.0	13.7	12.2	6.9
100–499[a]	24.2	29.4	30.1	21.5	27.6
500–999[a]	10.3	13.8	12.4	16.3	20.1
1,000 or more[a]	29.1	37.5	41.2	45.9	40.2
Valid total[b]	130	160	226	200	174
	(78.8%)	(90.4%)	(84.3%)	(95.7%)	(91.6%)
Missing cases[c]	35	17	42	9	16
	(21.2%)	(9.6%)	(15.7%)	(4.3%)	(8.4%)
Total number of *amakudari*	165	177	268	209	190
	(100%)	(100%)	(100%)	(100%)	(100%)

Source: Information on number of *amakudari* and *amakudari* destinations (company name) obtained from NPA (1963, 1972, 1982, 1992, 1995). Information on each company obtained from Nihon Keizai Shinbunsha (1963, 1972, 1982, 1992, 1995) and *Japan Company Handbook* (1982, 1992, 1995).
[a] Percentage *amakudari*—the number of *amakudari* in each category of company size as a percentage of the total number of *amakudari*.
[b] Valid cases are those companies for which we obtained information on company size.
[c] Missing cases are companies that received *amakudari* for which we could not identify company size.

percent compared to 40.2 percent among large firms (more than 1,000 employees).

An examination of the smallest and largest firms over time confirms the relationship between corporate size and *amakudari* placement. For smaller firms (fewer than one hundred employees), the percentage of *amakudari* ranges between 15 and 20 percent and dropped to 12.1 percent in 1995. Placements of *amakudari* were stable in middle-size (100–499 employees) firms at 20–30 percent during the same period. The larger middle-size firms (500–999 employees) increased their share of *amakudari* dramatically from 10.3 percent in 1963 to 20.1 percent in 1995. The share of *amakudari* among the largest firms (more than 1,000 employees) also increased from 29.1 to 40.2 percent. This expansion in the distribution of *amakudari* to the largest firms is not explained by an expand-

Table 3.6 *Amakudari* by Company Location

Company Location (Geographic Region)	1963	1972	1982	1992	1995
Kanto[a,b]	44.8	51.2	55.0	56.9	50.6
Non-Kanto[a]	55.2	48.8	45.0	43.1	49.4
Valid total[c]	148	164	251	200	176
	(89.7%)	(92.7%)	(93.7%)	(95.7%)	(92.6%)
Missing cases[d]	35	17	42	9	14
	(21.2%)	(9.6%)	(15.7%)	(4.3%)	(7.4%)
Total number of *amakudari*	165	177	268	209	190
	(100%)	(100%)	(100%)	(100%)	(100%)

Source: Information on number of *amakudari* and *amakudari* destinations (company name and location) from National Personnel Authority (1963, 1972, 1982, 1992, 1995).
[a] Percentage *amakudari*—the number of *amakudari* that went to companies in each region as a percentage of the total number of *amakudari*.
[b] Kanto refers to the greater Tokyo region, including Tokyo, Chiba, Gunma, Ibaraki, Kanagawa, Saitama, and Tochigi.
[c] Valid cases are those companies whose geographical locations we could locate.
[d] Missing cases refer to those companies whose geographical locations we could not locate.

ing relative employment in these firms, which was stable during this period. The data suggest an increasing concentration of *amakudari* placements in the larger firms.

Table 3.6 shows that company location and *amakudari* deviates from predictions by the resource dependency model. The Kanto area (the greater Tokyo region)[13] accounted for 44.8 percent of *amakudari* in 1963, but 50.6 percent in 1995. This pattern of *amakudari* placement has been relatively stable. *Amakudari* placements in the Kanto area have been consistently between 45 and 57 percent. Increasing *amakudari* placements outside Tokyo have not materialized. *Amakudari* placements are concentrated in Japan's center (Tokyo) and show no sign of the redistribution over time suggested by resource dependency.

Using a conservative estimate of *keiretsu* affiliation, table 3.7 examines the relationship between *amakudari* and *keiretsu* affiliation. In our data coding, less than five hundredths of 1 percent of

Table 3.7 *Amakudari* by *Keiretsu* Affiliation

	1963	1972	1982	1992	1995
Keiretsu-affiliated firms[a]	23.6	23.7	34.3	30.1	18.4
Nonaffiliated firms[a]	32.7	66.7	51.1	45.9	70.0
Semiprivate firms[a]	3.6	5.1	4.5	3.3	2.6
Missing cases (%)	43.6	9.6	14.6	20.1	8.9
Total number of *amakudari*	165	177	268	209	190

Source: Dodwell Marketing Consultants (1990); National Personnel Authority (1963, 1972, 1982, 1992, 1995); Nihon Keizai Shinbunsha ([*Kaisha nekan*] 1963, 1972, 1982, 1992, 1995; [*Kaisha sokan*] 1963, 1995; [*Kaisha sokan*: Mijojo] 1963, 1964, 1995).
[a] Percentage *amakudari*—the number of *amakudari* that went to *keiretsu*-affiliated firms, nonaffiliated firms, or semiprivate firms as a percentage of the total number of *amakudari*.
Information on the percentage of companies that are *keiretsu* affiliated or nonaffiliated is difficult to determine. According to *Industrial Groupings in Japan: The Anatomy of the Keiretsu*, in 1994–95 there were 2.2 million companies (excluding banks and insurance companies) of which 1,000, or 0.04 percent, were identified as belonging to the eight major (horizontal) industrial groups (Mitsubishi, Mitsui, Sumitomo, Fuyo, DKB, Sanwa, Tokai, and IBJ). Total employment for all companies was 37.3 million, of which 5.7 percent (or 2,109 million) is accounted for by the eight major industry groups (Dodwell Marketing Consultants 1994). For 1992, there were 34.5 million employees in 2 million companies. Of those, 5.6 percent (or 2 million employees) were accounted for the by eight major industrial groups (Dodwell Marketing Consultants 1992, 33). For 1982, there were approximately 2.8 million companies in Japan. Of these firms, about 6.2 percent of employment was accounted for by the major industrial groups (Dodwell Marketing Consultants 1982, 13). For 1973, estimates were 31.7 million Japanese employees and 2.0 million employees for major horizontal groupings (Dodwell Marketing Consultants 1973, 257).

firms were conservatively identified as *keiretsu*-affiliated firms through the 1980s and mid-1990s. *Keiretsu*-affiliated firms received 18–34 percent of *amakudari* placements between 1963 and 1995 (table 3.7). *Amakudari* to *keiretsu*-affiliated firms increased from 1963 to 1982, but declined to 18.4 percent in 1995. Although a disproportionate percentage of *amakudari* go to *keiretsu*-affiliated firms, the 1995 decline suggests a change in direction consistent with resource dependency predictions. *Keiretsu*-affiliated firms may have gained economic independence in the 1980s and become less receptive to *amakudari*.

Table 3.8 examines the distribution of *amakudari* by industries. In 1995, the agriculture, forestry, and fishery industries had no

Table 3.8 *Amakudari* by Industry

Industrial Sector	1963	1972	1982	1992	1995
Agriculture, forestry and fisheries[a]	3.0	0.6	1.9	1.0	0.0
Construction[a]	20.0	23.2	23.2	15.3	10.0
Manufacturing[a]	27.3	29.4	22.1	26.8	22.1
Utilities[a]	1.2	0.6	2.2	0.0	2.1
Transport and communication[a]	26.1	20.3	19.1	17.2	15.8
Trade, retail, and wholesale[a]	3.6	7.3	4.5	5.3	5.3
Banking and insurance[a]	15.2	15.3	16.9	23.0	25.3
Service[a]	2.4	3.4	10.1	12.0	19.5
Total number amakudari	165	177	267	209	190

Source: Prime Minister's Office (1990). Figures for *amakudari* do not always add up to 100 percent due to rounding. There are two missing cases in 1963.
[a] Percentage *amakudari*—the number of *amakudari* that went to a particular type of industry as a percentage of the total number of *amakudari*.

amakudari placements, and the utilities and the trade, retail, and wholesale industries accounted for only 2.1 and 5.3 percent of *amakudari*, respectively. In contrast, *amakudari* to transportation and communications accounted for 15.8 percent, to services 19.5 percent, and to banking and insurance 25.3 percent in 1995.

To control for industry growth, we checked employment data (ministry of Labor 1990, 1995). They show the share of employment in agriculture, which declined from 31.0 to 5.9 percent of overall employment over a thirty-year period while their share of *amakudari* declined from 3 percent in 1963 to zero in 1995. In contrast, expanding industries such as services, moving from 2.9 to 23.9 percent of employment during this period, increased their percentage of *amakudari* from 2.4 to 19.5 percent. There was an overall decrease in *amakudari* percentage in agriculture, transportation and communication, and construction. The manufacturing sector showed a slight decline. However, the banking and insurance and the service industries consistently increased their proportion of *amakudari* over time;

changes in these industries moved in the direction opposite that predicted by resource dependency.

The proportion of *amakudari* increased to large firms and were not concentrated in the non-Tokyo area but instead were concentrated in *keiretsu*-affiliated firms. In addition, *amakudari* placements to construction and to the agriculture, forestry, and fishery industries decreased; they increased in the service and the banking and insurance industries. *Amakudari* is concentrated more in larger, Kanto-based, and *keiretsu*-affiliated firms. The data we examined suggest *amakudari* is not a compensatory strategy of weaker firms but instead a way for larger powerful firms to maintain their positions. These findings further imply that *amakudari* is a power-based phenomenon rather than a market-based mechanism, as suggested by resource dependency.

These results are consistent with authors who contend that *amakudari* reflects elite movements within the iron triangle (Mulgen 1997; Wanner 2000; Prestowitz 1988). Resource dependency presumes the choosing capability of all ministries and corporations is equal and can be used to make firms more economically equal. This market equalization operates as if Hitachi and Sanwa Bank were equal to mid-size industrial and financial firms. Our results instead support a view of the institutional power of the larger industrial and financial firms. Further, these large firms relate to government through the most powerful ministries. It appears *amakudari* represents a disproportionate tie between the most powerful ministries and the larger *keiretsu* firms, Tokyo-based firms, and firms in the financial, service, and manufacturing industries.

Our results also support Ulrike Schaede's analysis of *amakudari* in the one hundred largest firms and reports by Cutts (1997) regarding *amakudari* concentration levels across different industries. Schaede found *amakudari* on the boards of over 75 percent of the expanding electronics, auto, steel, and construction firms among the one hundred largest firms, yet fewer than one-half of commercial banking, insurance, and investment banking firms had *amakudari* on their boards. This does not necessarily mean that *amakudari* are thin or inconspicuous in the financial sectors. Cutts (1997, 197) reported 6 percent of board-level executives in banking and securities industries in 1991 were ex-officials from either the MOF or Bank of Japan (BOJ).[14] This is a much higher level than the 2 percent found overall in the private sector. In 1994, *amakudari* from the MOF occupied the top position at the Tokyo Stock Exchange, Export-Import Bank of Japan, National Finance Corporation, Bank of Yokohama, and BOJ. In 1993, MOF *amakudari* occupied the top position at the Fair Trade Commission, Overseas Economic Cooperation Fund, and Japan Development Bank. Further, 26 percent of the presidents of Japan's 150 private banks had come either from the MOF or BOJ in 1993. This, of course, does not take into account the many MOF officials who serve as auditors, advisers to the board, and councillors to the board or the numerous officials who retire to lower administrative positions.

Amakudari and Regulation

The prevailing wisdom suggests a strong positive relationship between regulation and *amakudari*. By implication, if regulation were decreased or eliminated, *amakudari* would decrease or cease to exist. Regulation is viewed as creating the need for *amakudari* personnel to interpret regulations for private firms.[15] Continuing foreign pressures to lower trade barriers and deregulate domestic markets are seen as weakening the linkages between the bureaucracy and domestic markets. Increasing pressures to reduce the trade surplus, to ease inspection and certification rules for foreign goods, and to shift from a producer- to a more consumer-oriented society should undermine *amakudari* (Johnson 1974; do Rososario 1993; Schaede 1995; Farrell 1999). And Japan's possible decreasing need to protect its domestic industries should reduce the usefulness of *amakudari* to private firms.

For many authors, regulation and *amakudari* are the pathological outcomes of state intervention in the natural prerogatives of the market. Regulation is a government infringement on the self-regulating nature of private-sector firms, whereas *amakudari* compromises the autonomy of the labor market choices of private companies. *Amakudari* and regulation operate as hidden barriers to entry into lucrative Japanese markets or "a hindrance to the opening up of Japan (do Rosario 1993, 55)."[16]

For other authors, regulation is one mechanism used by government to stabilize the economy. Regulation is viewed as both the cause and consequence of the harmony and coordination between private interests and the bureaucracy. This argument suggests that *amakudari,* working in conjunction with industry regulation, provides the basis to stabilize sunset (or declining) industries. Contrary to this position, the evidence presented in the previous section does not confirm the notion that *amakudari* disproportionately go to sunset industries.

Still others point to a gap between the pressures for administrative reform and deregulation and the actual operational reform and deregulation of the number of licenses administered by the ministries (e.g., Carlile and Tilton 1998; Mulgen 1997; Wanner 2000). They suggest that the causal link between actual regulation and *amakudari* may be reversed. That is, *amakudari* mediates the relationship between formal deregulation initiatives and actual reductions in the number of operation regulations. Although media criticism has been continuous and increasing throughout the 1990s, the reforms have had the effect of increasing the MOF's power over the financial sector by enhancing the MOF's licensing authority and putting a premium on access to new regulatory information (Norville 1998, 128). The MOF's life-and-death authority was dramatized by the failure of large financial institutions such as Hokkaido Takushoku Bank and Yamaichi Securities Company in 1997. The ministry's threat to let the market punish the inefficient has enhanced its power over troubled financial institutions. Finally, the ministries' interests in protecting public corporations and the businesses' interests in protecting their sectors by keeping newcomers out of their markets provide a confluence of iron-triangle interests that frustrates deregulation initiatives.

The interpretation of the meaning of aggregate regulations is difficult. Our discussions with officials at the Management and Coordination Agency (MCA) led to questions about the measurement of regulation data. The number of regulations in an industry does not necessarily represent the degree of constraint on private-sector operations; the additional regulations may constitute repeals of previous regulations. Some regulations represent more intensive restrictions or constraints on private-sector operations, constraining activities more aggressively than others, but others vary in their scope or extent of application. This suggests that some regulations apply to broader or more narrowly defined sets of operations. This means that using the number of regulations administered by a ministry to measure the extent of constraint exercised over industry operations is questionable. Yet MCA officials indicated that these data represent the first attempt to systematically quantify regulation over time. Having stated our reservations, we now proceed to analyze this data and its correspondence with *amakudari*.

Table 3.9 shows that the number of regulations administered by twenty-three ministries and agencies increased from 1985 to 1994. There was an average increase of thirty-nine regulations per ministry and agency (a 19 percent increase) between 1985 and 1994.

Table 3.10 converts the data on the number of regulations to percentage changes and compares them with the percentage changes in the number of *amakudari* for the corresponding ministries and agencies, using NPA data for the same period (1985–94).

If the number of regulations and *amakudari* are directly related and not spurious, we expect changes in regulations to be positively related to changes in *amakudari*. Of the fourteen ministries and agencies for which we have data for changes in both *amakudari* and regulation between 1985 and 1994, only five changed in the predicted direction: Education, the MITI, Transport, the National Police Agency, and the Okinawa Development Agency. Eight ministries and agencies changed in the direction opposite to that predicted: the MOF, Health and Welfare, Posts and Telecommunications, Construction, Agriculture, Labor, the Management and Coordination Agency, and the Hokkaido Development Agency. No direction was apparent for the Science and Technology Agency.

The data in table 3.10 suggest that the regulation thesis has limited application to *amakudari*. *Amakudari* is associated with the number of regulations in the sectors regulated by the MITI, Education, Transport, Police, and the Okinawa Development Agency only. The MITI and Transport administer large numbers of regulations and place large numbers of *amakudari*. As they decreased their regulations between 1985 and 1994, they decreased the number of *amakudari* they placed. In contrast, the MOF, Construction, Agriculture, and Health and Welfare also administer large numbers of regulations, but as these ministries increased their numbers of regulations between 1985 and 1994, they decreased their *amakudari* placements. Again, this suggests *amakudari* placements might have a different logic for these ministries. Or, alternatively, the increased number of regulations does not represent the increased constraint over the operations of these industries; rather, the increased regulations are, in practice, repeals of existing regulations.

Table 3.9 Number of Regulations by Ministry and Agency[a]

Ministry/Agency	1985	1988	1991	1994
Prime Minister's Office	27	29	32	32
Fair Trade Commission	26	26	26	26
National Police Agency	81	97	99	144
MCA	29	29	34	35
Hokkaido Development Agency	26	28	31	31
Defense Agency	26	28	31	31
Economic Planning Agency	26	26	31	31
STA	218	263	298	301
Environment Agency	149	156	164	194
Okinawa Development Agency	27	37	32	32
National Land Agency	81	81	86	88
MOJ	146	148	154	172
Foreign Affairs	37	39	46	50
MOF	1,116	1,143	1,210	1,391
Education	310	317	312	327
MHW	936	985	1,106	1,246
MOA	1,263	1,270	1,315	1,419
MITI	1,870	1,863	1,916	1,769
MOT	2,017	1,977	1,966	1,700
MPT	265	379	308	291
Labor	532	563	565	629
MOC	742	776	842	879
Home Affairs	104	108	113	127
Total number	10,054	10,288	10,717	10,945

Source: Management and Coordination Agency (1995, app., 3).
[a] MCA, Management and Coordination Agency; MHW, Ministry of Health and Welfare; MITI, Ministry of International Trade and Industry; MOA, Ministry of Agriculture, Forestry, and Fisheries; MOC, Ministry of Construction; MOF, Ministry of Finance; MOJ, Ministry of Justice; MOT, Ministry of Transport; MPT, Ministry of Posts and Telecommunications; STA, Science and Technology Agency.

In the aggregate, neither the resource dependency nor the regulation thesis holds up under examination. A closer inspection of the data, however, suggests that both theses have merit when applied to certain ministries and industries. *Amakudari* from various ministries to the relevant industries operate with different logics. Regulation is one type of *amakudari* logic; resource dependency is another. Our analysis suggests that *amakudari* is a complex multidimensional

Table 3.10 Correspondence between Percentage Changes in Regulation and *Amakudari* Placements, 1985–1994[a]

Ministry/Agency	Number of Regulations[b]	Incidence of *Amakudari*[b]	Confirming
Education	0.05	0.18	Yes
MITI	−0.05	−0.25	Yes
MOT	−0.16	−0.45	Yes
National Police Agency	0.78	1.67	Yes
Okinawa Development Agency	0.19	1.00	Yes
MOF	0.25	−0.03	No
MHW	0.33	−0.50	No
MPT	0.10	−0.41	No
MOC	0.10	−0.52	No
MOA	0.12	−0.55	No
Labor	0.18	−0.75	No
MCA	0.21	−0.50	No
Hokkaido Development Agency	0.19	−0.80	No
STA	0.38	0.00	—

[a] Only fourteen ministries and agencies had information on both regulation and *amakudari*. MCA, Management and Coordination Agency; MHW, Ministry of Health and Welfare; MITI, Ministry of International Trade and Industry; MOA, Ministry of Agriculture, Forestry, and Fisheries; MOC, Ministry of Construction; MOF, Ministry of Finance; MOT, Ministry of Transport; MPT, Ministry of Posts and Telecommunications; STA, Science and Technology Agency.
[b] Percentage of change.

phenomenon. The MITI, Ministry of Tranport, National Police Agency, and even MOF (for which, remember, regulation increased while *amakudari* was close to being flat and *amakudari* placements to the banking and insurance industry expanded) operate according to the logic of regulation—*amakudari* results from the regulatory authority of these ministries because *amakudari* personnel are used to interpret regulations and to provide insurance against uncertainties. On the other hand, the Ministries of Construction, Agriculture, and Posts and Telecommunications showed decreasing *amakudari* but increasing regulation. This relationship does not support the regulation thesis, but it does not preclude the resource dependency thesis. In short, *amakudari* helps interpret regulations for some industrial sectors, but in other sectors it helps private companies gain strategic information and grants from the ministries.

Our examination of the overall trend in the incidence of *amakudari* (based on the NPA data) shows that the number of *amakudari* declined after 1985, in particular after 1995. But prevalence data from the boards of listed private firms indicates a stable distribution of *amakudari* at 2 percent over time. In addition, the distribution of *amakudari* among the one hundred largest firms was much higher. Our inspection of the prevalence data reveals a pattern that is not expected from the NPA data. Both the incidence and prevalence data on *amakudari* by ministry indicates that the *amakudari* networks are not a homogenous collection of ministries more or less equal to one another. Rather, there is a hierarchy of *amakudari* among ministries, with linkages between the bureaucracy and private sector manifesting different logics.

Our analysis suggests three elaborations of the structure and processes of *amakudari*. First, the MOF is a central point in the path of *amakudari* to the private sector. There is also a concentration of *amakudari* among three ministries (MOF including the Tax Agency, MITI, and Construction) throughout the period in both the incidence and prevalence data.

Second, our analysis of the resource dependency model suggests that *amakudari* is associated with larger firms, *keiretsu*-affiliated firms, firms located in the Kanto area, and firms in the banking, insurance, and service industries with expanding proportions of employment. *Amakudari* creates a linkage between the most powerful segments of the bureaucracy and the more established segments of the private sector. The dominant ministries (those having a large number of *amakudari*) place their ex-officials among the most powerful and well-situated corporations in the private sector. This substantiates suggestions that *amakudari* is "the glue of the iron triangle" (Prestowitz 1988, 117).

Finally, our analysis of the association of *amakudari* and regulation suggests the multidimensional logic of *amakudari*. The MITI, Education, Transport, the National Police Agency, and the Okinawa Development Agency operate with a regulation-*amakudari* logic, whereas other ministries follow the resource dependency logic. Clearly, there is a heterogeneity of relations between the ministries and the private sector.

Amakudari is one type of relationship in the multiplex of relationships between the bureaucracy and society. The decline in the number of *amakudari* since 1985 was a response to government reform and public criticism. Greater constraints exerted on *amakudari* placements to the private sector, in turn, led the ministries to substitute other landing positions (e.g., *yokosuberi*) for their retirees.

4 *Yokosuberi* and Public Corporations

Yokosuberi is the postretirement path of high-ranking bureaucrats to public corporations. Recall that there was a steep decline (see chap. 3) in the annual incidence of *amakudari* after 1985 (particularly after 1995), even though the prevalence rates of ex-bureaucrats on private-sector boards of directors were relatively high and stable; this raises the issue of other routes to the private sector. In this chapter, we explore the public sector, examining the discrepancy between the NPA incidence data and the total number of bureaucrats leaving the central ministries.

Approximately 1,700 high-ranking bureaucrats (those reaching the level of section chief or above) each leave the bureaucracy early (in their fifties) and take positions in the private and public corporations, industrial associations, or the political world.[1] Yet the NPA records only a fraction of that number. Where do these bureaucrats go upon retirement? The NPA reported sixty-two *amakudari* in 1999 and a record low forty in 2000, but these numbers do not include officials hired by public corporations. A government report published in December 2000 (reported in *Japan Times*, 22 December 2000) revealed that 538 high-ranking bureaucrats (at the level of division chief or above) retired between August 1999 and August 2000. Of these, 485 (90 percent) were hired within three months of retirement and 259 of those 485 (53.4 percent) took positions in public corporations as advisers, managing directors, and senior managing directors.

The public sector provides a context in which the ministries connect with the private sector. Many private firms rely on resources from public-sector corporations, which blurs the distinction between the public and private sectors. These resources include contracts, loans, subsidies, and regulatory protection that presage personnel movements from both the ministries and the public sector.

The public sector itself receives personnel from the ministries in the form of *yokosuberi*, which is less regulated and less visible than *amakudari*. An examination of this path allows the investigation of how the various ministries connect to the public sector. The public sector integrates the central ministries into society financially and politically. Public corporations are the "arms and legs" of the central ministries, funded by the central ministries and controlled through *yokosuberi* placements on their boards of directors. Their operating costs are estimated to be as high as 22 percent of GDP (Hayashi 1997, 195). *Yokosuberi* also represents an additional set of linchpins in the coordination and mediation of relations between ministries and the private sector.

The public sector has been the target of administrative reform. To reassure the public that something is being done, reform efforts have taken the form of symbolic gestures toward democratic and free-market restructuring with little content. We examine the extent to which efforts to reform the financing and administration of public corporations are simply *koromogae* (changing clothes).

This chapter examines two types of public corporations and the patterns of *yokosuberi* to each and then compares the patterns of *yokosuberi* and *amakudari*. Our case study, the Japan National Petroleum Corporation (JNPC), illustrates the matrix of organizations dependent on public corporations and the role of *yokosuberi* in linking the ministries, public corporations, and private-sector firms.

Rationale for Public Organizations

The public sector is lodged between the bureaucracy and the private sector and provides a linkage of control and coordination, money, and political influence. Scholars often overlook the Japanese public sector because it has little or no analog in the U.S. political economy. At best, the Japanese public sector is treated as a residual category and ignored. Alternatively, there is a tendency to treat the public sector as a pathological intervention into market operations because of popular laissez-faire notions of economics and a tradition of the separation of economic and political activities. Yet in Japan the public sector represents an instrument of the bureaucracy. What is

significant beyond formal and institutional interventions into the
private sector is how the public sector becomes a vehicle for the
close interaction among bureaucratic, political, and private-sector
interests.

Public corporations were created as a hybrid corporation (part
government, part private corporation), combining the advantages of
private-sector initiative and flexibility with government coordination and stability.[2] Initially, public corporations were established to
control and coordinate the economy in the war effort. Subsequent
impetus to create public corporations resulted from strict limits on
the size of government combined with renewed efforts to catch up
with the West. These functions included the provision of services
(e.g., telegraph and telephone service, railway transportation, and
international air transport), housing and highway construction,
promotion of small- and medium-size enterprises, and energy
development. They are more or less closely tethered to government
ministries, but operate with considerable independence from the
Diet. Specific ministries and specific public corporations are aligned
through *yokosuberi* to the boards of directors of public corporations.
These alignments follow from Japan's style of vertical administration (*tatewari gyosei*) and sectoralism. The important feature of
vertical administration is the twin process of competition among
ministries for independence while ministries work to ensconce themselves in sectors of Japanese society. Most ministries have territory
over which they exercise supervision, and public corporations are a
key ingredient of a ministry's territory. Conflicts between ministries
over jurisdictions (*nawabari arasoi*) are recognized as some of the
most significant features in the government (Johnson 1978, 182–83;
Keehn 1990).

Specific ministries supervise the business conduct of public corporations. The mode of ministry supervision and the power of public
corporations differ according to their functions.[3] One tool of control
and political independence is funding for public corporations, which
are financed by the national government primarily through the Fiscal
Investment and Loan Program (FILP) or *zaisei toushi* (commonly
referred to as *zaito*). FILP is often dubbed the second budget because
its amounts are approximately two-thirds the size of the formal
(general) budget. For example, FILP funds exceeded ¥400 trillion
in 1994.

FILP funds are collected from postal savings and welfare annuity insurance and are managed by the MOF's Trust Fund Bureau. The MOF lends the funds to public and private companies, mainly to promote the construction of houses and social infrastructure[4] (IPMS Group 1994, 104). FILP is insulated from many mechanisms of parliamentary supervision. For example, the lending programs of the *tokushu hojin* are not included in the government budget submitted to the Diet, providing the controlling ministries and public corporations with considerable policymaking freedom. Thus, the decision-making process is more dispersed and decentralized for FILP than for the regular national budget (Noguchi 1995, 262–68). This measure of independence from the Diet is also a source of the criticism about public corporations; for example, many public corporations outlive their original missions. Since the rising government deficit of the 1970s, the public sector has been subjected to a series of political efforts at reform and reorganization.

Yokosuberi is one tool of ministry control and accountability. Ministries also have the power to supervise the operations of public corporations, appoint or authorize the selection of directors to the boards, collect reports, and make inspections. Most public corporations must confer with the MOF concerning financial affairs. *Yokosuberi* placements operate as compliance mechanisms, linking public corporations to the central ministries by providing a tool for monitoring the operations of public corporations.

The public sector represents a confluence of interests as part of the complex apparatus that brings together the interests of bureaucrats, politicians, and business (the iron triangle), providing a formidable obstruction to deregulation and reform. Politicians lack enthusiasm for deregulation and reform because they depend on private-sector interests that have benefited from regulations administered by public corporations. These regulations provide selective advantages to big and small manufacturing, the service sector, and primary industry. These business interests rely on *zoku* politicians (policy specialists) to broker the maintenance and expansion of these benefits. Deregulation threatens the rights and benefits of these key private-sector political support groups, with the concomitant political costs.

For ministries, regulation represents a core element of bureaucratic control and ministry expenditures. Public corporations funded through FILP, general accounts, and special budgets provide substantial *yokosuberi* locations for top bureaucrats. Deregulation, in the form of the privatization of public corporations, reduces ministry control over industry, diminishes ministry budgets, and cuts back on the available *yokosuberi* posts for senior bureaucrats.

Public Organizations: The Hidden Aspects of the Bureaucracy

Public corporations are sometimes called *hi-eiri hojin* (nonprofit organizations) and *koeki hojin* (public organizations), but this distinction is ambiguous.[5] Public corporations are divided into three broad categories (see table 4.1). The first category contains two classes of special legal entities: *tokushu hojin* and *ninka hojin*. *Tokushu hojin*, for example, were established by a 1936 law and created by a special act of the Diet. The second category of public corporations contains *zaidan* and *shadan hojin* that are guided by Minpo, the civil code. The third category includes other public corporations that are created by specific laws, such as educational, medical, social welfare, and religious organizations. To this category, we also add *dokuritsu gyosei hojin* (independent administrative organizations), created by a 1999 law as part of administrative reform of 1996.[6]

Yokosuberi operates across these categories of public corporations. We focus here on *tokushu hojin* and on *zaidan* and *shadan hojin*. These two types of public corporations are empirically tractable (i.e., systematic data exist). *Tokushu hojin* are the most powerful elements in the public sector, but a comparison with the lesser *zaidan* and *shadan hojin* illustrates the *yokosuberi* paths among particular ministries.

Public corporations make the Japanese government appear smaller than it actually is. In 1995, the total number of public employees (*komuin*) of the central and local governments was 4.5 million—1.16 million for the central government and 3.34 million for the local governments (Gyosei Kanri Center 1996, 41). Many cross-national comparisons of the size of central governments as a percentage of total employment have ranked Japan at the bottom of all industrialized countries.[7] There are approximately 750,000 employees of public corporations: 550,000 in *tokushu hojin* and 200,000 in *zaidan* and *shadan hojin*. Even with the addition of these employees, Japan still ranks at or near the bottom compared to other Organization for

Table 4.1 Types of Public Corporations

	1996	1998	2000	2001	Legal Basis
Special legal entities[a]					
Tokushu hojin	92	85	—	77	1936 law
Ninka hojin	—	87	—	—	
Public corporations (narrowly defined)	26,089[b]	—	26,264	—	
Zaidan hojin	—	—	13,375	—	
Shadan hojin	—	—	12,889	—	
Other public organizations					
Social welfare					1951 social welfare law
Educational					1947 educational law
Religious					1951 religional organization law
Medical					1948 medical organization law
Dokuritsu gyosei hojin	—	—	—	57	1999 law

Source: Hayashi and Iriyama (1997, 6); Management and Coordination Ministry (2001, 2, 23); Matsubara (1995, 80).

[a] According to Matsubara (1995, 80), there is no substantial difference between *tokushu hojin* and *ninka hojin*. High-profile examples of *ninka hojin* include the Bank of Japan, pension funds for a variety of industrial groups, professional groups, and local government employee unions. *Ninka hojin* are not subject to inspection by the Management and Coordination Agency (see http://www.soumu.go.jp).
[b] Approximately 6,815 were established by central ministry approval.
[c] *Dokuritsu gyosei hojin* includes museums, medical, educational, and research institutions.

Economic Cooperation and Development (OECD) countries (Hayashi and Iriyama 1997).

A second important feature of public corporations is that the primary source of funding among the large *tokushu hojin* comes from FILP funds or *zaito*. In 2001, FILP funds exceeded ¥32 trillion or 6.5 percent of the GDP, down from 8.2 percent of the GDP in 1994

(Nihon Keizai Shinbunsha 2001, 29; Noguchi 1995, 267).[8] In no other industrial country do such huge public funds exist (Matsubara 1995). These funds are often not counted in comparative statistics on government disbursements or government costs as a percentage of GDP (Shibata 1993; Muramatsu 1997). Further, FILP's total operating costs represent a little over 11 percent of GDP; when loans, investments, subsidies, and other forms of income are included, the real total operating costs are approximately twice that estimate or almost 22 percent of GDP (Hayashi 1997, 195).

The flows of money and personnel are further obscured by the fact that many *tokushu hojin* have their own subsidiaries and affiliates. Some *tokushu hojin* have more than twenty subsidiaries, which are either public corporations (*zaidan* or *shadan hojin*) or private companies. Over this tangle of personnel, funding flows, and corporate affiliations hangs a financial structure that is enormous and opaque. The hidden aspects of public corporations compound the ambiguity in the kinds of public corporations. On the surface, public corporations represent a substantial extension of the bureaucracy in terms of personnel and budget; yet underneath, these attributes are obscure circuits of money and personnel.

Tokushu Hojin

There are seven classes of *tokushu hojin*: *kodan, gigyodan, koko, kinko* and *ginko, eidan, tokushu kaisha*, and other. The first *tokushu hojin* was created in 1922. After World War II, various *tokushu hojin* were established to exercise control over the economy (e.g., the Foodstuff Distribution Public Corporation). These were abolished when their missions were accomplished and the economic situation changed. Between 1946 and 1955, however, new large *tokushu hojin* were established, such as the Japanese National Railways (JNR) in 1949, the Japan Tobacco Corporation in 1949, the Nippon Telegraph and Telephone Corporation (NTT) in 1952, and Japan Airline Corporation (JAL) in 1953 (Management and Coordination Agency, 1995, 592). These operations had previously been under the direct management of the government but were spun off into the public sector. Additional infrastructural *tokushu hojin* (*kodan*) were established, such as the Electric Power Development Company in 1952 and Japan National Highway Corporation in 1956. Financial *tokushu hojin* (*koko* and *ginko*) were also established for aiding imports and exports, industrial development, small- and medium-size businesses, agriculture, forestry, fisheries, and housing construction (e.g., Japan Impor and Export Bank 1950; Japan Development Bank 1951; and Japan Housing Loan Corporation 1950). The number of *tokushu hojin* rose during the late 1950s and 1960s as the government created them to keep the central bureaucracy's size constant, from 46 *tokushu hojin* after the war to 113 by 1967. Several attempts to reorganize and restructure these organizations decreased the number to eighty-five in 1998 and seventy-seven in 2001. In 1986, the cabinet recommended that all *tokushu hojin* be subject to inspection by the MCA, but there was lax management of funds and limited disclosure of their operations. According to Satoru Matsubara (1995, 32), fifty-four out of ninety-two *tokushu hojin* did not make assessments of their business operations in 1991.

Tokushu hojin can be seen as a sphere of money and personnel, carved up among specific controlling ministries. Table 4.2 shows the breakdown of *tokushu hojin* operating costs by the top ten controlling ministries/agencies in 1995. The MOF accounts for the largest

Table 4.2 Scale of *Tokushu Hojin* by Controlling Ministry, 1995[a]

Rank	Entity	Total Operating Costs (trillions of yen)	Number of Employees
1	MOF	11 ($110 billion)	40,230
2	MOT	10 ($100 billion)	216,890
3	MITI	8.1 ($81 billion)	6,738
4	Small and Medium Enterprises Agency	8.1 ($81 billion)	8,205
5	MOC	8 ($80 billion)	31,682
6	MPT	7.6 ($76 billion)	214,335
7	MOA	5.8 ($58 billion)	7,306
8	Labor	5.7 ($57 billion)	21,586
9	Hokkaido Development Agency	3.1 ($31 billion)	288
10	MHW	3.0 ($30 billion)	9,538
Total		70.4[b] ($704 billion)	556,798
Total for all (92) tokushu hojin		106 ($1.06 trillion)	570,000

Source: Hayashi and Iriyama (1997, 6).
[a] In 1995 Japan's GDP was ¥488.5 trillion ($4.89 trillion). For simplicity of conversion, $1 to ¥100 is used. MHW, Ministry of Health and Welfare; MITI, Ministry of International Trade and Industry; MOA, Ministry of Agriculture, Forestry, and Fisheries; MOC, Ministry of Construction; MOF, Ministry of Finance; MOT, Ministry of Transport; MPT, Ministry of Posts and Telecommunications.
[b] This includes operating expenses, loans, investments in housing, land, facilities, and other subsidies.

share, followed by Transport, Construction, the MITI, and the Small and Medium Enterprises Agency. In 1995, the top ten ministries and agencies accounted for ¥70.4 trillion in operating costs and employed 556,000 people (out of a total of ¥106 trillion and 570,000 employees), representing 66 percent of the total costs of *tokushu hojin* and 98 percent of *tokushu hojin* personnel.

Ministry officials control appointments to the boards of directors of public corporations and thus we expect a high percentage of board members to be ex-ministry officials, *yokosuberi*. However, in 1979 the cabinet made a recommendation limiting *yokosuberi* to one-half the board positions of any *tokushu hojin*.[9] Since then, criticisms of *yokosuberi* to *tokushu hojin* have intensified, including the call for dismantling *tokushu hojin* and complete privatization. Table 4.3 shows a sharp decline in *yokosuberi* on the boards of directors of

Table 4.3 *Yokosuberi* to *Tokushu Hojin* (Board of Director Positions)

Year	Number of Tokushu Hojin[a]	Total Directors (a)	Number of Yokosuberi (b)	Yokosuberi (b/a) (%)
1967	38	276	214	77.5
1969	42	263	184	70.3
1971	43	255	188	73.7
1973	61	384	303	79.2
1975	66	433	350	80.8
1977	65	397	315	79.3
1979	75	454	353	77.7
1981	109	772	546	70.7
1983	99	727	477	65.6
1985	99	704	464	65.9
1987	87	670	430	64.2
1989	92	750	433	57.8
1991	92	764	435	56.9
1993	92	821	431	52.5
1998	85	811	359	44.3

Source: Seiroren (1994). *Seiroren Amakudari hakusho*. Values for 1998 from Seiroren 1994 internal document.
[a] Values for 1967–79 indicate the number of *tokushu hojin* that participated in Seiroren's survey.
Values for 1981–98 indicate the total number of *tokushu hojin*. The total number of *tokushu hojin* was 77 in 2001.

tokushu hojin from 77.5 percent in 1967 to 44.3 percent in 1998.[10] This pattern gives the appearance of conformity to the cabinet recommendation of 1979.

If we examine the mix of directors' backgrounds by class of *tokushu hojin*, we see considerable variation in *yokosuberi* and the degree of dependence on ministries (table 4.4). In 1998, the overall percentage of *yokosuberi* on the boards of 85 *tokushu hojin* was 44.3 percent, yet if we exclude Japan Railways (JR; formerly, JNR), the remaining seventy-nine *tokushu hojin* had 52.4 percent *yokosuberi*. If we exclude the group of twelve *tokushu kaisha*, the percentage of *yokosuberi* on the boards of the remaining seventy-three *tokushu hojin* was 60.6 percent. The mix of directors' backgrounds differs by type of *tokushu hojin*, indicating a varying degree of dependence of the *tokushu hojin* on the ministries. On one side, the twenty-nine *kodan* and *jigyodan* have approximately 70 percent of the board positions as *yokosuberi* from the central ministries. These are older public corporations and their sources of capital are closely tied to the central government (both FILP and subsidies from the general budget). On the other end of the continuum are *tokushu kaisha* such as JR. *Tokushu kaisha* are very much like ordinary stock-holding private firms except that the government has a controlling share. After World War II, the old Ministry of Railways (Testudo-sho) and JNR were created. JNR continued to assert its independence (and opposed *amakudari*) from the Ministry of Transport, which had replaced the Ministry of Railways. Members of the boards of directors from inside the companies (55 percent) dominate the boards of the *tokushu kaisha*, with as little as 12.9 percent coming from the central ministries.

The linkages between the ministries and *tokushu hojin* are more like latticework than the spokes of a wheel. Underneath this tightly laced relationship between the central ministries and *tokushu hojin* exists a complex web of *yokosuberi* relationships between specific ministries and specific *tokushu hojin*. Positions on the boards of directors are considered the property of a particular ministry and they are nonnegotiable. When one ex-bureaucrat leaves his board position, another ex-bureaucrat from the same ministry replaces him. Several ministries, however, may be present on the same board:

> informal norms have developed governing the assignments of available positions in a single corporation to various ministries. Sometimes these allocations are negotiated by the sponsoring ministry and

Table 4.4 Composition of Boards of Directors by Category of *Tokushu Hojin*, 1998[a]

	Number of *Tokushu Hojin*	Number of Directors	Origins of Directors					
			Central Ministries	Local Government	Internal	Private Sector	Other	N.A.
Kodan	12	111 (100)	80 (72.1)	6 (5.4)	22 (19.8)	0 (0.0)	3 (2.7)	0 (0.0)
Jigyodan	17	125 (100)	85 (68)	0 (0.0)	29 (23.2)	6 (4.8)	2 (1.6)	3 (2.4)
Koko	9	60 (100)	37 (61.8)	1 (1.7)	20 (33.3)	0 (0.0)	0 (0.0)	2 (3.3)
Special banks	3	30 (100)	11 (36.7)	0 (0.0)	16 (53.3)	0 (0.0)	3 (10.0)	0 (0.0)
Eidan	1	13 (100)	5 (38.5)	2 (15.4)	5 (38.5)	0 (0.0)	0 (0.0)	1 (7.7)
Tokushu kaisha	12	278 (100)	36 (12.9)	1 (0.4)	154 (55.4)	11 (4.0)	0 (0.0)	76 (27.3)
Other	31	194 (100)	105 (54.1)	8 (4.1)	47 (24.2)	5 (2.6)	5 (2.6)	24 (12.4)
Total	85	811 (100)	359 (44.3)	18 (2.2)	293 (36.1)	22 (2.7)	13 (1.6)	106 (13.1)
Excluding JR	79	643 (100)	337 (52.4)	18 (2.8)	189 (29.4)	17 (2.6)	13 (2.0)	69 (10.7)
Excluding all *tokushu kaisha*	73	533 (100)	323 (60.6)	17 (3.2)	139 (26.1)	11 (2.1)	13 (2.4)	30 (5.6)

Source: Seiroren 1998 internal document.
[a] Numbers in parentheses are percentages.
JR, Japan Railways (there are six JR); N.A., not assertained.

the Budget Bureau of the Ministry of Finance when the proposal to set up a new corporation comes under budgetary review. For example, out of eleven executive positions in the Housing Loan Corporation (president, vice-president, seven directors, and two auditors), six are reserved for *amakudari* [*yokosuberi*] bureaucrats: the Ministry of Construction controls the presidency, Finance names the vice-president, Construction supplies two directors, and the Prime Minister's Office and the Economic Planning Agency are allowed to send one director each. (Johnson 1978, 112)

Thus a particular ministry does not necessarily have exclusive control over a particular *tokushu hojin*.

To investigate these complex relations between the central ministries and *tokushu hojin*, we ranked the ministries by the distribution (allocation) of *yokosuberi* to the boards of directors for all ninety-two *tokushu hojin* in 1995 (table 4.5). Some *tokushu hojin* receive *yokosuberi* from only a single ministry, whereas others receive *yokosuberi* from multiple ministries. When a board of directors of a *tokushu hojin* has *yokosuberi* from multiple ministries, one ministry's *yokosuberi* may dominate the board or possibly no one ministry dominates the board.

Table 4.5 shows the three types of ministry control over a *tokushu hojin* board. First, a ministry participates in the board of directors of a *tokushu hojin* through *yokosuberi* on the board. The percentage of *yokosuberi* placements by a ministry on any board indicates the scope of the relationship between the particular ministry and *tokushu hojin*; for example, the Ministry of Transport participates on the boards of directors of twenty-one *tokushu hojin*, meaning it has the broadest scope of participation with its ex-officials sitting on the largest number of *tokushu hojin*. Second, a ministry may dominate a board of directors by controlling the majority of positions for a particular *tokushu hojin*. The Ministry of Transport dominates sixteen of the twenty-one *tokushu hojin* in which it participates. Third, a ministry may monopolize all the positions on the board of directors of a *tokushu hojin*: Transport monopolizes the boards of directors of fourteen of the twenty-one *tokushu hojin* in which it participates. The values for dominates and monopolizes give the best sense of the degree of control over *tokushu hojin*. The large number listed for the MOF's participation and the small numbers for dominating and monopolizing suggest the ministry's primary roles are related to the flow of financing, whereas other ministries'

Table 4.5 *Tokushu Hojin* by Ministry Control, 1995[a]

Rank	Ministry/Agency	Number of *Tokushu Hojin* That the Ministry		
		Participates	Dominates	Monopolizes
1	MOT	21	16	14
2	MITI	18	13	10
3	MOF	14	4	4
4	MOA	13	8	7
5	MOC	11	7	4
6	MHW	9	7	5
7	Education	8	8	7
8	Labor	6	5	5
	STA	6	6	4
	MPT	6	4	4
11	National Land Agency	4	3	0
12	Home Affairs	3	2	1
13	Economic Planning Agency	2	2	2
	Foreign Affairs	2	2	1
	Environment Agency	2	2	0
	MCA	2	1	0
17	Hokkaido Development Agency	1	1	0
	Okinawa Development Agency	1	1	0

Source: Management and Coordination Agency (1996).
[a] MCA, Management and Coordination Agency; MHW, Ministry of Health and Welfare; MITI, Ministry of International Trade and Industry; MOA, Ministry of Agriculture, Forestry, and Fisheries; MOC, Ministry of Construction; MOF, Ministry of Finance; MOT, Ministry of Transport; MPT, Ministry of Posts and Telecommunications; STA, Science and Technology Agency.

yokosuberi on these boards administer the policy directions of *tokushu hojin*.

When the domain of operations of a *tokushu hojin* cuts across the functions of different ministries (e.g., highways and airports are jurisdictions of both the Ministries of Construction and Transport), detailed and thorough negotiations occur before any public corporation structure is set. "The allocation usually depends on each ministry's relation to the sponsoring ministry and on the jurisdiction of the new public corporation" (Johnson 1974, 113).[11] Vice ministers from multiple ministries make sure their ministry gets its share of positions when a new public corporation is created. The purpose of participation by multiple ministries on a board is twofold. First, operations will be smoother, especially when the domain of operations of the public corporation has mixed functions. Second, this mixture of *yokosuberi* from different ministries on the same *tokushu hojin* board represents a larger issue involving the nature of relationships between ministries and public corporations. *Yokosuberi* to *tokushu hojin* is neither homogeneous nor random, nor is this *yokosuberi* distribution the exclusive linkage between the controlling ministry and the *tokushu hojin*. Rather, the data in table 4.5 suggest a distribution of *yokosuberi* to *tokushu hojin* that is a combination of exclusive and mixed relationships. In the latter case, the boards of directors of these *tokushu hojin* provide locations for multiple ministries to work out their interests. These board locations also include representatives of other interests.

The distribution of *yokosuberi* by economic and social ministries sheds light on whether *yokosuberi* is an alternative to *amakudari* for the social ministries. Table 4.6 provides a ranking of ministries and agencies by the number of *yokosuberi* they place. It shows the relatively stable dominance of the economic ministries over time. In 1973, the economic ministries (such as the MITI, Agriculture, and MOF) accounted for the largest share of *yokosuberi* placements, yet the social ministries (such as Construction, Education, the Prime Minister's Office, the National Police Agency, and Labor) ranked fourth, fifth, eighth, ninth, and tenth in *yokosuberi* placements. In subsequent years, the distribution was similar (see table 4.7).

Recall that between 1991 and 1998 the total number of *amakudari* declined, as reported by NPA (see chap. 3); however, during this period the total number of *yokosuberi* to *tokushu hojin* increased for both economic and social ministries (table 4.6). This suggests that *yokosuberi* to *tokushu hojin* represents an alternative (but interdependent) route for placing retirees from the central ministries.

Table 4.6 addresses another hidden aspect of public corporations— the reorganization of *tokushu hojin*. The number of *tokushu hojin* declined from 109 in 1982 to 85 in 1998. Media and politicians criticized *yokosuberi* and pressed for the reorganization and even elimination of *tokushu hojin* whose functions were deemed no longer relevant. Yet, as the number of *tokushu hojin* declined, the

Table 4.6 *Yokosuberi* by Ministry[a]

Ministry/Agency	1973	1982	1991	1998
Economic Ministries				
MITI	43 (1)	55 (1)	36 (2)	41 (1)
MOF	33 (3)	39 (3)	26 (3)	36 (2)
MOA	41 (2)	43 (2)	41 (1)	32 (3)
MOT	14 (7)	23 (7)	17 (6)	28 (4)
STA	7	15 (9)	8	16 (10)
Economic Planning Agency	5	7	7	7
Social Ministries				
MOC	31 (4)	31 (4)	20 (4)	28 (4)
Education	19 (5)	27 (5)	16 (7)	22 (6)
Labor	10 (10)	19 (8)	12 (8)	19 (7)
National Land Agency	0	11 (10)	10 (10)	19 (7)
MHW	5	9	10 (10)	17 (9)
Police Agency	11 (9)	6	4	9
Home Affairs	9	8	6	6
PMO	13 (8)	8	12 (8)	1
Other				
MPT	0	2	5	15
MOJ	0	0	1	0
Foreign Affairs	8	7	8	12
Defense Agency	1	3	0	2
Environment Agency	0	4	4	2
Local government agencies	16 (6)	26 (6)	18 (5)	15
Others	15	28	19	36
Total (a)	281	371	280	373
Number of *tokushu hojin* (b)[b]	61	109	92	85
Average *yokosuberi* per board (a/b)	4.6	3.4	3.0	4.4

Source: Seiroren. 1994; *Seiroren Amakudari Hakusho* and Seiroren 1998 internal documents.

[a] Economic and social ministries are arranged using Garon's (1987) distinction. Numbers in parentheses indicate rank. MHW, Ministry of Health and Welfare; MITI, Ministry of International Trade and Industry; MOA, Ministry of Agriculture, Forestry, and Fisheries; MOC, Ministry of Construction; MOF, Ministry of Finance; MOJ, Ministry of Justice; MOT, Ministry of Transport; MPT, Ministry of Posts and Telecommunications; PMO, Prime Minister's Office; STA, Science and Technology Agency.

[b] Value for 1973 is a sample of *tokushu hojin*. All others are total populations.

Table 4.7 *Yokosuberi*, Ranking Summary[a]

Rank	1973	1982	1991	1998
1	MITI	MITI	MOA	MITI
2	MOA	MOA	MITI	MOF
3	MOF	MOF	MOF	MOA
4	MOC	MOC	MOC	MOT, MOC
5	Education	Education	Local government	
6	Local government	Local government	MOT	Education
7	MOT	MOT	Education	Labor, Land Agency
8	PMO	Labor	Labor; PMO	
9	Police Agency	STA		MHW
10	Labor	Land Agency	Land Agency; MHW	STA

[a] MHW, Ministry of Health and Welfare; MITI, Ministry of International Trade and Industry; MOA, Ministry of Agriculture, Forestry, and Fisheries; MOC, Ministry of Construction; MOF, Ministry of Finance; MOT, Ministry of Transport; PMO, Prime Minister's Office; STA, Science and Technology Agency.

total number of *yokosuberi* increased, suggesting an expansion in board size. As shown in the bottom portion of table 4.6, sixty-one *tokushu hojin* had an average of 4.6 *yokosuberi* in 1973; in 1998, the average was still 4.4. As the number of *tokushu hojin* decreased, the average size of the boards of directors of the remaining corporations expanded, bringing the percentages down but maintaining the number of landing spots for retiring bureaucrats. A closer look at the reorganization that brought the number of *tokushu hojin* down from ninty-two in 1991 to eighty-five in 1998 reveals the merger of *tokushu hojin* rather than their elimination. Nine *tokushu hojin* were merged into four new and one existing *jigyodan*, one research institute was moved back into the Ministry of Health and Welfare, and one was privatized.

Zaidan and *Shadan Hojin*

Zaidan and *shadan hojin* are lower in profile than *tokushu hojin*. They are smaller than *tokushu hojin* in number of employees and capital but are more numerous. There were 26,089 *zaidan* and *shadan hojin* in 1996 and 26,264 in 2000 (see table 4.1), employing 200,000 people or 0.4 percent of Japan's total employees. Its operating costs accounted for 4.4 percent of GDP in 1995 (Prime Minister's Office 1998, 90). These are a group of substantial organizations whose policies, personnel, and budgets have only been disclosed in the mid-1990s.[12] In many ways, *zaidan* and *shadan hojin* can be seen as the fine tentacles that secure their ministries in the public and private sectors.

The relation of *zaidan* and *shadan hojin* to the central ministries is complex and contingent. This complexity results from how a corporation is established and financed and whether *yokosuberi* are on its board of directors. To establish a *zaidan* or *shadan hojin*, it is necessary to receive approval from either the central or local government. For example, the Children's Future Zaidan is a *zaidan hojin* approved by the Ministry of Health and Welfare. *Zaidan hojin* carry out educational, social, and cultural functions, whereas *shadan hojin* tend to carry out promotional activities for interest groups and industry and regional associations.[13] Examples of *shadan hojin* include JNPC, approved by the MITI; the International House of Japan, approved by the MITI; and Japan Promotion of Ships, approved by the Ministry of Transport.

Of the 26,089 *zaidan* and *shadan hojin* in 1996, 6,815 (26.1 percent) were established by central governmental approval; the remainder were established by local governments. The composition was similar in 2000. Of the 26,264 *zaidan* and *shadan hojin* in 2000, 7,154 (27.2 percent) were established by central government approval. These *zaidan* and *shadan hojin* were not required to disclose their operations to the public until 2001.[14] In contrast, *tokushu hojin* have always been required to do so and their operations have been reviewed annually by the Management and Coordination Agency, although the extent of disclosure has varied over time. Thus, *zaidan* and *shadan hojin* were beyond public scrutiny, and *tokushu hojin* were much more easily subjected to political debate and public criticism because of the accessibility of information.

Table 4.8 summarizes the number of *zaidan* and *shadan hojin* established by central government approval between 1992 and 2000. The Ministry of Education, for example, approved a total of 1,821 *zaidan* and *shadan hojin* by 2000, giving the ministry a broad reach

Table 4.8 *Zaidan* and *Shadan Hojin*

Ministry/Agency of Approval	Number		
	1992	1996	2000
Education	1,699	1,792	1,821
International Trade and Industry	881	908	903
MOT	819	848	849
MOF	747	798	716
MHW	545	573	566
MOA	492	496	491
Labor	420	440	448
MOC	320	336	345
Foreign Affairs	236	243	238
MPT	217	227	220
MOJ	295	135	136
STA	112	124	128
Home Affairs	72	74	76
Prime Minister's Office	70	74	82
Environment Agency	52	64	73
Police Agency	45	51	52
National Land Agency	40	41	42
MCA	29	31	31
Economic Planning Agency	29	30	29
Defense Agency	23	22	23
Hokkaido Development Agency	7	8	10
Okinawa Development Agency	4	3	3
Total	6,674[a]	6,815	7,154

Source: Prime Minister's Office (1998, 235); Management and Coordination Ministry (2001, 25, 85).
[a] Number for 1992 is authors' estimate. MCA, Management and Coordination Agency; MHW, Ministry of Health and Welfare; MITI, Ministry of International Trade and Industry; MOA, Ministry of Agriculture, Forestry, and Fisheries; MOC, Ministry of Construction; MOF, Ministry of Finance; MOJ, Ministry of Justice; MOT, Ministry of Transport; MPT, Ministry of Posts and Telecommunications; STA, Science and Technology Agency.

over religious, ceremonial, educational, arts, and cultural organizations in the public sector. Although the total number of *zaidan* and *shadan hojin* approved by the economic and social ministries are similar, *zaidan* and *shadan hojin* are important avenues of embedding for the social ministries.

The composition of the boards of directors of *zaidan* and *shadan hojin* indicates the embeddedness of specific ministries (table 4.9). Not all *zaidan* and *shadan hojin* have boards of directors to receive *yokosuberi*. Of the 6,815 corporations approved by the central ministries and agencies, 2,483 (36.4 percent) had *yokosuberi* among

Table 4.9 Ranking of Ministries by *Yokosuberi* to *Zaidan* and *Shadan Hojin*[a]

Rank	Ministry	Corporations with *Yokosuberi* 1996	2000	Rank	Ministry	Number of *Yokosuberi* 1996	2000
1	MITI	320	311	1	MOA	900	707
2	MOA	311	288	2	MITI	661	622
3	Education	303	303	3	MOT	556	530
4	MHW	248	230	4	MOC	501	481
5	MOC	176	179	5	Education	507	476
6	MOT	214	168	6	MHW	553	453
7	Foreign Affairs	129	119	7	Labor	283	353
8	Labor	128	85	8	Foreign Affairs	270	224
9	MPT	86	65	9	MPT	211	156
10	MOF	94	37	10	MOF	183	78[b]

Total number of *zaidan* and *shadan* with *yokosuberi* (a)	2,483	2,056		Total number of *yokosuberi* for 10 top ministries	4,625	4,126
Total number of *zaidan* and *shadan* (b)	6,815	7,154		Total number of *yokosuberi* (c)	7,080	4,327
Yokosuberi (%) (a/b)	36.4	28.7		Total number of board of directors (d)	150,395	154,454
				Yokosuberi (%) (c/d)	4.7	2.8

Source: Prime Minister's Office (1998); Management and Coordination Ministry (2001, 113, 119, 122).
[a] MHW, Ministry of Health and Welfare; MITI, Ministry of International Trade and Industry; MOA, Ministry of Agriculture, Forestry, and Fisheries; MOC, Ministry of Construction; MOF, Ministry of Finance; MOT, Ministry of Transport; MPT, Ministry of Posts and Telecommunications.
[b] MOF ranked 10th in 1996, but 13th in 2000. Defense Agency, with 124 *yokosuberi*, ranked 10th in 2000.

their directors in 1996; however, the percentage of *zaidan* and *shadan hojin* with *yokosuberi* decreased to 2,056 out of 7,154 corporations (28.7 percent) in 2000. If we break down the number of *zaidan* and *shadan hojin* with *yokosuberi* by controlling ministry (columns 3 and 4 of table 4.9), the top two ministries are economic ministries (MITI and Agriculture), followed by the social ministries (Education, Health and Welfare, and Construction). Comparing the number of *zaidan* and *shadan hojin* with *yokosuberi* between 1996 and 2000, a notable decline occurred in the Ministry Agriculture, MPT, and MOF.

A closer look at *yokosuberi* to these 2,483 *zaidan* and *shadan hojin* shows the total number of *yokosuberi* positions at 7,080, accounting for 4.7 percent of the total number of board members among *zaidan* and *shadan hojin* in 1996 (i.e., 7,080 *yokosuberi* among 150,395 directors). However, the percentage of *yokosuberi* decreased to 2.8 percent in 2000. Still, given the large number of *zaidan* and *shadan hojin*, they provide a large number of *yokosuberi* positions for retired bureaucrats from the central ministries. The top ten ministries together have over 4,000 positions.

An examination of ministry rankings by number of *yokosuberi* positions indicate, again, the dominance of three economic ministries (Agriculture, MITI, and Transport). Four social ministries (Health and Welfare, Education, Construction, and Labor) follow. The social ministries show a relatively strong presence in the use of *zaidan* and *shadan hojin* for *yokosuberi*, but the economic ministries also claim a large share of *yokosuberi* placements in *zaidan* and *shadan hojin*. In short, there is only weak evidence to support the distinctive use of *yokosuberi* to *zaidan* and *shadan hojin* in the two types of ministries.

There was a dramatic decline in the total number of *yokosuberi* among *zaidan* and *shadan hojin* from 7,080 in 1996 to 4,327 in 2000 (table 4.9). This decline in the total number of *yokosuberi* is nearly 39 percent. In contrast, the total number of *yokosuberi* among the ten top ministries decreased from 4,625 in 1996 to 4,126 in 2000, or only 11 percent. This indicates that the reduction took place mostly among peripheral ministries and agencies and that the ten top ministries were much less affected in the overall reduction in the number of *yokosuberi*.

Another reason for the sharp decline in the number of *yokosuberi* may lie in the elimination of nonpaid board-of-director positions. Not all board-of-director positions among *zaidan* and *shadan hojin*

are paid. They are divided into regular (*jokin riji*) and nonregular
(*hijokin rijii*) positions—regular positions get paid but nonregular
positions do not. Table 4.10 distinguishes the total number of directors from the number of regular (paid) directors. Theoretically, all
directors provide a basis for embedding a ministry in society, but the
paid regular directorships provide the ministry with landing spots for
its retirees.

In 1996, one-third (2,483) of the 6,815 *zaidan* and *shadan hojin*
approved by central ministries had regular, paid director positions.
The distinction between the number of *zaidan* and *shadan hojin* with
yokosuberi and the total number of regular (paid) positions on these
boards indicates, again, the dominance of three economic ministries
(Agriculture, MITI, and Transport). The Ministries of Construction,
Labor, and Health and Welfare follow (table 4.10). Although the Prime
Minster's Office provided the information for regular and nonregular

Table 4.10 Ranking of Ministries by *Yokosuberi* among *Zaidan* and *Shadan
Hojin*, 1996[a]

Rank	Ministry	Total Number of *Yokosuberi*	Number of Paid *Yokosuberi* Positions
1	MOA	900	297
2	MITI	661	254
3	MOT	556	185
4	MHW	553	85
5	Education	507	48
6	MOC	501	158
7	Labor	283	144
8	Foreign Affairs	270	27
9	MPT	211	69
10	MOF	183	55
Total number for 10 top ministries		4,625	1,322
Total number of *yokosuberi*		7,080	

Source: Prime Minister's Office (1998).
[a] The total number of *zaidan* and *shadan hojin* was 6,815 in 1996 (see table 4.9).
The total number of *zaidan* and *shadan hojin* with paid (regular) director positions
was 2,483. MHW, Ministry of Health and Welfare; MITI, Ministry of International
Trade and Industry; MOA, Ministry of Agriculture, Forestry, and Fisheries; MOC,
Ministry of Construction; MOF, Ministry of Finance; MOT, Ministry of Transport;
MPT, Ministry of Posts and Telecommunications.

yokosuberi positions among *zaidan* and *shadan hojin* for 1996, the Ministry of Management and Coordination (MMC; a new ministry that combines MCA, Home Affairs, and Posts and Telecommunications) did not disclose such information for 2000. This is ironic because the cabinet in 1991 approved a set of criteria for the disclosure of administrative information, with the then MCA (currently MMC) taking a leading role in the promotion of the disclosure of information by ministries and agencies (IPMS Group, 1994, 95). The dramatic reduction in the total number of *yokosuberi* from 1996 to 2000 might have resulted from the elimination of *yokosuberi* in nonpaid director positions and not from paid director positions. Although such a scenario is entirely possible, we have no data to verify it.

Comparison of *Yokosuberi* and *Amakudari*

Table 4.11 ranks ministries by the number of placements on the boards of directors of private and public organizations. In general, the economic ministries dominate all three retirement paths but there are interesting variations in the patterns. First, the MITI ranks third in the *amakudari* categories but first or second in the *yokosuberi* categories. The MOF is first in *amakudari*, second in *yokosuberi* to *tokushu hojin*, a distant tenth to *zaidan* and *shadan hojin* in 1996. If there was an erosion of the MOF's ability to keep *amakudari* (in its broad sense), the erosion took place first in the peripheral locations. Second, social ministries such as Labor, Health and Welfare, and Education rank no better than fifth for *tokushu hojin* and fourth for *zaidan* and *shadan hojin*. The only social ministry that stands out is the Ministry of Construction—it is second for private-sector *amakudari*, fourth in *yokosuberi* to *tokushu hojin*, and fourth in *yokosuberi* to *zaidan* and *shadan hojin*.

In general, these patterns of descent from the ministries make sense when we consider the general functions of *tokushu hojin* and *zaidan* and *shadan hojin*. *Tokushu hojin* are the "arms and legs" of the central ministries, involved in large-scale operations such as economic and infrastructural development (e.g., transportation, communications, and providing goods and services that the private sector eschews). They interface with both the financial and commercial segments of the private sector. *Tokushu hojin* board positions are

Table 4.11 Ministries with the Top Ten Placements: *Amakudari* and *Yokosuberi*[a]

Rank	Amakudari (Private Sector)			Yokosuberi to Tokushu Hojin, 1998	Yokosuberi to Zaidan and Shadan Hojin, 1996
	1994	1998	1999		
1	MOF[b]	MOF	MOF	MITI	MOA
2	MOC	MOC	MOC	MOF	MITI
3	MITI	MITI	MITI	MOA	MOT
4	MOT	MOT	MOT	MOC	MHW
				MOT	
5	MOA	MOA	MOA		Education
6				Education	MOC
7				Labor	Labor
				Land	
8					Foreign Affairs
9				MHW	MPT
10				STA	MOF

Source: Amakudari data for 1994 from Toyo Keizai Shinposha (1995); for 1998 from Toyo Keizai Shinposha ([Kigyo] 2000); for 1999 from NPA (1999).
[a] MHW, Ministry of Health and Welfare; MITI, Ministry of International Trade and Industry; MOA, Ministry of Agriculture, Forestry, and Fisheries; MOC, Ministry of Construction; MOF, Ministry of Finance; MOT, Ministry of Transport; MPT, Ministry of Posts and Telecommunications; STA, Science and Technology Agency.
[b] Ranking for MOF includes placements by the National Tax Agency.

reserved for ex-officials from the financial and commercial ministries. In contrast, *zaidan* and *shadan hojin* are the "feet and hands" of the central ministries, representing a different class and scale of public corporations, intersecting with a different segment of society, and producing a different type of embeddedness. *Zaidan* and *shadan hojin* primarily operate educational, social, cultural, and promotional activities. The economic ministries place their retirees directly onto the boards of private corporations and *tokushu hojin*, whereas the social ministries are more embedded in the myriad small and diverse *zaidan* and *shadan hojin*. The economic ministries dominate placements to boards of directors in the private sector and in the more prestigious and lucrative segments of the public sector (*tokushu hojin*), whereas the social ministries' primary outlets are the boards of directors of *zaidan* and *shadan hojin* and even there they do not dominate the retirement path. Our analysis identifies the multilayered linkages created by *amakudari* and *yokosuberi*.

Tokushu Hojin Reform: *Koromogae?*

There has been a series of *tokushu hojin* reorganizations and reforms since the 1980s. Many characterize the administrative reform of the 1980s as revolutinary. Three huge *tokushu hojin* (NTT, JNR, and Japan Tobacco), for example, were reorganized and privatized, although not completely.[15] When he took office in April 2000, Prime Minister Junichiro Koizumi made *tokushu hojin* reform as one of his top priority in an effort to reduce the government debt that increased to ¥666 trillion in 2001 (approximately 135 percent of GDP) as the result of economic stimulus packages introduced in the late 1990s.[16] As of 2002, his cabinet intended to reform forty-six *tokushu hojin*, either by merging thirty-eight with others, privatizing them, or transferring them to new public corporations (*dokuritsu gyosei hojin*). These corporations included the Government Housing Loan Corporation, Japan Regional Development Corporation, Japan Scholarship Foundation, Japan Highway Corporation, Metropolitan Expressway Corporation, Hanshin Expressway Corporation, Honshu-Shikoku Bridge Authority, Urban Development Corporation, JNPC, and Airport Corporations.

In 2001, FILP funds exceeded ¥32 trillion, corresponding to 39 percent of the general government budget (Nihon Keizai Shinbunsha 2001, 29). The total debt accumulated by seventy-seven *tokushu hojin* was ¥250 trillion with interest payments of ¥5.3 trillion yen, which was annually subsidized from taxes (Iwami 2001, 26; Nihon Keizai Shinbunsha 2001, 5). The Japan Highway Corporation, directly controlled by the Ministry of Construction, carried a debt of ¥26 trillion and received annual subsidies of ¥300 billion just to pay interest on the debt (Iwami 2001, 59). Kansai Airport Corporation, which constructed a new airport near Osaka in 1995, carried a debt of ¥1.2 trillion (Nihon Keizai Shinbunsha 2001, 63). JNPC had accumulated a debt of ¥2.3 trillion, with ¥190 billion in unrecoverable loans (Nihon Keizai Shinbunsha 2001, 130).[17]

The case of JNPC highlights the intricate relations among public corporate deficit, *amakudari* and *yokosuberi*, vested interests, and the frustrations of reform. It is indicative of the operation of a personnel circuit between the MITI and private corporations that is entrenched because of ministry control and the special interests of politicians in trading pork for votes.

JNPC (formerly the Japan Development of Petroleum Corporation) was created as a *tokushu hojin* in 1967 with the goal of drilling crude oil wells and securing an oil supply for the Japanese domestic market. After the oil shocks of 1973 and 1979, its mission was expanded to include oil storage in addition to oil exploration. JNPC dramatically increased Japan's oil reserves. At the time of the first oil shock, Japan had oil stores to supply the nation for two weeks. In 1994, the stores of private companies and public corporations combined could provide a 154-day supply for the country (Iwase 1997, 106).

Oil exploration is a risky and costly business. The probability of finding oil is three in one thousand. Finding it usually costs ¥1–1.5 billion on land and ¥2–4 billion in the seabed (Iwase 1997, 107). JNPC conducts oil exploration by giving money to nearly 120 private Japanese companies that have cooperative oil-exploration projects in thirty countries. JNPC and a private company typically set up a new oil-exploration company by putting up the initial capital.[18] This company explores for oil, and when oil is found, the company imports it to Japan. This method is known as "one project, one company," meaning one specific company is created for oil exploration in a specific area. The company is disbanded if the project is unsuccessful; however, the company is not required to repay the loan if the venture ends in failure. Of the forty-five private companies funded by the JNPC to explore for oil, thirty-nine companies had more than 50 percent of their initial capital provided (Iwase 1997, 110).

The logic is straightforward. JPNC is a *tokushu hojin* controlled by the MITI. It funds and underwrites private oil-exploration companies for risky drilling ventures. The private companies then use these funds to undertake cooperative ventures with other companies to explore for oil. JNPC itself and the private corporations it funds become locations for *yokosuberi* and *amakudari* from the MITI. Public corporations such as JNPC fund and regulate private corporations in regard to oil exploration and storage. JNPC had 138 private companies and one public corporation (*zaidan hojin*) that were affiliated in 2001. Since its establishment, JNPC has created 293 companies; 200 of these had been disbanded by 2000. Only eleven of the ninety-three remaining companies reported net operating gains (Nihon Keizai Shinbunsha 2001, 132). The MITI and JNPC enjoy selective advantages in terms of funding and regulation to these private corporations. The private corporations, in turn, provide *amakudari* landing spots for MITI officials, and JNPC provides *yokosuberi* landing spots. For example, seven of the companies affiliated with JNPC provided fourteen board-of-director positions to MITI ex-bureaucrats. This is an example of the complex apparatus between the ministry and the private sector, in which public corporations provide intermediate landing spots between the bureaucracy and the private sector.

The ministries are responsible for the supervision of the public corporations they themselves established, including the oversight of business operations, use of loans, compensation for services, and the appointment of directors to the boards. Public corporations, however, use accounting methods that differ from the conventional accounting methods used in private firms, making records difficult for outsiders to understand. The annual inspection of their business operations by the MCA, the extent of oversight, and public disclosure of financial information have varied over time. The lax monitoring of business operations by the ministries and the incautious use of public money by *tokushu hojin* came to light in December 1997. Kazuo Ishigaki, a Diet member from the Liberal Party (Jiyuto) raised questions about the financial operations of JNPC. The issue was then picked up by Mitsuo Horiuchi, then a MITI minister, an accounting expert and former chairman of the Fuji Kyuko Railway Company. As late as September 1999, the MITI denied any mismanagement at JNPC. Instead, the MITI blamed unexpected market changes such as the plunge in oil prices since the 1980s and the surging value of the yen for its failings. In February 2000, a panel of experts examining JNPC called for greater transparency. The absence of accountability of *tokushu hojin* such as JPNC reflects the seniority influence that retired bureaucrats (*yokosuberi* and *amakudari*) have over serving bureaucrats. The administrative ties make it difficult for current MITI bureaucrats to inspect and monitor the operations of JNPC and oil-exploration companies run by senior ex-MITI bureaucrats.

Tokushu hojin represent the vital interests of their controlling ministries, *zoku* politicians, and business interests. The money available through FILP and the number of *amakudari* and *yokosuberi* posts solidified the ties among segments of the petroleum industry, *zoku* politicians, and the MITI. This explains why it is so difficult to reform *tokushu hojin*—the ministries, *zoku* politicians, and business are all against any type of reform.

When *tokushu hojin* are reformed, it often takes the form of *koromogae* (simply changing clothes)—they are merged with other *tokushu hojin*, moved from one class of *tokushu hojin* to another, or changed to another type of public corporation. In essence, their functions do not change fundamentally but give the appearance of change. For example, during the *tokushu hojin* reform of 1999, the total number of *tokushu hojin* went down from eighty-one to seventy-eight. The elimination of just three entities was accomplished in the following complex, costly way. Six were reorganized into three new *tokushu hojin*, five were merged with three existing *tokushu hojin*, and one was transformed into three new *tokushu hojin*. All these changes produced the elimination of just one board of director position (Nihon Keizai Shinbunsha 2001, 16).

It has long been argued that a real *tokushu hojin* reform will not take place unless FILP (*zaito*) is reformed. Under FILP, the MOF controls the funds collected from postal saving and welfare annuity insurance and lends funds to public corporations. The amount of money in FILP, the absence of accountability, and limited information disclosure make *tokushu hojin* a hotbed for collusive ties and *amakudari* destinations. And although FILP was supposedly reformed in April 2001, most observers suggest little will change in the funding mechanisms of *tokushu hojin*. The new reformed *zaito* system replaced the MOF by MPT, which is housed in the newly merged MMC,[19] and the funds are invested by MPT in the financial market. In principle, it forces *tokushu hojin* to seek loans from the financial markets. The goal of abolishing the old *zaito* system is to make *tokushu hojin* more accountable for the management of money (*jishu unyu*).

As in the past reforms of *tokushu hojin*, the reorganized FILP provided a loophole. It allowed financially troubled *tokushu hojin* to use either *zaito* bonds (*zaitosai*, government bonds specifically issued for funding *tokushu hojin* projects in the form of loans) or *zaito kikansai* (loans from the private market, where the loan is guaranteed by the government). *Zaito kikansai* works just like a loan from a private lender except that its repayment is guaranteed by the government. *Zaito kikansei* is issued with interest rates determined in the market, but the interest rates for *zaito* bonds are lower. Simply put, it is easier and cheaper for *tokushu hojin* to use *zaito* bonds than *zaito kikansai*. Only 3 percent of *zaito* funds came from *zaito kikansai* and the remaining 97 percent were derived from *zaito* bonds after the reform (Nihon Keizai Shinbunsha 2001, 32)—in essence, no fundamental change occurred.

In short, given the vested interests of bureaucrats, politicians, and private firms, much of *tokushu hojin* reform, including the restriction of *amakudari* (in its broad sense), have either ended in deadlock or been postponed. When *tokushu hojin* were reformed, they were often transferred to a new entity with only the appearance of change. Political resistance from ministries, *zoku* politicians, and business interests lead *tokushu hojin* to be renamed, but to maintain the same three-way relations and the same mechanism of financing.

This chapter begins with the paradox of numerous senior bureaucrats leaving the central ministries but with their whereabouts not accounted for in the NPA data. *Yokosuberi* to public corporations provides a solution to the administrative constraint on bureaucrats (the two-year waiting period) moving from ministries directly into the private sector. All *tokushu hojin* receive *yokosuberi*, and *yokosuberi* to *tokushu hojin* accounts for nearly 45 percent of all positions on *tokushu hojin* boards of directors. A hierarchical pattern of *yokosuberi* exists. Three economic ministries—the MITI, MOF, and Agriculture—dominate *yokosuberi* to *tokushu hojin* just as they dominate *amakudari* to the private sector; Agriculture, MITI, and Transport dominate *yokosuberi* to *zaidan* and *shadan hojin*. But this placement pattern is not exclusive. Many boards of directors of public corporations have representatives from several ministries. Ministry control over a *tokushu hojin* is a matter of degree and their boards are possible sites of interministry negotiation, communication, and coordination.

These mixed boards of directors modify notions that public corporations are the exclusive extension of a controlling ministry's influence in the form of vertical administration and exclusive sectoralism. Instead of the direction of influence being like the spokes of a wheel, boards with *yokosuberi* from different ministries exhibit a relationship more like a lattice, with the mixed boards allowing a diffusion of control and responsibility with no privileged alignments with the ministries. This imagery reveals an enigma of Japanese administration.

Public corporations mediate, through multilayered personnel circuits, the relations between ministries and the private sector. *Yokosuberi* networks represent another manifestation of the vertical administration and sectoralism of Japanese administration by linking specific ministries to public corporations. The contrast between *yokosuberi* to *tokushu hojin*, and *yokosuberi* to *zaidan* and *shadan hojin* illustrates the multilayered character of the relations spreading out across the public and private sectors. The boards of directors of *zaidan* and *shadan hojin* are tentacles into Japanese society, binding together central and local governments and private-sector representatives. The economic ministries dominate *yokosuberi* to these boards, but *yokosuberi* to *zaidan* and *shadan hojin* provide the largest avenue of retirement for ex-bureaucrats from the social ministries.

Our case study of JNPC illustrates the circuits of personnel relations among the ministries, public organizations, and private corporations bound by special political interests. JNPC provides a bridge between the MITI and the private sector through *yokosuberi* and *amakudari*. *Yokosuberi* and *amakudari* are two circuits of ministry embeddedness (*yokosuberi* from the MITI to JNPC and *amakudari* from the MITI to the private corporations funded by JNPC). This embeddedness fuses the interests of the ministry with private and political interests and accounts for the resistance to administrative reform that takes the form of *koromogae*. Recategorizing or renaming financially troubled *tokushu hojin* such as JNPC does not substantially change the circuit of *amakudari* and *yokosuberi* that connects the ministries with the private sector. The reduction in the number of *zaidan* and *shadan hojin* and the dramatic reduction of *yokosuberi* to the boards are a real reduction of the overall *amakudari* network, but our suspicion is that the eliminated *yokosuberi* were unpaid positions (the 2000 data do not disclose whether the reductions in *yokosuberi* were regular director position).

Yokosuberi to public corporations should be viewed as interdependent with *amakudari* placements, providing flexibility under pressure through its circuits and layers. The scope and flexibility of the *yokosuberi* pathways suggest alternative routes for officials not included in the NPA incidence data. A clearer picture of the retirement patterns of bureaucrats emerges from examining *amakudari* and *yokosuberi* patterns together. *Yokosuberi* is a key component of bureaucratic retirement and an alternative path interdependent with *amakudari*. *Zaidan* and *shadan hojin* appear to serve as a buffer zone when *amakudari* (in its broad sense) to public corporations comes under pressure. So far, ministries have surrendered *yokosuberi* positions, but the decline has occurred more substantially in the peripheral locations of *zaidan* and *shadan hojin* than in *tokushu hojin*.

5 *Wataridori* and Private and Public Corporations

This chapter identifies the overall interdependence of elite movements connecting the central ministries with the private and public sectors through the circuit of *wataridori*, reemployment subsequent to the first reemployment position after leaving the ministry (i.e., second or subsequent *amakudari* or *yokosuberi*). High-level bureaucrats, moving out of central ministries, may look forward to two, three, or even four high-level positions in the public and private sectors. In a sense, counting *amakudari* to the private sector and *yokosuberi* to the public sector separately masks the underlying indirect structure of *wataridori*. *Wataridori* also raises new issues about the *amakudari* structure and the processes that create and recreate its structure.

The examination of the indirect route or circuit of *wataridori* clarifies the structure of interinstitutional movements of elites and plays up the consciously coordinated collaboration of elites in the maintenance of the institutionalized elite power structure. *Amakudari* placements are often described as informal, temporally discrete events, yet the empirical examination of *wataridori* reveals that *amakudari* and *yokosuberi* are parts of multiple sequenced events taking place over time. *Amakudari* and *yokosuberi* placements, as components of *wataridori*, are consciously calculated, ministry-level operations necessary for maintaining a reemployment circuit involving elite positions across the private and public sectors.

In this chapter we first examine the hierarchical character of the relationship between Japanese bureaucracy and society in terms of both direct links created through *amakudari* and *yokosuberi* and indirect links created through *wataridori*. We present the structural and processual features of *wataridori* by examining the logistical and coordinated process of placement and the strict adherence to position ranks and then the controversial financial compensation accumulated through *wataridori*.

Review of the Literature

The literature on *wataridori* is thin and this chapter may be the first systematic empirical examination of *wataridori* in English. Johnson (1978, 110) writes of ex-bureaucrats moving from one government corporation to another, but does not use the term *wataridori*. Inoki (1995) examines the correspondence between ministry rank and the total amount of time spent in retirement positions. Japanese sources include Seiroren (1992) and Cho (1995). Seiroren's survey of seventy-seven *tokushu hojin* in 1979 found that 117 of the 454 directors on the boards of *tokushu hojin* were *wataridori*. Cho's questionnaire survey of 331 ex-bureaucrats found these officials moved to their second *amakudari* job (i.e., their first *wataridori* position) within five to six years (Cho 1995, 89). Funaki (1997) writes of *wataridori* positions corresponding to the status of positions of exit at the time of retirement.

The examination of *wataridori* reveals certain misconceptions about and extensions of *amakudari* as representing the embeddedness of the bureaucracy in Japanese society (cf. Evans 1995).[1] "Embeddedness" here simply means "connection to." *Amakudari* provides channels of communication that increase the stability and effectiveness of state policy. Using *amakudari* as a measure of embeddedness implies that *amakudari* is a broad set of simple relationships between the bureaucracy and other sectors. However, this conception ignores the way each relationship fits into a more holistic pattern or structure of relationships (Granovetter 1990). *Amakudari* as a measure of embeddedness reduces to its dyadic form.[2] In contrast, the examination of *wataridori* reveals a more elaborate structure than has been previously recognized. *Wataridori* represents not only the relationship between ministry and location of first reemployment, but also the indirect relationships between the two.

The analysis of *wataridori* again reveals the hierarchy of ministries in the coordination and management of *amakudari* and *yokosuberi;* the MOF, MITI, Construction, Agriculture, and Transport dominate the *amakudari* and *yokosuberi* networks (see chaps. 3–4). The use of *amakudari* as a measure of embeddedness implies a kind of equality in the network, in which all ministries and agencies participate. *Wataridori* is more challenging because it requires ministry coordination. Thus, we use the ratio of *wataridori* to *amakudari* to indicate a ministry's coordination and orchestration of the reemployment processes of its ex-officials beyond their first reemployment as a more stringent measure of ministry capacity. If "the reemployment of higher civil servants in high posts within the private sector (*amakudari*) is perhaps the best unobtrusive indicator of relative bureaucratic power vis-à-vis other ministries" as Okimoto suggests, we may ask how much more precise *wataridori* is as a measure of ministry power (Okimoto 1988, 319).

The analysis of *wataridori* also expands our recognition of processual features of *amakudari* between two points (the ministry and the private corporation). Rather than seeing *amakudari* as a temporally discrete position with no history[3] or larger processual logic, *wataridori* highlights the use of the same positions and the temporal movement of the same people by ministries over time. *Wataridori* as a scheduled sequence of events avoids the reductionist use of *amakudari* and points to the more formal, institutional, yet calculated and conscious features of reemployment of ex-bureaucrats.

Amakudari placements are both informal (i.e., not codified) and institutionalized (part of the operational routine of an organization). But "informal" implies spontaneous and unconscious (Roethlisberger and Dickson 1939; Selznick 1948; 1949).[4] Institutionalization implies stable routine operations that are taken for granted, unconscious, and without rational interests or agency (Zukin and DiMaggio 1990; Powell and DiMaggio 1991), thus suggesting that *amakudari* is a type of spontaneous, unconscious, non-self-interested, and routinized procedure. The examination of *wataridori* suggests a logic of conscious, calculated, yet bounded rationality.[5]

Wataridori as a Stable Structure

Examining *wataridori* as an extension of *amakudari* and *yokosuberi* emphasizes the interdependence of these two and highlights *wataridori*'s distinctiveness as a route to the private sector and circuit within the public sector, as graphically presented in figure 1.1. *Wataridori* reveals the stratification of the ministries based on their ability to sustain the reemployment placements of *wataridori* over time. This stratification or hierarchy involves a small subset of ministries, similar to the patterns of *amakudari* and *yokosuberi*.

Direct and Indirect Relationships

The prevalence data in table 5.1 show *amakudari* and *wataridori* in 1994. The table decomposes *wataridori* into a family of paths distinguished by an intermediate stop between ministry and board positions in private firms. There were 873 *amakudari* out of the 42,625 directors among 2,220 firms, or 2 percent of the directors on private boards. As shown in the aggregate totals at the bottom of table 5.1, 280 of the 873 (32.1 percent) *amakudari* officials moved through the *wataridori* route to the boards of private firms. Note that the overwhelming proportion of these *wataridori* cases came from the public sector. Of the 280 *wataridori*, 277 (178 plus 15 plus 84) moved to private firms through the public sector (*tokushu hojin, zaidan* and *shadan hojin*, and quasi-governmental enterprises), and three were from the private sector and educational institutions.

This indirect route to the boards of private firms is the result of the two-year waiting period imposed on high-ranking bureaucrats before they take jobs in the areas they had supervised or regulated. This prohibition can be lifted when the director general of the relevant ministry requests and receives permission to do so from the NPA. Because only a fraction of those moving through the NPA are top-level bureaucrats, only a few top-level bureaucrats take *amakudari* to private firms directly upon retirement. Instead, they take their first position in the public sector, and then after the two-year limit has expired, they move to the boards of private firms. This indirect route invites closer examination.

The legal restriction selectively obstructs top-level bureaucrats (at the rank of section chief and above) from taking private-sector positions (*amakudari*) immediately upon retirement. The operative condition of the restriction is areas they supervised (five years prior to retirement). The higher the rank of a bureaucrat, the broader the area under his or her supervision and the more likely the legal restriction is to be in effect upon his or her retirement. This suggests that the NPA data used in chapter 3 are disproportionately loaded with mid-level bureaucrats. Thus, the 32 percent *wataridori* identified in table 5.1 probably represents a group that differs from the other *amakudari* on the boards, either by higher bureaucratic rank or supervisory

Table 5.1 *Amakudari* and *Wataridori* to Boards of Private Firms, 1994[a]

Originating Entity	Total Number of Amakudari (a)	Wataridori Path[b]					Number of Wataridori (b)	Wataridori/ Amakudari (%) (b/a)	Wataridori/ Total (%) (b/c)
		1	2	3	4	5			
MOF	213	58	3	20	0	0	(81)	38.0	28.9
MOC	180	42	3	13	0	0	(58)	32.2	20.7
MITI	115	34	1	16	2	0	(53)	46.0	18.9
MOT	70	14	2	22	0	0	(38)	54.3	13.6
MOA	58	17	0	5	0	0	(22)	37.9	7.9
Tax Agency	84	0	0	2	0	0	(2)	2.3	7
National Police Agency	43	1	3	0	0	1	(5)	12.0	1.8
MPT	28	5	1	4	0	0	(10)	35.7	3.6
Defense Agency	22	2	2	1	0	0	(5)	22.7	1.8
Hokkaido Development Agency	8	1	0	0	0	0	(1)	12.5	4
Board of Audit	5	2	0	0	0	0	(2)	40.0	0.7
Prime Minister's Office	1	0	0	0	0	0	(0)	0	0
Fair Trade Commission	1	0	0	0	0	0	(0)	0	0
Economic Planning Agency	0	0	0	0	0	0	(0)	0	0
Defense Facilities Administration Agency	4	0	0	0	0	0	(0)	0	0
STA	1	0	0	0	0	0	(0)	0	0

Environment Agency	2	0	0	0	0	0	(0)	0	0
National Land Agency	4	2	0	1	0	0	(3)	75	1.1
MCA	2	0	0	0	0	0	(0)	0	0
Ministry of Education	1	0	0	0	0	0	(0)	0	0
MHW	6	0	0	0	0	0	(0)	0	0
Social Insurance Agency	0	0	0	0	0	0	(0)	0	0
Food Agency	1	na	na	na	na	na	(na)	na	na
MOJ	7[c]	0	0	0	0	0	(0)	0	0
Committee for the Inquest of Prosecution	9[d]	0	0	0	0	0	(0)	0	0
Ministry of Foreign Affairs	1	0	0	0	0	0	(0)	0	0
Maritime Safety Agency	3	0	0	0	0	0	(0)	0	0
Ministry of Labor	3	0	0	0	0	0	(0)	0	0
Ministry of Home Affairs	1	na	na	na	na	na	(na)	na	na
Total	873[e]	178	15	84	2	1	280 (c)	32.1	100

Source: Toyo Keizai Shinposha (1995).

[a] MCA, Management and Coordination Agency; MHW, Ministry of Health and Welfare; MITI, Ministry of International Trade and Industry; MOA, Ministry of Agriculture, Forestry, and Fisheries; MOC, Ministry of Construction; MOF, Ministry of Finance; MOJ, Ministry of Justice; MOT, Ministry of Transport; MPT, Ministry of Posts and Telecommunications; na, not applicable; STA, Science and Technology Agency.

[b] Path 1, move from a ministry to *tokushu hojin* and then to the private sector.
Path 2, move from a ministry to *zaidan-shadan* and then to the private sector.
Path 3, move from a ministry to quasi-governmental entities and then to the private sector.
Path 4, move from a ministry to a private firm and then to another private firm.
Path 5, move from a ministry to an educational institution and then to the private sector.

[c] The original source reported total *amakudari* for the Ministry of Justice as 4 but gives 7 entries under MOJ.

[d] The original source reported total *amakudari* for the Committee for the Inquest of Prosecution as 8; however, there are 9 entries.

[e] There were 873 *amakudari* out of the 42,625 of the directors among 2,200 firms combined or 2 percent of the private boards.

experience. They were blocked from moving directly into the private sector and from substantially higher salaries, yet got there later through *wataridori*.

Wataridori represents a family of paths or circuits distinguished by an intermediate stop. As shown in table 5.1, there are five theoretically possible paths between the ministry of origin and the board of a private firm.

Path 1 is a movement from a ministry to a *tokushu hojin*, then to a private corporation.

Path 2 is a movement from a ministry to a *zaidan* or *shadan hojin* and then to a private company.

Path 3 is a movement from a ministry to a quasi-governmental entity (such as the Bank of Japan, BOJ) and, then to a private company.

Path 4 is a movement from a ministry to a private firm and then to another private company.

Path 5 is a movement from a ministry to an educational institution and then to a private corporation.

Initially striking in table 5.1 is the prominence of path 1, through the large public *tokushu hojin*. If we include *wataridori* who came through *zaidan* and *shadan hojin*, the move through the public sector accounts for almost 99 percent of *wataridori*. *Tokushu hojin* and quasi-governmental entities offer high-status *yokosuberi* positions for top-level bureaucrats.

Figure 5.1 decomposes *wataridori* into two primary linkages: linkage 1 is from the ministries to the boards of public corporations (*yokosuberi*); linkage 2 is from public corporations to private-sector boards. The boards of directors of public corporations are the intermediate step in the indirect (structural) relationship indicated by the boldface arrow labeled *wataridori*. These public-sector boards are locations through which personnel move. Theoretically, these boards are also locations from which personnel originate and then move to private-sector boards (linkage 2, direct relations). In addition, these boards may represent terminal landing spots for civil servants originating from the central ministries (*yokosuberi*). Yet *wataridori* also takes place within public corporations. This is linkage 3, which occurs when ex-bureaucrats move from a ministry to a public corporation and then on to other public corporations.

Table 5.2 summarizes the prevalence data of ex-bureaucrats on the boards of private corporations who began their careers at *tokushu*

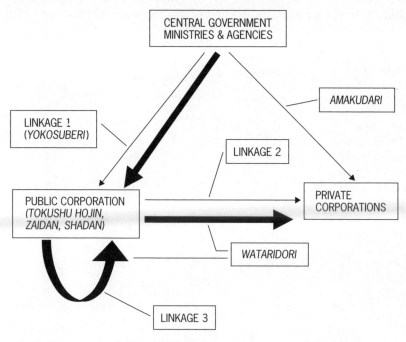

Figure 5.1 Structural Embeddedness

hojin or the BOJ (a quasi-governmental agency) and then took an intermediate position before moving to a private firm (linkage 2 in figure 5.1). Originating from the *tokushu hojin* or BOJ is a less prevalent *wataridori* path than originating from the central ministries/agencies. About 0.1 percent of private-sector board positions are occupied by people who originated in *tokushu hojin* or quasi-public organizations (532 out of 42,625 of the private board positions). This rate of *wataridori* is considerably lower than expected because there are no specific legal restrictions on postretirement employment of *tokushu hojin* and BOJ officials. But personnel originating from BOJ and *tokushu hojin* are not Type I civil servants. They are involved in an *amakudari*-like process, although under our definition they are technically not *amakudari*.[6] Nevertheless, the comparison of the movement of personnel in this route with *amakudari*, *yokosuberi*, and *wataridori* originating from the ministries is illustrative of the hierarchical or vertical nature of networks in Japanese society.

Table 5.2 Personnel Movements to Private-Sector Boards of Directors from *Tokushu Hojin*

Originating Entity	Total Number of *Amakudari* (a)	Path[a] 1	2	3	Number of *Wataridori* (b)	*Wataridori/ Amakudari* (%) (b/a)
Bank of Japan	107	1	7	0	8	7.5
Japan Highways Public Corp.	59	4	5	0	9	15.3
Norin Chukin Bank[b]	46	0	0	0	0	0
Housing Loan Corp.	41	0	0	0	0	0
Japan Development Bank	14	0	0	1	1	7.1
Japan National Railways	103	0	26	0	26	25.2
Japan Tobacco	11	0	0	0	0	0
Total	532	5	38	1	44	8.3

Source: Toyo Keizai Shinposha (1995, 772, 774).
[a] Path 1, move from *tokushu hojin* to *zaidan-shadan* and then to a private corporation.
Path 2, move from *tokushu hojin* to other public corporation (including another *tokushu hojin*) and then to a private corporation.
Path 3, move from *tokushu hojin* to a private corporation and then to another private corporation.
[b] Privatized in 1986.

Table 5.2 indicates that BOJ and just three *tokushu hojin* (Japan Highways Public Corp.; Japan Development Bank, JDB; and JNR) account for all forty-four *wataridori*. The overall share of *wataridori* among these public corporations is 8.3 percent, which is substantially lower than the 32 percent for the central ministries. *Tokushu hojin* and other quasi-governmental corporations are therefore not effective launching pads for *wataridori*-like reemployment on the boards of private firms compared to the central ministries. The fact that there are no legal restrictions on reemployment from *tokushu hojin* and quasi-governmental agencies further suggests the weakness of postretirement placements in these types of organizations for access to some of the best *wataridori* positions. The share of *wataridori* to *amakudari* indicates the capacity of ministries as well as public corporations to deploy and redeploy these people in the field. The rankings of these ministries and corporations also illustrate the hierarchical feature of personnel movements in Japanese society.

Table 5.3 presents the *yokosuberi* and *wataridori* traffic between the central ministries and the boards of directors of sixty-one public corporations (mostly *tokushu hojin*) based on Seiroren's (1992) survey. There were 354 board of director positions in the sixty-one corporations in 1991; 280 of these positions (79.1 percent) were filled by ex-bureaucrats from the central ministry (*yokosuberi*) and 81 (22.9 percent) were *wataridori*. Of the 280 *yokosuberi*, 81 (28.9 percent) were *wataridori*, meaning that 81 ex-bureaucrats had previously been on the boards of other *tokushu hojin*. Compared to *amakudari* to the private sector, there are no substantial legal restrictions on movements from the ministries to *tokushu hojin*, except for the 1979 Diet regulation restricting ex-bureaucrats to fewer than 50 percent of the director positions on the boards of *tokushu hojin* and to *wataridori* practice only when necessary. But recall that, these restrictions were not immediately followed (see chap. 4); ex-bureaucrats held over 50 percent of the director positions until the mid-1990s when the appearance of compliance was created by reorganizing *tokushu hojin* entities.

Structure of Wataridori *by Ministry*

There is a curious feature of *wataridori* that bears on the embeddedness of the Japanese ministries. Table 5.1 shows the ministries that use the *wataridori* route most frequently. The overall average (the share of *wataridori* to *amakudari*) in 1994 was 32.1 percent, but 54.3 percent of the Ministry of Transport's *amakudari* to the boards of private firms came through *wataridori*. For the MITI, it was 46 percent and for the MOF and Agriculture, it was 38 percent. In fact, *wataridori* to top positions in private firms seems to be almost the exclusive domain of six ministries: Transport, the MITI, the MOF, Agriculture, the MPT, and Construction.

Ranking the ministries according to their percentage of *wataridori* to overall number of *wataridori* by ministries (far right column of table 5.1) provides another measure of the use of the *wataridori* route. The MOF (28.9%), Construction (20.7%), the MITI (18.9%), Transport (13.6%), and Agriculture (7.9%) together account for 90 percent of all *wataridori* to private-sector boards. If we add the MPT (3.6

Table 5.3 Top Ten *Wataridori* by Ministry among *Tokushu Hojin*, 1991[a]

Rank	Ministry/Agency	Number of Yokosuberi (a)	Number of Wataridori (b)	Wataridori (%)		Positions Held					
				(b/a)	(b/d)	2	3	4	5	6	7
1	MITI	36	23	63.9	28.4	11	8	3	0	0	1
2	MOC	20	11	55.0	13.4	8	1	2	0	0	0
3	MOF	27	9	33.3	11.1	6	2	0	1	0	0
4	STA	8	7			7	0	0	0	0	0
4	MOA	41	7	17.1	8.6	6	1	0	0	0	0
6	MOT	21	6	28.6	7.4	4	2	0	0	0	0
6	MHW	10	6	60.0	7.4	5	1	0	0	0	0
8	Education	16	4	25.0	4.9	3	1	0	0	0	0
9	Labor	12	3	25.0	3.7	1	2	0	0	0	0
10	Home Affairs	7	2	28.6	2.5	1	0	0	1	0	0
11	Others	82	3	3.7	3.7						
Total		280 (c)	81 (d)		28.9 (d/c)						

Source: Seiroren (1992).

[a] Based on a survey of sixty-one public corporations conducted by Seiroren in 1991 with 354 board of directors. Public corporations participating in the survey included *tokushu hojin* and their affiliates. These corporations are also called government-related organizations. The official count of *tokushu hojin* for 1991 was 92, with 777 board of director positions. MHW, Ministry of Health and Welfare; MITI, Ministry of International Trade and Industry; MOA, Ministry of Agriculture, Forestry, and Fisheries; MOC, Ministry of Construction; MOF, Ministry of Finance; MOT, Ministry of Transport; STA, Science and Technology Agency.

percent), we can say that six ministries account for 94 percent of all *wataridori* to the boards of private firms. The *wataridori* path is not evenly distributed across ministries; it is hierarchical and dominated by a handful of ministries. Taken together, these two measures of a ministry's capacity to find serial reemployment for its retirees indicate that five or six ministries have the capacity to move their ex-officials continuously to private-sector boards. The same ranking of five ministries accounts for *wataridori* within public corporations. As table 5.3 shows, the MITI, Construction, the MOF, Agriculture, and Transport monopolize the continuous circuit connecting the ministries and the public sector.

Table 5.4 summarizes *amakudari* and *wataridori* traffic through the three links among the ministries, public corporations, and private firms. The top panel of the table presents the ranking of *amakudari* and *wataridori* by ministry. We see the number of ex-bureaucrats on the boards of private firms who got there indirectly (*wataridori*) in 1994, with the overall average of 32.1 percent, indicating nearly one in three *amakudari* took the indirect route of *wataridori*. The middle panel of table 5.4 summarizes the third component of the three linkages specified in figure 5.1—the relationship between the ministries and the boards of public corporations. The overall ratio of *wataridori* to *yokosuberi* in 1991 was 28.9 percent, indicating the strength of this link in the broader *amakudari* pattern. What is striking about this portion of the table is that this path, like the one between the ministries and private-sector boards, is dominated by the same five ministries: the MITI, Construction, the MOF, Transport, and Agriculture.

The bottom panel of table 5.4 indicates that 8.3 percent of top-ranking personnel who moved to the boards of private firms from public corporations in 1994 came to these positions indirectly. Compared to the *wataridori* patterns originating from the central ministries (28.9 percent), these public corporations are weaker in their ability to serially reemploy their top personnel.

In summary, the data in table 5.1 indicate that *amakudari* constitutes 2 percent of the board of directors and that 32 percent of *amakudari* came through the indirect route, *wataridori*. Five ministries (MOF, Construction, MITI, Transport, and Agriculture) represent 90 percent of all *wataridori* to the boards of directors of these private firms. In addition, 28.9 percent of *yokosuberi* to public corporations

Table 5.4 Overall Comparisons[a]

Rank	Entity	Number of Amakudari (b)	Rank	Entity	Number of Wataridori (a)	Rank	Entity	Wataridori (% of Amakudari) (a/b)
Amakudari and Wataridori to Private-Sector Firms, 1994								
1	MOF	213	1	MOF	81	1	MOT	54.3
2	MOC	80	2	MITI	58	2	MITI	46.1
3	MITI	15	3	MOF	53	3	MOF	38.0
4	TA	84	4	MOA	38	4	MOA	37.9
5	MOT	70	5	MOT	22	5	MPT	35.7
						6	MOC	32.2
							Overall	32.1
Yokosuberi to Public Corporations and Wataridori within Public Corporations, 1991								
1	MOA	41	1	MITI	23	1	STA	87.5
2	MITI	36	2	MOC	11	2	MITI	63.9
3	MOF	27	3	MOF	9	3	MOC	55
4	MOT	21	4	MOA	7	4	MOF	33.3
5	MOC	20	5	MOT	6	5	MOT	28.6
						6	MOA	17.1
							Overall	28.9
Personnel Movement from Public Corporations to Private Firms, 1994								
1	Bank of Japan	107	1	Japan Railways	26	1	Japan Railways	25.2
2	Japan Railway	103	2	Japan Highway	9	2	Japan Highway	15.3
3	Japan Highway	59	3	Bank of Japan	8	3	Bank of Japan	7.8
4	Norin Chukin Bk.	46	4	Norin Chukin Bk.	0		Norin Chukin Bk.	0
5	J. Housing Corp.	41	5	J. Housing Corporation	0		J. Housing Corporation	0
							Overall	8.3

Source: Toyo Keizai Shinposha (1995); Sairoren (1992).

[a] Calculations by authors. MITI, Ministry of International Trade and Industry; MOA, Ministry of Agriculture, Forestry, and Fisheries; MOC, Ministry of Construction; MOF, Ministry of Finance; MOT, Ministry of Transport; MPT, Ministry of Posts and Telecommunications; STA, Science and Technology Agency; TA, Tax Agency.

were *wataridori* within the public corporations, dominated by the same five ministries. These five ministries accounted for 78 percent of all *wataridori*. Thus, *wataridori* to top corporate positions (private or public) is monopolized by a handful of ministries, making *wataridori* a severely stratified route to the public sector. These ministries are capable of keeping their retirees in multiple positions over time. The paths through *tokushu hojin* and other public corporations are the most frequented *wataridori* paths from the ministries to private firms, showing the prevailing indirect route between the ministries and the boards of directors of private firms.

Ministry Rank, Amakudari *Position, and* Wataridori *Distance*
We suggest that *wataridori* are likely to be higher-ranking ex-bureaucrats moving through the reemployment process. Is a bureaucrat's rank at the time of retirement systematically related to his rank in his postretirement positions? What are the characteristics of this relationship and how is it accomplished?

The examination of *wataridori* patterns reveals a logistical process, a pattern of supply and resupply of personnel managed by the ministries. The rank of the retiring bureaucrat determines the appropriate first *amakudari* (or *yokosuberi*) position as well as subsequent *wataridori* landing spots. The process is logistical in that it represents the coordinated distribution of placements into the private and public sectors. The fact that *amakudari* placement is often to a position vacated by an ex-civil servant from the same ministry illustrates its logistical character. Interviewees described how they went to a private firm and then to an affiliate of that company; in their first and sometimes their subsequent reemployment positions they took the place of other ex-officials from the same ministry.

The rank of the retired civil servant affects the rank of the first position of placement (*amakudari* or *yokosuberi*) and the number of *wataridori* positions (distance). Some authors contend that the higher a bureaucrat's position in the ministry at the point of retirement, the higher the rank of the *amakudari* destination (for both the private and public sectors). Preretirement rank correlates with postretirement rank (which is intuitively reasonable). Interviews with *amakudari* officials from the MOF confirmed this relationship at least for the MOF. According to one interviewee, high-ranking officials at the MOF (at the rank of bureau chief or above) typically take their first

amakudari position in a *tokushu hojin*, but lower-ranking MOF officials (below bureau chief) take their first *amakudari* in a *zaidan* or
shadan hojin, which is lower in prestige and compensation than
tokushu hojin. Similarly, Ishizawa (1995, 87) illustrates how *amakudari* is governed by strict principles of rank at the MOF. The top
amakudari position for bureaucrats retiring from the MOF is the governor of the BOJ. Past patterns reveal that the MOF's retiring bureaucrats and those moving up from within the BOJ alternate in the top
position. In addition, the director/chairman position of the JDB is
reserved for bureaucrats who reach the vice minister position in the
MOF. Next in line is the director/chairman of the Export-Import
Bank of Japan, and then the National Financial Corporation (Kinyu
Koko). Further down the status hierarchy are the director/chairman
of the Japan Finance Corporation for Small Business, Shoko Chukin
Bank, Housing Loan Corporation, and Norin Gyogyo Kinyu Koko.
Those bureaucrats ending their careers as bureau chiefs typically
descend to *riji* (director) positions of *tokushu hojin*.

In addition to the strict correspondence between ministry career
rank and reemployment rank, ministry rank affects the distance, or
length of time of reemployment as measured by the seriality of reemployment. For example, ministry rank at retirement is positively
related to the number of positions received by an ex-bureaucrat, but
there is a decay function in the quality of positions from the first to
subsequent *wataridori* positions. Thus, the third position is somewhat inferior to the first, but still within the range of positions seen
as appropriate for someone of a particular retirement rank. A retired
vice minister takes a very high position with a public corporation
(e.g., president or managing director), but he is more likely to be managing director instead of president in his second reemployment position, and definitely more likely to be managing director in his third
reemployment.[7]

Inoki (1995) best illustrates the relationship between ministry
rank at the time of retirement and length of reemployment ("flying
time"). Although a retired vice minister may find placement in appropriate positions until he is seventy or older (fifteen years of "flying
time"), a person who retires as section chief may find appropriate
employment in only one or two positions (or three to six years). Inoki
implies that when ministry reemployment efforts cease, the retired
official must rely on his own resources and contacts to find further
employment. Thus, another facet of the *wataridori* network is the

decay function of rank of exit to rank of placements over a sequence of *wataridori* positions.

This discussion indicates the dimensions of the systematic character of *wataridori*, better specifying the pattern of elite interinstitutional movements. First, *wataridori* manifests a logistical process of placing bureaucrats in positions vacated by an earlier retiree from the same ministry. Second, the rank of the bureaucrat at retirement largely determines the rank and status of his first and subsequent retirement positions. Third, the sequence of retirement positions manifests a decay function from the first through subsequent positions. Fourth, some positions are alternately occupied by retiring officials from different ministries or public corporations. And finally, the length of reemployment of retired bureaucrats is positively correlated with their rank at the time of retirement.

Wataridori as a Process: Organization and Coordination

Demonstrating the dominance of five ministries over the *wataridori* movement and the correspondence among the rank at retirement, the position of placement, and longer "flying time" begs the question of how *amakudari* or *wataridori* movements are created and recreated over time. Our descriptions of structural patterns of *wataridori* so far lack an explanation of who arranges these reemployment movements and how those arrangements are made (Johnson 1974 and Cho 1995 are exceptions). The characterizations of *amakudari* as carefully institutionalized and informal suggest spontaneous unconscious and non-self-interested practices that are also somehow autogenerated and reproduced; they lack explanatory power. In our view, *amakudari* processes (in its broad sense) are institutionalized in that these movements are carefully calculated and consciously managed, but they are also routinized and coordinated strategies of the ministries. Our interview data combined with the ethnographic literature provide insights into these processes and refract light onto the more demanding *wataridori* process.

Amakudari arrangements are not individual arrangements but are ministry-level processes operating out of specific positions and certain administrative units. A recently promoted vice minister was described as under "compelling obligation to find suitable positions" for those retiring from his ministry (Johnson 1974, 940). The key man in each ministry who is responsible for orchestrating *amakudari* placements is the *kanbocho* (chief of the secretariat), a position equivalent in rank to the most senior bureau chief. This position is a stepping stone to the vice ministership. Johnson points out that *amakudari* decisions are not centrally planned for all ministries but emanate from each ministry with a high-ranking bureaucrat specifically responsible for creating and orchestrating these decisions. There has, however, been little if any examination of the extent and variation of these processes.

Our interviews indicate that each ministry personnel office has a list of companies and positions accumulated over time, suggesting that *amakudari* (in its broad sense) is an orderly blueprint of positions in the field, not an informal process. The personnel office of a ministry maintains contact with the companies on its list to make *amakudari* arrangements for its soon-to-be-retiring bureaucrats. Sometimes companies contact ministries to request *amakudari* placements.

In chapter 2 we discuss features of the coordination of *amakudari* placements. Ethnographies of the MOF indicate that there are over 19,000 *amakudari* destinations for MOF bureaucrats, most in entities that received subsidies or funds from the MOF or its National Tax Agency. Private companies receive *amakudari* in the hope of receiving information, money, and regulatory considerations. *Amakudari* and *wataridori* positions open when a company is under stress. The MOF gains control of banks in trouble, devises a rescue plan, and sends *amakudari* and *wataridori* into the bank to implement the plan. Once a position has been granted to the MOF, it is added to the portfolio of the MOF's positions and it is difficult for the receiving company to terminate it.

Who makes these arrangements depends on the rank of retiring officials, but the placement of top-level bureaucrats is almost always handled by the *kanbocho*, along with a committee of bureau chiefs and currently retired *amakudari* and *wataridori*, including retired vice ministers. For example, Cho's (1995) survey of 331 ex-officials indicates that for officials retiring to the highest positions, those of the board of directors (*daihyo* and *fuku-daihyo*)[8] are handled by the *kanbocho* of the ministry of exit. Retirements to lower administrative positions (e.g., *senmu*, *jomu*, *hiratori*, *jokansa*, and *kansa*) are sometimes handled by the *kanbocho*, but are also handled at lower levels (by a bureau chief) of the ministry. Thus, the rank of the *amakudari* position is closely related to the rank of the person making the arrangement.

In addition to the logistical process shown in the correspondence among the ministry rank, reemployment rank, and the rank of the ministry personnel making the arrangement, there is concern for an appropriate match. The process reveals the beliefs, norms, and expectations of ministry officials. The *amakudari* placement, the second job of a civil servant, is often to a position vacated by an ex-civil servant—most typically from the same ministry, with both retirees moving simultaneously. This pattern brings personal pressure on each occupant of that position. For example, Cho (1995) found that ex-civil servants who inherited these positions from their predecessors felt obliged to do good work (for the private firms) so their positions could be handed over to their successors. The ex-bureaucrats take the role of the stewards of such positions.

In our interview, a *wataridori* official who went to a private construction company and then to an affiliate of that construction company expressed similar beliefs. In addition, he emphasized the importance of the appropriateness of a position for an ex-official. Like many of his colleagues, this interviewee had inherited his first *amakudari* position from another retired official from his agency. But in his case, this arrangement was made informally through the vacating ex-bureaucrat. Once this informal arrangement was made (by the interviewee, the vacating ex-bureaucrat, and the company), the private company approached his agency to say they were interested in having the interviewee join the company. The interviewee indicated the agency personnel thought long and hard about the "appropriateness" of this match, by which he meant the personality, style, and culture of the company. This thinking involves an agency's concern that future placements to that position and that corporation depend on the good fit of any present placement. The current match must be good because it will affect the agency's ability to place retirees in the future.

This continuous movement and the appropriateness of the fit of the ex-official to the position is one reason *kanbocho* offices periodically hold study group meetings to give ex-bureaucrats opportunities for access to the latest news, information, and events. These meetings are geared to prevent ex-bureaucrats from becoming obsolete commodities. The smooth continuation of *amakudari* and *wataridori* directly translates into survival for the ministries. Through *amakudari*, *yokosuberi*, and *wataridori*, the ministries continue to promote new blood inside the ministry and receiving companies can economize their linkages with the government (especially the costs incurred in dealings with the central ministries). Our interviews, however, did not confirm this conception of continuous education but instead indicated that many *amakudari* officials' value to private companies is based on personal skills and social contacts (human and social capital) and not on current inside knowledge of ministry operations. The difference involves different types of *amakudari*. Some officials are valued for their knowledge of the inner workings of their home ministry (MOF), whereas others tend to be valued for their skills and experience (MITI).

Financial Compensation

The tension between the institution of *amakudari/wataridori* and the exclusion of nonelites forms the basis for important political issues. This tension takes the form of criticism of *wataridori* by labor organizations as obstructing members from the opportunity to participate as board members of *tokushu hojin*. Essentially, this truncates the promotion ladder. The issue of participation and *wataridori* is particularly intense over the placement of ex-bureaucrats on the boards of public organizations. Seiroren (1992) focuses on the practice of repeated *yokosuberi* (*wataridori*) to *tokushu hojin* and the lump-sum payment given to ex-bureaucrats on their departure from each position.

Financial compensation for *yokosuberi* and *wataridori* comes in two forms: salary and lump-sum payments. The salaries of bureaucrats, compared to their private-sector counterparts, are low. According to a NPA report (1995), the highest-ranking bureaucrat (administrative rank 11) received ¥590,000/month in 1995, whereas someone of lower rank in the private sector received ¥890,000/month in 1993. *Yokosuberi* to *tokushu hojin* provides salaries comparable to what ex-bureaucrats received in their last ministry position (Inoki 1995). *Amakudari* salaries in the private sector, however, are consistent with industry standards. The salaries of bureaucrats increase by 50 percent with *amakudari* to the private sector. The political issue of *wataridori* is not salary but the potential accumulation of lump-

Table 5.5 Average Lump-Sum Payments by *Tokushu Hojin*, 1991[a]

Controlling Entity	Number of *Tokushu Hojin* Surveyed	Number of *Yokosuberi* Involved	Average Job Tenure (months)	Average Lump-Sum Received (yen)
MOC	2	7	52.6	20,540,000[b]
MOA	9	14	44.6	14,150,000
STA	3	8	45.0	16,050,000
MOF	5	17	38.4	13,520,000
Education	3	6	43.7	13,520,000
MITI	5	13	44.5	13,680,000
Labor	2	5	42.4	13,450,000
MHW	3	4	47.5	13,430,000
Foreign Affairs	2	4	52.0	15,620,000
Economic Planning Agency	1	2	65.5	21,960,000
MOT	1	3	51.2	17,120,000
Average			45.0	14,500,000
Range			38–66	$134,300–219,600

Source: Seiroren (1992, 51).
[a] MHW, Ministry of Health and Welfare; MITI, Ministry of International Trade and Industry; MOA, Ministry of Agriculture, Forestry, and Fisheries; MOC, Ministry of Construction; MOF, Ministry of Finance; MOT, Ministry of Transport; STA, Science and Technology Agency.
[b] $205,400.

sum pensions collected from the chain of *wataridori* reemployment positions that make up an ex-civil servant's retirement compared to the regular employees of the *tokushu hojin*. Table 5.5 indicates the average lump sum paid to *yokosuberi* officials at *tokushu hojin* by the ministries.

The issue of lump-sum compensation involves the formula used to calculate this severance compensation. According to Seiroren (1992, 150), board-of-directors' retirement lump-sum payments are determined by the following formula: Monthly pay × 0.36 × Number of months served. The 0.36 multiplier was changed from 0.45 in 1978 and from 0.70 in 1970. In other words, lump-sum pensions to board members were cut almost by one-half from 1970 to 1978. The retirement pensions of the regular employees of *tokushu hojin* are determined by a different formula: Monthly pay × Number of years served. The comparison of lump-sum payments for *tokushu hojin* board members with those of regular employees is instructive for understanding the tension between the labor organization and *wataridori*. Although the multiplier of 0.36 reduces the monthly pay function for calculating pensions, the fact that the board member's pay function is based on the number of months worked rather than years exaggerates the pension benefits. Despite some variation by ministry of origin, as shown on average in table 5.5, *yokosuberi* officials stayed on the job at *tokushu hojin* for forty-five months and received ¥14,500,000 ($145,000) as their one-time lump-sum payment when they left the position.

To examine the nature of *wataridori* more fully, Seiroren (1992) examined 103 cases of *wataridori* (eighty-one current and twenty-two retired cases) in 1991 (table 5.6). The survey indicates that of the eighty-one then-current *wataridori*, almost one in three (32.1 percent) moved within and among *tokushu hojin* three or more times. One person moved more than seven times. If we assume the average rate ($145,000) of lump-sum pensions, we can say that almost 68 percent (67.9 percent) were in positions to have received at least $290,000 in pensions and one person was in a position to have received over $1 million in lump-sum compensation. Among those *wataridori* who retired from *tokushu hojin* (those who left employment in this type of organization), over one in five (22.7 percent) had moved within and around *tokushu hojin* three or more times. The

Table 5.6 Number of *Wataridori* Moves within *Tokushu Hojin*, 1991[a]

| | N | Number of Moves | | | | | |
		2	3	4	5	6	>7
Current *wataridori*	81	55	18	5	2	0	1
	(100)	(67.9)	←		(32.1)		→
Retired *wataridori*	22	17	2	1	2	0	0
	(100)	(77.3)	←		(22.7)		→

Source: Seiroren (1992, 56, table 3.13).
[a] Values in parentheses are percentages.

two most mobile had five moves or five positions at *tokushu hojin* after leaving the central ministry.

These cases of accumulated lump-sum payments have invited criticisms of *wataridori* processes. The problem is both substantial and symbolic. Career *tokushu hojin* employees resent the placement of ex-bureaucrats on their boards of directors and the discriminary lump-sum retirement payment. The discriminatory formula for lump-sum retirement pay is substantial in that it better compensates exbureaucrats than career *tokushu hojin* personnel for time served. However, the number of payments to ex-bureaucrats is irrelevant to total compensation. Lump-sum payments for six years at one *tokushu hojin* is equivalent to three two-year stays at three different *tokushu hojin*. The symbolic issue comes from the placement of ex-bureaucrats on the boards of directors to the neglect of internal promotions and the discriminatory lump-sum compensation reminds career employees of their second class status. The lump-sum payment differentials are just one of the myriad issues involving retired ministry personnel that incite popular criticism because they both challenge the legitimacy of the process and have not been readily disclosed in a timely fashion by ministry officials.

The examination of *wataridori* provides a description of the structure and process of serial reemployment of top-level bureaucrats. *Wataridori* accounts for a significant proportion of *amakudari* positions in the private sector. The recognition of the differences between *amakudari* and *wataridori* and between *yokosuberi* and *wataridori* highlights the indirect path or what network analysts call the structural embeddedness of the ministries in the private sector. *Amakudari* (the direct path to the private sector) and *yokosuberi* (the direct path to the public sector) reveal the relational aspect of the embeddedness of the bureaucracy in the private and public sectors, but they do not provide the larger structural picture. These structural features come to light when the indirect path (*wataridori*) and the status hierarchy of ministries involved in *wataridori* are scrutinized. For example, *wataridori* ending in private-sector positions are higher-status bureaucrats than those who go directly (*amakudari*) to the private sector. The hierarchical nature of *wataridori* indicates a variation in ministry power or organizational capacity. The same five ministries (MOF, MITI, Construction, Transport, and Agriculture) that dominate the *amakudari* and *yokosuberi* networks also lead in *wataridori* placements. Thus, *wataridori* is a function of a ministry's capacity to mobilize influence, and *wataridori* positions are related to bureaucratic rank at the time of retirement. Only five ministries have developed the institutional apparatuses (specialized and dedicated personnel coordination functions) necessary to allow the ministry sponsorship of serial reemployment of their retirees. *Wataridori* processes are social processes creating and recreating personnel movements. They are institutionalized, strictly coordinated, logistical, and driven by the status of the retiring bureaucrat and the capacities of the ministry.

As is *amakudari* and *yokosuberi*, *wataridori* is not about the person who is reemployed but the position that the person occupies. Yet *wataridori* is not simply about a single position but about the chain, sequence, or circuit of positions occupied by ex-civil servants, which represents ministry turf. As these ex-bureaucrats move out of one position and on to another, they often replace retired bureaucrats from the same ministry. Simultaneously, their previous positions are taken by other retired bureaucrats from the same ministry. This lock-step movement of personnel has a sense of circuit as both structure and process, and also of space and time. Space is the process of the movement or flow of personnel from the government to and through other sectors of Japanese society—the retirement process of the civil servant does not stop at the first job taken after leaving the ministry; it may go on for several more positions. Time is indicated with the retirement of civil servants around age fifty-five and employment continuing through age sixty-five, seventy, or longer.

There are important theoretical issues raised by the study of *wataridori*. The creation and reproduction of *wataridori* is difficult to characterize with the available concepts. As our analysis indicates, the examination of the process of creation and recreation of *wataridori* is neither formal (in the sense of codified, explicit, and enforced by law) nor informal (in the sense of spontaneous and unconscious). *Wataridori* appears to exemplify a hybrid process. We first organized our exposition of *wataridori* around the notions of structure and process; however, our analysis makes it apparent that the imagery of structure and process does not capture the coordinated movement over time. It may be better captured in the concept of circuit—the combination of structure and process over time.

6 *Seikai Tensin*: Movement to the Political World

This chapter examines *seikai tensin*, the movement of bureaucrats to the political world.[1] The three previous chapters addressed the movement of resources and personnel from the ministries to the private and public sectors. In the larger political economy, this movement is shaped and guided by parliament. Diet members enact legislation to facilitate and obstruct this flow of resources and personnel; they are often called on to address conflicting interests and negotiate the direction of these resources and personnel. Given the pivotal position of the Diet in the movement of personnel, it is important to understand the integration of the bureaucracy and parliament.

The early academic literature on Japanese political economy recognized the importance of networks in producing a homogeneity of outlook and common orientation among the institutional elites. At its broadest conception, these networks provide the structural substance of a power structure based on an association of bureaucratic, political, and business elites, or the iron triangle. Iron triangle invokes an image of a high level of integration and coordination among elites that dominate policymaking to the exclusion of other groups.[2] Since the 1970s, however, a wave of reaction to the image of Japan as a monolithic elitist society emerged, emphasizing instead the fluid and processual nature of politics, the fragmentation of interests, and the greater differentiation of politicians and political decision making from the bureaucracy.

Authors writing from both perspectives recognize *seikai tensin* as evidence of elite integration, but argue over its contemporary relevance. We believe the movement of bureaucrats to politics as a form of elite integration is a matter of degree and has varied over time and by political position. In this chapter, we examine the prevalence of ex-bureaucrats in high-profile political positions including the prime ministership, the cabinet, and elected positions in the Lower House (the House of Representatives) of the Diet[3] and present systematic data on the relationship between the polity and bureaucracy to map the degree and location of differentiation versus integration or variation versus stability between the two institutions. We analyze the change in the degree of integration of the ministries and politics as indicated by the pattern of *seikai tensin* in national political office since World War II and explore the stratification of *seikai tensin* by ministry.

Review of the Literature

Scholars agree on the importance of *seikai tensin* as a measure of elite integration but disagree on the extent and location of this integration as it has developed over time. One group emphasizes a general integration between bureaucratic and political elites (cf. Scalapino 1968; Johnson 1974), which is expressed as the "fusion" of the two (Pempel 1998) or "corporate cohesion" of the state (Evans 1995). A second group postulates a differentiation or cleavage between bureaucrats and politicians (Fukui 1977; Samuels 1987; Allinson 1989; Calder 1993; Richardson 1997; Schwartz 1998).

The first set of scholars assumes that elite groups are united in both purpose and action, participate in most important decisions, and exclude nonelites from major political decisions (Alford and Friedland 1985). Bureaucrats and politicians are seen as two sides of the iron triangle and *seikai tensin* represents the uniting of the two. Ex-bureaucrats occupying the prime ministership or positions in the cabinet and the Lower House are key indicators of elite participation in major policy decisions. The patterns of *seikai tensin* over time bear on the validity of this type of elite participation.

Elite integration may be natural for a country such as Japan, where bureaucratic power and elite integration have a long history. Bureaucrats moving into political parties served to strike a balance between dictatorship and mass participation and provided a basis for a guided democracy in the first few decades after the Meiji Restoration in 1868 (Scalapino 1968, 249–91).[4] After World War II, the bureaucracy rose in institutional stature and ex-bureaucrats were seen to contribute to the political stability of the war-damaged country (Johnson 1975).

The Occupation affected the influence of bureaucracy in postwar recovery and postoccupation industrial policy. The bureaucracy was the primary recruiting ground for party [LDP] leadership between 1955 and 1980 (Kawakita 1989).

The conservative party (LDP) was closely intertwined with the bureaucracy in the early postwar era through its recruitment of high-level bureaucrats. Ex-bureaucrats (*seikai tensin*) have constituted a significant percentage of LDP, Diet and cabinet members, and prime ministers (Curtis 1988; Rothacher 1993). This personnel relationship was supplemented by other sources of bureaucratic influence on the legislative process, including the ability of bureaucrats to write legislation that could pass the Diet (Johnson 1982; Kerbo 2000), their control of information and technical expertise in the early stages of policymaking (Curtis 1988; Richardson 1997), and their involvement in policy deliberations and policy advisory councils (Kawakita 1989). The fusion between bureaucrats and politicians takes place in their close working relations in a number of circumstances including *shingi kai* (policy deliberation councils) and consultations of bureaucrats to *seimu chosa kai* (study groups) of members of the upper and lower houses of the Diet (Kawakita 1989, 142, 197).

Authors in the second group view the central government as an arena of contested institutional power and reject the monolithic notion of an iron triangle. These scholars emphasize the formal differentiation of the state, competition and conflict within the bureaucracy (e.g., vertical administration and turf battles), and the factional nature of party politics (Allinson 1989; Samuels 1987; Fukui 1977; Calder 1993; Richardson 1997; Broadbent 1998; Schwartz 1998).[5]

For example, the notion of "mixed pluralism" (Muramatsu 1981) refers to the influence bureaucrats, private interests, and *zoku* politicians wield within highly differentiated and vertically administered sector bound policy spheres. *Zoku* politicians are LDP career politicians who are trained to tackle the policy issues of specific ministries. The emergence of the expert *zoku* politician is assumed to be evidence of two important features: that the initiatives of the bureaucracy and its power over the LDP are not all there is to policymaking and that the legislature and bureaucracy operate independently and hence conflict and compete. Michio Muramatsu and Ellis Krauss argue that "the bureaucracy is the pivot around which the policy making alliances are formed on a particular issue" (1984, 516–54).

Into these sectors emerge subgovernments of collaboration, negotiation, conflicts, cooperation, and cooptation involving relevant ministries, *zoku* politicians, and pertinent sector interests. The interface of the LDP and business interests involves *zoku* politicians, in particular, the LDP's Policy Affairs Research Council (PARC). LDP politicians have gained policy expertise, becoming more involved in policymaking and developing closer ties with interest groups to obtain political funds and votes (Schoppa 1991; Sato and Matsuzaki 1986). According to Yung Park (1986), policymaking migrated from the bureaucracy to the LDP, especially to PARC, during the 1970s. PARC committees provide LDP politicians with opportunities for experience early in their careers and with a continuous flow of staff, information, and technical expertise that relieves the politicians' dependence on bureaucrats. The emergence of *zoku* politicians is said to have led to the the end of iron triangle politics and created a steadily more competitive polity in the 1980s and 1990s (Allinson 1993, 17–49). Thus, although ex-bureaucrats dominated the prime ministership, key cabinet posts, and major leadership positions in the private sector in the 1950s and 1960s, by the 1970s ex-bureaucrats were almost shut out of top positions in favor of men groomed from within. The rise of *zoku* politicians within the LDP led to greater merit-based competition, recruitment, and promotion.

Explanations of the Changing Pattern of *Seikai Tensin*

The notion of the decline of *seikai tensin* has led to several alternative and somewhat complementary explanations suggesting various points of change: the rise of the *zoku* politician, generational changes in faction leaders, the increasing enforcement of the LDP seniority system, and the rise of the hereditary politician.

Rise of Zoku *Politicians*
The rise of *zoku* politicians beginning in the late 1960s was presumed to have changed the balance of power between politicians and bureaucrats and led to the demise of *seikai tensin* by the 1970s (Uchida 1993; Sato and Matsuzaki 1986; Park 1986; Mabuchi 1997; Richardson 1997). Their emergence is attributed to the long LDP rule and the routinization of office-holding in the party. *Zoku* politicians (policy specialists operating within the LDP's PARC) gain experience and

expertise in the policy process through their participation in research groups, Diet councils, and commissions and through appointments to parliamentary vice ministerships and to high-ranking party and cabinet minister positions. The experience and expertise of *zoku* politicians made the LDP both more factional and more independent of the bureaucracy. For example, Bradley Richardson contends that since World War II "the party had replaced the bureaucracy as policy innovator and agenda setter until its recent loss of power. Finance Ministry officials have reportedly lamented that the Government-LDP Consultative Council had become the 'real Budget Bureau,' and the party's Tax-Reduction-Problem Subcommittee the 'real Tax Bureau.' The ability of the LDP to overrule Finance Ministry budget decisions supposedly exemplified these changes. A belief that LDP *zoku* were growing in influence was an integral part of this argument" (1997, 125).

The explanation of the demise of *seikai tensin* based on the development of technical expertise by *zoku* politicians is not without its critics. Some authors suggest that *zoku* politicians are not powerful enough to shift the balance of influence between bureaucrats and politicians (Inoguchi and Iwai 1987; Sato and Matsuzaki 1986; Keehn 1990; Ishizawa 1995). Takashi Inoguchi and Tomsaki Iwai's (1987) study of *zoku* politicians' participation in ten cases of policymaking finds mixed results on the direction of influence. In some cases the *zoku* shaped and guided the policy process, but in other cases a bureaucrat–private interest alliance prevailed. Inoguchi and Iwai (1987) argue for the resilience of the bureaucracy and characterize the Japanese polity as bureaucracy-led mass-inclusionary pluralism (*kanryoshudo taishu hokatsu-gata tagenshugi*), but still suggest the demise of a cohesive iron triangle, reflected in their notion of mass-inclusionary pluralism. Taking the long view, Inoguchi and Iwai contend that the decline of bureaucratic power in the 1970s and 1980s was temporary. Similar to Inoguchi and Iwai, Edward Keehn (1990, 1028–29) suggests that, rather than a relationship of competition and domination between bureaucrats and politicians, the relationship between *zoku* politicians and bureaucrats is more one of reciprocal patronage. *Zoku* politicians act as proxies, protecting and advancing their ministry's or agency's interests in return for access to the resources of that ministry or agency. They "carry forward the bureaucrat's battles, on the latter's behalf, in the political arena" (Keehn 1990, 1029).

Thus the development of technical expertise by the *zoku* may have neither shifted the balance of influence between the LDP and the bureaucracy nor eroded the position of *seikai tensin* politicians (Inoguchi and Iwai 1987; Keehn 1990). To make matters more complicated, Seizaburo Sato and Tetsuhisa Matsuzaki (1986) bring up the problem of measuring who exactly qualifies as a *zoku* politician. These basic issues of definitions and measurement are not settled, and no one has taken the next step to present evidence on this presumed inverse relationship between *zoku* and *seikai tensin* politicians. The rise of the *zoku* politicians has not been firmly measured, and the relationship between *zoku* and *seikai tensin* is at best a correspondence in time and not causally established. Yet, the suggestion is that *zoku* politicians began to undermine *seikai tensin* politicians as early as the 1960s.

Changes in Faction Leadership
The second explanation of the decline of *seikai tensin* politicians focuses on a generational change in the faction leaders within the LDP. The patron-client relationship between factional bosses and their followers became weaker in the 1980s due to a generational change in the leaders (Curtis 1988, 81). Faction leaders in the 1980s inherited their factions; gone were those entrepreneurial old-line party bosses who had built the factions. In the early postwar period, the factions had been smaller and more numerous. Each faction involved an inner core of loyal followers marked by a strong patron-client (*oyabun-kobun*) relationship in which the faction leader provided political funds and access to party posts in return for support and votes.

The generational change in leadership is particularly relevant to the postwar Yoshida School, which built its faction bases on the recruitment of ex-bureaucrats. *Seikai tensin* came to prominence in the postwar era through the active recruitment of bureaucrats by Shigeru Yoshida of the Liberal Party (1945–55); the Liberal Party merged with the Progressive Party in 1955 to form the Liberal Democratic Party. Yoshida, out of the MOF, recruited prime ministers Hayato Ikeda, Takeo Fukuda, and Eisaku Sato from the Ministry of Railways (today, the Ministry of Transport). Ikeda later recruited Masayoshi Ohira and Kiichi Miyazawa from the MOF. Yet, with Yoshida's passing and a split in the faction, the *seikai tensin* politicians lost their advocacy and factional base. The Yoshida School of elite bureaucrats split into the Ikeda and Sato factions in 1956–57, and in the 1990s the legacy of the Yoshida School is represented by the Miyazawa faction of the LDP, which passed from Ikeda to Miyazawa via Ohira and Zenko Suzuki.[6] According to Albert Rothacher (1993, 14–15), the decline of *seikai tensin* politicians should be clearly reflected among the prime ministers of the 1980s.

Enforcement of Liberal Democratic Party Seniority

The third explanation of the decline of *seikai tensin* relates to the internal organization of the LDP. In the 1970s, the factions became larger and were reduced to only four, due in part to changes in political funding. Some call this change the "Tanaka effect," referring to the money politics that became prevalent around Kakuei Tanaka's ascendance to power. The changes in the number of factions and their size corresponded to changes in the system of promoting LDP members to cabinet posts and other high-level party and political offices. These changes, in turn, led to important changes in the backgrounds of politicians recruited into LDP Diet membership. According to this logic, this effect should be apparent in the early 1970s.

In the 1950s and 1960s, a large proportion of party funds was garnered by the faction leader and distributed to his followers. In 1976, a revision of the laws regulating political contributions made it impossible for faction leaders to raise and control large portions of political funds on their own (Curtis 1988, 84). This law had the effect of decentralizing the networks of political fund-raising, diminishing the importance of the big business establishment (*zaikai*), and increasing the importance of provincial interests as a source of political financing. This decentralization of fund-raising moved the funding pattern away from the factional leaders and ex-bureaucrats, who were tied to central sources of support, and toward the professional politicians with strong local ties. Thus, changes in the factional composition within the LDP and changes in the funding networks weakened the bases of ex-bureaucrats connected to the political resources in the central government. According to Curtis (1988) this effect should be apparent by the late 1970s.

Another factor that led to the decline of *seikai tensin* was the increasing importance of seniority within the LDP. In the early postwar period, several *seikai tensin* politicians were able to start their political careers in their mid-forties, after a first career in the bureaucracy, and still become prime minister. In other words, there was considerable room on the fast track. Since the early 1970s, specifically since the Tanaka prime ministership of 1972–74, the accelerated career track has been almost eliminated. Little or no credit is given for time served in the bureaucracy, Upper House, or local political offices (e.g., governorship), as had been routine in the earlier period. LDP party members are all required to move up the same seniority ladder (Sato and Matsuzaki 1986).

In the late 1990s, it took twenty-five to thirty years of career experience in party politics to rise to the level of prime minister.[7] This suggests the impossibility for any bureaucrat of seeking a second career in a high political position. *Seikai tensin* prime ministers have become the exception since the 1980s. An individual must win political office continuously from approximately age thirty-five on to be considered for the prime minister position late in his career. The arithmetic of the LDP's seniority system diminishes the probability of *seikai tensin* politicians achieving high political office.

Rise of Hereditary Politicians

The fourth explanation for the decline of the *seikai tensin* politician involves the corresponding rise of the hereditary politician (*seshu giin*), someone who has inherited family wealth (*kaban*), reputation (*kanban*), and a political network and social organization (*jiban*).[8] These resources are then directly converted into election to office. Technically, hereditary politicians include adopted sons, sons-in-law, and even nephews and brothers. The rise of the hereditary politician builds on the previous explanation based on the importance of seniority (Uchida 1993; Rothacher 1993). The increasing enforcement of seniority rules within the LDP, coupled with the decentralization of political fund-raising, has contributed to the success of homegrown hereditary politicians.

> The LDP's seniority system, which today requires some four or five re-elections (that is, some 20 years in the Diet) in order to be considered for a first cabinet post, has worked against senior bureaucrats choosing a political secondary career [*seikai tensin*], and has benefited the young sons of established politicians who were able— unlike any of their peers—to enter parliament on [the] strength of inherited *jiban*, *kaban* and *kanban*, and to rise in the LDP's parliamentary pecking order with [their] first ministerial appointments in

their mid-fifties (at an age when elite bureaucrats begin to retire).
(Rothacher 1993, 52)

The enforcement of seniority put a premium on the early start of a
political career. In short, the LDP's career requirements and the
decentralization of political fund-raising gave an advantage to those
with strong local ties to the private sector.

The rise in the number of high-profile politicians who are hereditary politicians is noteworthy. Within the LDP, these include, for
example, former and current prime ministers Kiichi Miyazawa,
Junichiro Koizumi, Ryutaro Hashimoto, and Keizo Obuchi and
foreign minister Yohei Kono. In the Democratic Party, Tsutomu Hata
(ex-prime minister) and, in the Liberal Party, Ichiro Ozawa are hereditary politicians. Between elections in 1983 and 1986,

> the second-generation [hereditary] phenomenon has closed off oppor-
> tunities for other ambitious politicians to get into the Diet, but it has
> brought greater diversity in career backgrounds and life experience to
> the LDP's Diet member contingent and has played a role in giving the
> party a more modern look. Japan's emergence as a world economic
> power has forced even the LDP's most parochial Diet members to
> become more aware of international affairs, and the party as a whole
> has slowly been becoming more "internationalist," a popular word in
> present day Japan. But this is especially true for second-generation
> politicians, particularly salarymen who have worked for banks,
> trading companies, and other corporations involved in international
> business and have spent time working abroad. Many of these politi-
> cians convey a more cosmopolitan image than an earlier generation
> of LDP politicians or the present generation of largely union-based
> opposition party politicians. And they appeal to a young and urban
> electorate party for that reason. (Curtis 1988, 97)

To Gerald Curtis, hereditary politicians represent "diversity of
career" and an appealing cosmopolitan image; there is no suggestion
of the emergence of a new ensconced elite.

The four explanations of the decline of *seikai tensin* politicians
suggest changes in different political offices and in the timing of those
changes. The generational change among politicians suggests the
decline of *seikai tensin* in the prime ministership in the 1980s. The
rise of *zoku* politicians suggests a general decline of *seikai tensin*
arguably to the Diet from the late 1960's to the late 1970s. And the

rise of the hereditary politician suggests the decline of *seikai tensin* in Diet membership in the mid- to late 1970s. We next investigate *seikai tensin* patterns among prime ministers and cabinet, Diet, and LDP members and their correspondence with changes in other institutional patterns to suggest other explanations.

Data on Political Officeholders

To systematically examine the demise of *seikai tensin*, we assembled data at four levels of political office: prime minister, cabinet posts, Lower House LDP membership, and Lower House membership generally over selected times since World War II. In addition, we included two other related features of each politician's background: graduation from the University of Tokyo and family background (to reveal hereditary politicians). The possible limitations of this design are that other political positions may capture change at different times, results from the years not sampled may differ or change the interpretation of the overall trend. Having said that, we proceed with the information we could practically collect.

Prime Ministers
Table 6.1 lists the names, age at election to the prime ministership, terms in office, and career and family backgrounds of postwar prime ministers. There have been twenty-eight prime ministerships (but twenty-seven prime ministers); ten (35.7 percent) were *seikai tensin*: Kijuro Shidehara, Shigeru Yoshida (twice), Hitoshi Ashida, Nobusuke Kishi, Hayato Ikeda, Eisaku Sato, Takeo Fukuda, Masayoshi Ohira, and Kiichi Miyazawa.[9] These nine prime ministers held office for almost twenty-nine of the fifty-six years between 1945 and 2002 (or 348 months out of 677 months) or for over 51.4 percent of the period. If the placement and tenure of ex-bureaucrats in the prime ministership is an indication of the integration of the bureaucracy and polity, then the influence of ex-bureaucrats has been significant. Of these nine prime ministers, four were from the MOF, four from the Ministry of Foreign Affairs, and one each from the Ministry of Commerce and Industry (later changed to the MITI) and the Ministry of Railways (later changed to the Ministry of Transport). In the early postwar years, most *seikai tensin* prime ministers came from the Ministry of Foreign Affairs, but after 1960 they came from the MOF.

But it is the pattern of change over this period that is the issue. Since Suzuki's election in 1980, only one prime minister has had a background in the bureaucracy, Kiichi Miyazawa. He came from the MOF and served as prime minister from November 1991 until August 1993. Between 1946 and 1980, eight ex-bureaucrats occupied nine prime ministerships, serving 327 months out of 418, or 78.2 percent of the period. In contrast, from 1980 to 2002, a period of twenty-two years, or 261 months, Miyazawa, the only *seikai tensin* prime minister, served 21 months (8 percent) of the total period. Thus, the data support the notion that *seikai tensin* politicians declined among prime ministers after 1980.

In addition, table 6.1 shows the number of years each prime minister served in the Diet before taking office and his age at the time of appointment to the prime ministership. The increasingly strict enforcement of the LDP seniority system, it has been argued, is a cause to the decline of *seikai tensin*. Before Tanaka, prime ministers had come to office with fewer years of experience in the Diet. For example, Yoshida had less than one year of experience in the Diet before his first prime ministership. We might dismiss this as purely the result of conditions in the immediate postwar era, but before Tanaka prime ministers averaged fewer than twelve years of experience in the Diet. From Tanaka's prime ministership to Junichiro Koizumi's, the average experience has more than doubled to thirty years. During the early postwar period, the LDP's promotion system made it practical for elite bureaucrats to have full careers in the bureaucracy, retire in their mid- to late forties, and begin their second careers in politics as *seikai tensin* politicians. In point of fact, Yoshida left the bureaucracy at the age of sixty to begin his political career, and Sato retired from the bureaucracy at forty-eight. All of Sato's successors, however, have had at least twenty-two years of Diet experience and three had over thirty-five years. The two *seikai tensin* politicians to become prime minister in the late 1970s, Fukuda and Ohira, retired from the bureaucracy at the ages of forty-five and forty-one, respectively. Miyazawa, the only *seikai tensin* politician to become prime minister in the 1990s, left the bureaucracy at the age of thirty-four and then spent thirty-eight years in the Diet before becoming prime minister at the age of seventy-two. This pattern of the changing seniority profile indicates the more limited possibilities for *seikai tensin* politicians to gain the prime ministership.

Table 6.1 Career Backgrounds of Japanese Prime Ministers 1945–2002[a]

Name	Age[b]	Term of Office (year/month/day)	Duration (months)	Time in Diet (years)
N. Higashikuni	58	1945/8/17 to 1945/10/09	2	0[c]
Kijuro Shidehara	73	1945/10/09 to 1946/05/22	7	0
Shigeru Yoshida	68	1946/5/12 to 1947/5/24	12	0
Tetsu Katayama	60	1947/5/24 to 1948/3/10	10	17
Hitoshi Ashida	61	1948/3/10 to 1948/10/15	7	16
Shigeru Yoshida	71	1948/10/15 to 1954/12/10	74	0
Ichiro Hatoyama	71	1954/12/10 to 1955/12/23	24	39
Tanzan Ishibashi	72	1956/12/23 to 1957/2/25	2	9
Nobusuke Kishi	61	1957/2/25 to 1960/7/19	41	15
Hayato Ikeda	61	1960/7/19 to 1964/11/09	52	11
Eisaku Sato	63	1964/11/9 to 1972/7/7	92	15
Kakuei Tanaka	54	1972/7/7 to 1974/12/9	29	25
Takeo Miki	67	1974/12/9 to 1976/12/24	24	37
Takeo Fukuda	71	1976/12/24 to 1978/12/7	24	24
Masayoshi Ohira	68	1978/12/7 to 1980/6/12	18	26
Zenko Suzuki	69	1980/7/17 to 1982/11/27	29	33
Yasuhiro Nakasone	64	1982/11/27 to 1987/11/6	59	35
Noboru Takeshita	63	1987/11/6 to 1989/6/2	19	29
Sosuke Uno	67	1989/6/3 to 1989/8/10	2	29
Toshiki Kaifu	58	1989/8/10 to 1991/11/5	26	29
Kiichi Miyazawa	72	1991/11/5 to 1993/8/9	21	38
Morihiro Hosokawa	55	1993/8/9 to 1994/4/27	8	22
Tsutomu Hata	59	1994/4/28 to 1994/6/29	2	25
Tomiichi Murayama	70	1994/6/30 to 1996/1/11	18	22
Ryutaro Hashimoto	59	1996/1/11 to 1998/7/30	31	33
Keizo Obuchi	61	1998/7/30 to 2000/4/05	20	35
Yoshiro Mori	63	2000/4/05 to 2001/4/26	12	31
Junichiro Koizumi	59	2001/4/26 to	12	29
Total			677[e]	

Source: J. P. Tsushinsha (1996); Nihon Seikei Shinbunsha (1997, 1998, 1999, 2000, 2001); Nichigai Associates (1990). The duration for Koizumi is as of April 2002.

[a] MCI, Ministry of Commerce and Industry (precursor to MITI); MFA, Ministry of Foreign Affairs; MITI, Ministry of International Trade and Industry; MOF, Ministry of Finance; MOR, Ministry of Railways (Tetsudo-sho); na, not available.

[b] Age at the beginning of the prime ministership.

[c] "Zero" in time spent in the Diet means no prior experience as an elected office holder in the Diet.

[d] Nakasone was a civil servant (Home Ministry), but left the bureaucracy after six years and entered politics when he was twenty nine years old.

[e] *Seikai tensin* of 348 months (total number of months occupied by ex-bureaucrat prime ministers).

The data in table 6.1 thus reflect the increasing strictness of the LDP seniority system. All prime ministers served at least twenty-two years in the Diet. The more general pattern indicates that a potential prime minister serves in the Diet between twenty-five and thirty years. Such seniority requirements make it increasingly difficult for bureaucrats to retire after a full career, around forty-five to fifty, and

Career Background	Time in Bureaucracy (years)	University Graduated	Family Background
Military		Army	
Bureaucrat (MFA)	1895–na	Tokyo	
Bureaucrat (MFA)	1906–39	Tokyo	Father was politician
Politician		Tokyo	
Bureaucrat (MFA)	1912–32	Tokyo	Father was politician
Bureaucrat (MFA)	1906–39	Tokyo	Father was politician
Politician		Tokyo	Father was politician
Journalist		Waseda	
Bureaucrat (MCI)	1920–41	Tokyo	E. Sato, brother
Bureaucrat (MOF)	1925–47	Kyoto	
Bureaucrat (MOR)	1938–48	Tokyo	N. Kishi, brother
Businessman			
Politician		Meiji	Brothers were politicians
Bureaucrat (MOF)	1929–50	Tokyo	
Bureaucrat (MOF)	1936–51	Hitotsubashi	
Interest group (fisheries)		Tokyo Suisan	
Politician[d]		Tokyo	
Prefectural assemblyman		Waseda	
Politician			Grandfather was mayor
Politician		Waseda	
Bureaucrat (MOF)	1942–52	Tokyo	Father was politician
Politician		Sophia	
Politician		Seijo	Father was politician
Politician		Meiji	
Politician		Keio	Father was politician
Politician		Waseda	Father was politician
Politician		Waseda	Father was politician
Politician		Keio	Father was politician

then go through the seniority ladder to become a candidate in their seventies. Miyazawa is the exception that highlights the rule.

The pattern of prime ministers after World War II also illustrates the importance of coming from a political family. The enforcement of the LDP seniority system places a premium on starting young and on the access to money and political resources. An individual's access to existing political resources from his family (money, organization, and reputation) mitigates obstacles for new politicians. It is striking that thirteen of twenty-seven prime ministers (48.1 percent) were hereditary politicians (table 6.1).[10] Nine of the twenty-seven prime ministers had fathers who were politicians, Sosuke Uno's grandfather was a politician, and three prime ministers had brothers who were politicians (Kishi and Sato, themselves, were brothers). In each case, the inheritance of wealth, political organization, and reputation was passed to the candidate. There appears to be a steady stream of hereditary politicians in the office of prime minister after World War II. Between 1945 and 1956, three of the seven prime ministers were hereditary politicians. During 1957–77, there were three hereditary politicians, but the brothers Kishi and Sato together occupied almost eleven of those twenty years. During 1978–1989, there were no prime ministers with hereditary backgrounds. But during 1989–2002 seven of the ten prime ministers were hereditary politicians.

Table 6.1 also indicates that the benefits of coming from the bureaucracy were compounded by the advantages of inheriting the money, organization, and reputation of family politicians through the first twenty years of the postwar era, up through Sato's administration. Five of the seven *seikai tensin* prime ministers were also hereditary politicians. In 1980–2002, however, the overlap between *seikai tensin* and hereditary politicians has all but disappeared (again Miyazawa is the exception). This suggests that the advantages of being an ex-bureaucrat and second-generation politician do not seem to overcome the increasing seniority requirements. Thus, the links between paths of *seikai tensin* and hereditary politicians have unraveled, differentiating the two paths to political careers after 1980.

The examination of a third feature, educational background, may shed light on the pattern of *seikai tensin* and hereditary politicians becoming prime minister. We might automatically assume that *seikai tensin* politicians are Todai graduates because *seikai tensin* politicians tend to have successful bureaucratic careers and a successful bureaucratic career is more likely for a Todai graduate. Seven of the nine postwar *seikai tensin* prime ministers were Todai graduates. Only Ikeda and Ohira did not graduate from Todai. This draws a clear line from Todai through the bureaucracy to the top political position—prime minister. There is little other pattern, however, to be seen over time. Of the thirteen prime ministerships occupied by a hereditary politician, six were occupied by Todai graduates. This pattern is strongest in the first twenty-five years (1946–72), when five—all Todai graduates—of the eleven prime ministers were hereditary politicians. From Tanaka to Koizumi, eight hereditary politicians became prime minister, but only one, Miyazawa, was a Todai graduate. Thus, the institutional mechanism of Todai graduation as a dominant credential for top politicians has declined with a corresponding diversity in the educational backgrounds of prime ministers. Pedigree was not the same after Tanaka.

Cabinet Positions

Next we examine the pattern of *seikai tensin* politicians occupying cabinet positions.[11] Table 6.2 presents information on the names, ministry of origin (*seikai tensin*), and ages of the prime minister and his cabinet members for selected years. Table 6.3 provides a summary of the backgrounds of cabinet members. In his 1953 cabinet, Yoshida included four *seikai tensin* politicians in addition to himself, accounting for five of the twenty cabinet positions. The Ikeda cabinet of 1963 was the peak of *seikai tensin* representation with eleven *seikai tensin* politicians out of twenty-one positions, or 52.4 percent of the cabinet. Although there has been considerable fluctuation, the representation of ex-bureaucrats has been fairly stable, between 25 and 30 percent over time.

There is a clear decline in the percentage of Todai graduates in the cabinet, from a high of 61.9 percent in 1963 to a low of 27.8 percent in 2001 (table 6.3). The monopoly of Todai graduates in the 1960s gave way to a level more comparable to two other elite features by the middle of the 1980s. The decline of Todai representation is not necessarily a result of the decline in ex-bureaucrats, but it is closely related. Considering the elite cachet of Todai graduation, this declining percentage indicates an alternative trend that might represent either the rise of democratic politics or the reversal of democracy with the rising popularity of hereditary politicians. This declining percentage of Todai graduates in cabinet members mirrors the pattern observed in table 6.1 for the prime ministers. There has been a growing differentiation in the educational backgrounds of both prime ministers and their cabinet members.

The percentage of hereditary politicians in each of the cabinets we sampled rises over the years (table 6.3). Starting at only 10 percent of the members of the Yoshida cabinet of 1953, the proportion of hereditary politicians gradually increased to 44 percent of the positions in

Table 6.2 Cabinet Members and Their Career Backgrounds for Selected Years[a]

1953	Age	1963	Age	1972	Age	1983	Age
Yoshida (MFA)	75	Ikeda (MOF)	64	Tanaka	54	**Nakasone**	65
Inukai	77	**Kaga** (MOF)	74	Tanaka	68	**Sumi** (MOL)	63
Okazaki (MFA)	56	Ohira (MOF)	53	Ohira (MOF)	62	**Abe**	59
Ogasawara	68	Tanaka	45	**Aichi**	na	Takeshita	59
Ohdatsu (HM)	61	**Nadao** (MHA)	64	**Okuno** (MHA)	59	Mori	46
Kusaba	58	**Kobayashi** (MPT)	64	**Saito** (Labor)	63	Watanabe	51
Uchida	73	**Akagi**	59	Kanemaru	58	Yamamura	50
Okano	63	**Fukuda**	61	Nakasone	54	Okonogi	55
Ishii	64	Ayabe	73	**Shintani** (MPT)	70	**Hosoda** (MOT)	71
Tsukada	49	**Koike** (MPT)	60	Kuno	62	Okuda	56
Kosaka	51	**Ohashi** (MHW)	59	Kato	67	Sakamoto	60
Totsuka (HM)	62	Kono	53	**Fukuda** (MOF)	67	Mizuno	58
Fukunaga	43	**Hayakawa**	47	Esaki	57	Tagawa*	65
Kimura	67	**Kurogane** (MOF)	53	Nikaido	70	Fujinami	51
Ando	77	Noda	68	Tsubokawa	70	**Nakanishi** (MOA)	68
Ogata	65	**Sato** (MOT)	62	Kosaka	60	Inamura	66
Ohno, B.	63	**Fukuda** (MFA)	57	**Maeda** (MPT)	62	**Kurihara**	63
Ohno, S.	58	**Miyazawa** (MOF)	44	Miki	65	Kohmoto	72
Tsukada	55	**Furuno**	54	Yamahara	57	Ueda (MOC)	69
Tanaka (MR)	52	Yanamura	55	Komiyama	45	**Gotoda** (MHA)	69
		Hayashi	na	**Yamashita** (MOF)	51	Mizuhhira	51
						Fujimori (MHW)	58
						Horiuchi	53

Source: Nihon Seikei Shinbunsha (1984, 1994, 1999, and 2002); Nichigai Associates (1990, 1999).
[a] The number of cabinet positions has varied over time (see table 6.3). In addition, the number of cabinet positions and the number of cabinet members are not always the same because the same position may be held by two people or one person may occupy two positions. Graduates of the University of Tokyo are printed in bold. Former bureaucrats are indicated by their origin of ministry in parenthesis. HM, Home Ministry; MHA, Ministry of Home Affairs; MHW, Ministry of Health and Welfare; MITI, Ministry of International Trade and Industry; MOA, Ministry of Agriculture, Forestry, and Fisheries; MOC, Ministry of Construction; MOF, Ministry of Finance; MOJ, Ministry of Justice; MOT, Ministry of Transport; MPT, Ministry of Posts and Telecommunications; MR, Ministry of Railways.

the 2001 Koizumi cabinet. Hereditary politicians have been widely caricatured as not being motivated in their "educational performance and achievement" and tend to graduate from private universities (Rothacher 1993, 51; Uchida 1993). Thus, the rise in hereditary politicians can be related to the definite decline in Todai graduates serving in cabinet positions.

1993	Age	1998	Age	2001	Age
Hosokawa	55	Obchi	61	Koizumi	60
Hata	58	Nakamura	64	Fukuda	65
Fujii (MOF)	61	Takamura	56	Omi	69
Akamatsu (Labor)	64	**Miyazawa** (MOF)	81	**Yanazawa** (MOF)	66
Obuchi	63	**Arima** (Education)	68	Takenaka	50
Hatake	65	**Miyashita** (MOF)	71	Ishihara	44
Kumagai	53	**Nakagawa**	45	**Murai** (MITI)	64
Itoh	65	**Yosano**	60	Nakatani	43
Kanzaki (MOJ)	50	Kawasaki	51	**Katayama** (HA)	66
Sakaguchi	59	Noda	38	**Moriyama** (Labor)	66
Igarashi	68	Amari	49	Tanaka	57
Sato	51	Sekiya	60	Shiokawa	78
Takemura (MHA)	59	Nishida	70	**Toyama** (Education)	62
Ishida	63	Nonaka	75	Sakaguchi	67
Uehara	61	Ohta	53	Takebe	60
Nakanishi	52	Inoue	78	Hiramuma	62
Kubota (MOL)	69	Hitaiga	74	Ougi	67
Eda	52	**Sakaiya** (MITI)	63	Kawaguchi (MITI)	60
Hironaka	59	Takeyama	65		
Ohide	71	Manabe	63		
Hatoyama	47	Ohmori	61		
Ishihara (MHA)	67	**Yanagisawa**	63		
Yamahana	57	Suzuki	50		
		Uesugi	56		
		Furukawa (MHW)	64		

Lower House Membership

Arguments about the background characteristics of politicians often extend to LDP Diet members or to Diet members as a whole. Tables 6.4 and 6.5 compare the patterns of *seikai tensin*, Todai graduates, and hereditary politicians for LDP members of the Lower House and the entire membership of the Lower House. Table 6.4 summarizes

Table 6.3 Summary of Cabinet Members and Their Backgrounds

	1953	1963	1972	1983	1993	1998	2001
Cabinet size[a]	20	21	21	23	23	25	18
Seikai tensin	5 (25.0)	11 (52.4)	7 (33.3)	6 (26.1)	6 (26.1)	5 (20.0)	6 (33.3)
Todai graduates	9 (45.0)	13 (61.9)	9 (42.9)	8 (34.8)	7 (30.4)	7 (28.0)	5 (27.8)
Hereditary[b]	2 (10.0)	3 (14.3)	3 (14.3)	6 (26.1)	6 (26.1)	11 (44.0)	8 (44.4)

[a] Number refers to cabinet members with valid data. The total number of cabinet members was 21 in 1953 and 1963, 24 in 1972; 23 in 1983; 24 in 1993; 25 in 1998, and 18 in 2001. Numbers in parentheses are percentages. Our numbers are smaller because data were missing for some cabinet members.
[b] Hereditary politicians are those with family members in political office, including grandparents, fathers-in-law, spouses, siblings, and uncles.

LDP members and their background characteristics for selected elections of between 1953 and 2000. We supplemented our data with estimates from other sources to better identify the patterns. These data from other sources indicate slightly higher percentages, but suggest the same pattern as our data.[12]

Table 6.4 indicates an increase, not a decline, in the percentage of *seikai tensin* LDP Lower House members from 1953 to 2000. According to our calculations (shown in boldface), LDP Diet members with bureaucratic backgrounds range from a low of 18 percent in 1953 to a high of 23.5 percent in 2000. An examination of the percentage of *seikai tensin* for all Lower House members reflects stability over time (see table 6.5). The percentage of Lower House Diet members with bureaucratic backgrounds was 13.9 percent in 1953 and 15.8 percent in 2000. The data for both LDP Lower House members (table 6.4) and all Lower House members (table 6.5) indicate a pattern of increase or stability in *seikai tensin* membership.

Turning to educational background in table 6.4, the percentage of Todai graduates among LDP members was 24.4 percent in 1953 and 25.6 percent in 2000. Between these elections, the highest level of Todai graduates occurred in 1967 when fully one-third (33.8 percent) of all LDP members were alumni. If we consider the entire postwar period, the percentage of Todai graduates is relatively stable, but rose above 30 percent during the 1967, 1972, and 1983 elections. It is only in the shorter time frame that the percentage of Todai graduates appears to be on the decline. The stability of *seikai tensin* and Todai graduates among the LDP members of the Lower House throughout the postwar era lends support for the continuing integration between

Table 6.4 Background of Liberal Democratic Party Members of the Lower House[a]

Election Date (year/month/day)	Number of LDP	Seikai Tensin	University of Tokyo Graduates	Hereditary Politicians[b]	Data Source
1947/4/25	120 (Liberal Party)	17 (14.2)			(I)
	106 (Progressive)	8 (7.5)			(I)
1949/1/23	261 (Liberal Democratic)	44 (16.8)			(I)
	75 (Democratic)	13 (17.3)			(I)
1953/4/19	237 (Liberal)	58 (24.5)			(I)
	76 (Progressive)	14 (18.4)			(I)
	283 (Liberal + Progressive)[c]	**51 (18.0)**	69 (24.4)	18 (6.4)	(II)
1958/5/22	298	79 (26.5)			(I)
1967/1/29	278	**58 (20.9)**	**94 (33.8)**	**52 (18.7)**	(II)
1972/12/10	282	**56 (19.9)**	**88 (31.2)**	**68 (24.1)**	(III)
1983/12/18	236[d]	**49 (18.5)**	**75 (31.8)**	**99 (37.4)**	(III)
1986/7/6	304	70 (23.6)	67 (22.6)	115 (38.7)	(III)
	297	67 (22.6)		133 (44.8)	(IV)
1993/7/18	226	**51 (22.6)**	**52 (23.0)**	**89 (39.3)**	(II)
2000/6/25	238	**56 (23.5)**	**61 (25.6)**	**76 (31.9)**	(II)

Source: (I) Scalapino and Masumi (1962, 2–3, app. table 3); (II) Chikako Usui's calculation based on Nihon Seikei Shinbunsha (1968, 1973, 1984, 1994, 2001); Nichigai Associates (1990, 1999); (III) *Asahi shinbun* (8 July 1986, p. 9); (IV) Uchida (1989, 162).

a Numbers in parentheses are percentages. Boldface values are from our calculations.

b Hereditary politician (*seshu giin*) are to those who inherit political machinery from their parents (including adoptive parents and fathers-in-law) and other family members.

c There were 309 members of the Liberal and Progressive Parties, but data are missing for 26 cases. Thus, the percentages are calculated based on 283 (309 minus 26).

d There were 240 LDP members, but data are missing for 4 cases. Thus, the percentages are calculated based on 236 (240 minus 4).

Table 6.5 Backgrounds of All Lower House Members[a]

Election Date (year/ month/day)	Lower House Total	Seikai Tensin	University of Tokyo Graduates	Hereditary Politicians[b]	Data Source
1947/4/25	466				(I)
1953/4/19	431[c]	60 (13.9)	100 (23.2)	22 (5.1)	(II)
1967/1/29	483	63 (13.0)	114 (23.6)	61 (12.6)	(II)
1972/12/10	491	59 (12.0)	108 (22.0)	77 (15.7)	(II)
1983/12/18	508	55 (10.8)	97 (19.1)	119 (23.4)	(II)
1993/7/18	511	79 (15.5)	94 (18.4)	123 (24.1)	(II)
1996/10/20	500	74 (14.8)		122 (24.4)	(III)
2000/6/25	480	76 (15.8)	100 (20.8)	117 (24.4)	(II)

Source: (I) Asahi Shinbunsha (1970, 327); (II) Chikako Usui's calculation based on Nihon Seikei Shinbunsha (1954, 1968, 1973, 1984, 1994, 1997, 2001); Nichigai Associates (1990, 1999); (III) *Asahi shinbun* (21 October 1996, p. 3).
[a] Numbers in parentheses are percentages.
[b] Hereditary politicians (*seshu giin*) are those who inherit political machinery from their parents (including adoptive parents and fathers-in-law) and other family members.
[c] There were 461 members of the Lower House, but data were missing for 30 cases. Thus the percentages are calculated based on 431 (461 minus 30).

Todai and the Diet at the level of LDP Lower House members. The percentage of Todai graduates for all Lower House members (table 6.5), however, indicates some decline over time, from 23.2 percent in 1953 to 20.8 percent in 2000, with a lows of 18.4 percent in 1993.

There is a high and (overall) increasing concentration of hereditary politicians among LDP Lower House members from 6.4 percent in 1953 to 31.9 percent in 2000. Between these years, there was a dramatic increase from the 1950s to the early 1990s and a sharp decrease from 1993 to 2000. The percentage of hereditary politicians for all Lower House members (table 6.5) demonstrates a pattern of increase with slightly lower percentages from the 1950s to the early 1980s, reaching a plateau thereafter at 23–24 percent.

Another measure of potential change involves newly elected LDP Lower House members (table 6.6) and Lower House members generally (table 6.7). This measure should be sensitive to changing circumstances when the prevalence measure used in tables 6.4 and 6.5 might be a function of incumbency. If, for example, *seikai tensin* con-

Table 6.6 Backgrounds of Newly Elected Liberal Democratic Party Members of the Lower House[a]

Election Date (year/ month/day)	Lower House LDP Members	*Seikai Tensin*	University of Tokyo Graduates	Hereditary Politicians[b]
1967/1/29	47	11 (23.4)	13 (27.7)	14 (29.8)
1972/12/10	42	5 (11.9)	9 (21.4)	8 (19.0)
1983/12/18	41	9 (22.2)	9 (22.0)	12 (29.3)
1993/7/18	30	6 (20.0)	6 (20.0)	9 (30.0)
2000/6/25	37	7 (18.9)	14 (37.8)	9 (24.3)

Source: Nihon Seikei Shinbunsha (1968, 1973, 1984, 1994, 2001); Nichigai Associates (1990, 1999); Toyo Keizai Shinposha (2000).
[a] Numbers in parentheses are percentages. Tabulations by Chikako Usui.LDP, Liberal Denocrtic Party.
[b] Hereditary politicians (*seshu giin*) are those who inherit political machinery from their parents (including adoptive parents and fathers-in-law) and other family members.

Table 6.7 Backgrounds of Newly Elected Members of the Lower House[a]

Election Date	Lower House Members	*Seikai Tensin*	University of Tokyo Graduates	Hereditary Politicians[b]
1967/1/29	137	13 (9.5)	21 (15.3)	21 (15.3)
1972/12/10	129	5 (3.9)	20 (15.5)	12 (9.3)
1983/12/18	130	10 (7.7)	14 (10.8)	15 (11.5)
1993/7/18	135	9 (6.7)	18 (13.3)	12 (8.9)
2000/6/25	126	19 (15.1)	28 (22.2)	26 (20.6)

Source: Nihon Seikei Shinbunsha (1968, 1973, 1984, 1994, 2001); Nichigai Associates (1990, 1999); Toyo Keizai Shinposha (2000).
[a] Numbers in parentheses are percentages. Tabulations by Chikako Usui.
[b] Hereditary politicians (*seshu giin*) are those who inherit political machinery from their parents (including adoptive parents and fathers-in-law) and other family members.

stitutes 25 percent of the LDP membership in a given year but only 10 percent of the newly elected politicians are *seikai tensin* in the same election year, the percentage of new members is below replacement level, indicating a future decline in *seikai tensin*. Conversely, if the percentage of newly elected *seikai tensin* is similar to the preva-

lence percentage of *seikai tensin*, the percentage is sufficient for
stable replacement, indicating a future stability of *seikai tensin*.
This logic assumes that newly elected political seats are evenly
distributed across electoral blocs. If newly elected politicians are
concentrated in certain blocs, it does not predict future changes in
the composition of the elite background characteristics (*seikai
tensin*, Todai graduate, or hereditary politician). For example, in the
1993 election when the dominance of the LDP was broken for
the first time since 1953, there were only thirty LDP members who
were newly elected in the Lower House (table 6.6). Of those
thirty, six (20 percent) were *seikai tensin*. Because the prevalence
of *seikai tensin* politicians among LDP members of the Lower
House was 22.6 percent in 1993 (table 6.4), we expect a slight decline
in the prevalence of *seikai tensin* among the LDP members in the
next election. To the contrary, the prevalence of *seikai tensin*
members within the LDP actually rose to 23.5 percent in 2000
(table 6.4). Similarly, the percentage of newly elected hereditary
politicians was consistently below replacement level from 1972 to
1993 (table 6.6). Yet from the prevalence data in tables 6.4 and 6.5
it is clear that the percentage of hereditary politicians continued to
increase in the 1983 and 1993 elections. The prevalence percentages
in tables 6.4 and 6.5 do not correspond well with the replacement
level indicated in table 6.6. It is more likely that a rapid turnover of
electoral seats is concentrated in urban areas rather than rural districts. In the urban districts, turnover rates are high (incumbency is
very low), whereas in the rural areas where elite credentials are tied
to political officeholding, turnover rates are low (incumbency is
high). Thus, the overall prevalence percentages shown in tables 6.4
and 6.5 are not highly correlated with the percentage changes in elite
background characteristics among the newly elected politicians (table
6.6).

Tables 6.8 and 6.9 show the ministry or agency of origin for LDP
Lower House members and all Lower House members for selected
postwar years. In table 6.4, our data showed that the percentage of
seikai tensin was steady between 18 and 23.5 percent for 1953–2000
period. Within this stable percentage we find an interesting distribution of ministries of origin for these *seikai tensin* politicians. If, as
some suggest, the bureaucracy is the recruiting ground for politicians,
only a handful of ministries provide fertile soil. The MOF has been
the source of the most *seikai tensin* over time, providing 101 of 392

Table 6.8 Ministry of Origin for *Seikai Tensin*: Liberal Democratic Party Members of the Lower House[a]

Ministry of Origin	1953	1967	1972	1983	1993	2000	Total
MOF	5	14	19	16	20	17	91
Home Affairs	24	15	14	5	6	4	68
MITI	4	7	4	5	5	12	37
MOA	5	5	4	4	7	6	31
MOC	0	0	1	4	5	7	17
Foreign Affairs	6	3	1	2	3	1	16
MOT	2	5	4	2	0	1	14
Labor	0	2	3	6	1	2	14
MPT	4	1	3	1	0	0	9
MHW	0	3	1	1	2	2	9
National Police Agency	0	0	0	2	1	2	5
Defense	0	1	1	1	0	0	3
Education	1	0	0	0	0	0	1
Others	0	2	1	0	1	2	6
Total	51	58	56	49	51	56	321

Source: Nihon Seikei Shinbunsha (1973, 1983, 1993, 2001).
[a] MHW, Ministry of Health and Welfare; MITI, Ministry of International Trade and Industry; MOA, Ministry of Agriculture, Forestry, and Fisheries; MOC, Ministry of Construction; MOF, Ministry of Finance; MOT, Ministry of Transport; MPT, Ministry of Posts and Telecommunications.

seikai tensin Lower House members and 91 of 321 *seikai tensin* LDP members. The Ministry of Home Affairs was by far the largest supplier in the 1950s and 1960s. The MITI, Agriculture, and Construction show signs of increase over time, which does not support the view that the rise of *zoku* politicians has diminished the need for the ex-bureaucrat's information and technical skills. Instead of a zero-sum relationship, this suggests a positive-sum relationship between LDP *zoku* politicians and ex-bureaucrats from these ministries. The contention that the number of *zoku* politicians rose through the 1970s and 1980s, obviating the need for ex-bureaucrats in the Diet, is called into question.

In addition, tables 6.8 and 6.9 show that the fusion of the bureaucracy and Diet is based on only a few ministries. The MOF, Home

Table 6.9 Ministry of Origin for *Seikai Tensin* Lower House Members[a]

Ministry of Origin	1953	1967	1972	1983	1993	2000	Total	Percentage
MOF	6 (1)	14 (3)	19 (4)	17 (5)	25 (7)	20 (4)	101 (24)	23.8
Home Affairs	24 (1)	17 (1)	14 (3)	5 (1)	8	5	73 (6)	8.2
MITI	6	7	4	5 (3)	10 (1)	15 (3)	47 (7)	14.9
MOA	5	5	4 (1)	4 (1)	12 (1)	11 (2)	41 (5)	12.2
Foreign Affairs	9 (2)	4	1	3 (1)	5 (1)	4	26 (4)	15.4
MOC	0	0	0	4	9	10	23	
MOT	3	6	5	3	0	1	18	
Labor	0	2	3 (1)	6	1	4 (1)	16 (2)	12.5
MPT	5 (1)	1	4	1	2	0	13 (1)	7.7
MHW	0	3 (1)	0	2 (1)	2 (1)	2	9 (3)	33.3[b]
National Police Agency	0	0	0	2	1	3	6	
Defense	0	1	1	1	1	0	4	
Education	1	0	0	0	1	0	2	
Others	1	3	4	2	2	1	13	
Total	60	63	59	55	79	76	392 (52)	13.3

Source: Nihon Seikei Shinbunsha (1973, 1983, 1993, 2001).
[a] Numbers in parenthesis indicate *seikai tensin* politicians who are also hereditary. MHW, Ministry of Health and Welfare; MITI, Ministry of International Trade and Industry; MOA, Ministry of Agriculture, Forestry, and Fisheries; MOC, Ministry of Construction; MOF, Ministry of Finance; MOT, Ministry of Transport; MPT, Ministry of Posts and Telecommunications.
[b] Number are too small to draw substantial interpretation.

Affairs, the MITI, and Agriculture are important suppliers of *seikai tensin*. In 2000 these four ministries accounted for 69.6 percent (39 of 56) of *seikai tensin* LDP politicians and 67.1 percent (51 of 76) of the *seikai tensin* members of the Lower House. Taking the broader view, we see that the MOF, Home Affairs, the MITI, and Agriculture accounted for 71 percent (227 of 321) of all *seikai tensin* LDP Lower House members for the selected years. These same four ministries accounted for 66.8 percent (262 of 392) of all *seikai tensin* Lower House members for those years. There is a competitive hierarchy in the production of *seikai tensin*.[13] Further, table 6.9 reveals an unusual overlap of the two background characteristics—twenty-four of the 101 (23.8 percent) *seikai tensin* politicians from the MOF were also hereditary politicians.

Table 6.10 demonstrates one element of fusion between the LDP and the ministries. The total number of *seikai tensin* remained relatively stable across elections, but the hierarchy of ministries of origin changed for these politicians. The Ministry of Home Affairs was the dominant supplier of ex-bureaucrats to Lower House political offices for the LDP in the 1950s and 1960s. However, by the 1972 election

Table 6.10 *Seikai Tensin* among Liberal Democratic Party Members of the Lower House by Originating Ministry[a]

Rank	Ministry	Number of *Seikai Tensin* Elected	Percentage
1953 Election			
1	Home Affairs	24	47.1
2	Foreign Affairs	6	11.8
3	MOF	5	9.8
4	MOA	5	9.8
5	MITI	4	7.8
6	MPT	4	7.8
	Total	51	100
1967 Election			
1	Home Affairs	15	25.9
2	MOF	14	24.1
3	MITI	7	12.1
4	MOA	5	8.6
5	MOT	5	8.6
	Total	58	100
1972 Election			
1	MOF	19	33.9
2	Home Affairs	14	25
3	MITI	4	7.1
4	MOA	4	7.1
5	MOT	4	7.1
	Total	56	100
1983 Election			
1	MOF	16	32.7
2	Labor	6	12.2
3	MITI	5	10.2
4	Home Affairs	5	10.2
5	MOA	4	8.2
	Total	49	100
1993 Election			
1	MOF	20	39.2
2	MOA	7	13.7
3	Home Affairs	6	11.8
4	MITI	5	9.8
5	MOC	5	9.8
	Total	51	100

Table 6.10 *Continued*

Rank	Ministry	Number of *Seikai Tensin* Elected	Percentage
2000 Election			
1	MOF	17	30.4
2	MITI	12	21.4
3	MOC	7	12.5
4	MOA	6	10.7
5	Home Affairs	4	7.1
	Total	56	100

[a] Total is the number of *seikai tensin* politicians elected in a given election year. MITI, Ministry of International Trade and Industry; MOA, Ministry of Agriculture, Forestry, and Fisheries; MOC, Ministry of Construction; MOF, Ministry of Finance; MOT, Ministry of Transport; MPT, Ministry of Posts and Telecommunications.

MOF was the top ministry of origin for *seikai tensin* among the LDP Lower House members and maintained that dominance through the election of 2000.

Interpretation of the Data

Our data show that integration of the bureaucracy and political office, as measured by *seikai tensin*, depends on the level of political office examined. There has been a decline in *seikai tensin* in the post–World War II prime ministerships—there was only one ex-bureaucrat prime minister from 1980 to 2002, although over 50 percent of prime ministers from 1945 to 2002 were *seikai tensin*. The number of *seikai tensin* cabinent members appears stable—six (33.3 percent) cabinet members in 2001 were *seikai tensin* politicians, up from 1998 but indicative of a stable range since 1953. There appears to be no correspondence between the supposed rise in *zoku* politicians and the change in percentage of *seikai tensin* politicians in either cabinet positions or LDP and general Lower House members. The fabric of cohesion between the bureaucracy and political office, as represented by *seikai tensin*, appears to be frayed at the top (prime minister) but resilient at the levels of cabinet and LDP membership.

Over time the MOF and Ministry of Home Affairs have had far and away the most *seikai tensin* politicians in the Lower House. However, Home Affairs representatives are declining, reflecting the breakup of the once-dominant ministry. The data for the later years indicate that the MOF, the MITI, Agriculture, and Construction are better represented in the Lower House by their ex-bureaucrats. The ascendancy of Agriculture and Construction representatives corresponds to their increasing reputation as influenced by politicians and private interests. A stable institutionalized path appears to operate at the level of cabinet and Lower House membership, with the threads provided by the MOF, Home Affairs, the MITI, Agriculture, and Construction.

There has been a significant decline in the share of Todai graduates among prime ministers and cabinet members since the 1970s, but stability among LDP Lower House members. And there is a significant rise in the percentage of hereditary politicians at all levels of political office. The Yoshida faction, known to actively recruit ex-bureaucrats, dominated the early postwar prime ministerships, but after 1980 the percentage of hereditary politicians exceeded that of *seikai tensin* or Todai alumni. Because we are dealing with small numbers of prime ministers and cabinet members, it is possible that these patterns reflect the political fortunes of the Yoshida-Miyazawa faction and not necessarily a structural change.

What is interesting, however, is the relative stability of the twin credentials of *seikai tensin* and Todai graduation as a percentage of LDP Lower House membership. The data do not support contentions that there has been a decline in *seikai tensin*. At the level of the Lower House, *seikai tensin* and a Todai diploma continue to provide a cachet, showing a substantial fusion of a Todai education, the bureaucracy, and political office among the LDP membership. More specifically, this is a fusion of Todai, the MOF, and LDP membership. Thus, in the 1970s and 1980s this fusion was split at the level of prime minister, declined at the level of cabinet membership, but continued at the level of LDP Lower House membership. This suggests a decentralization of cohesive, stable, structured relations of influence among Todai, the bureaucracy, and political office.

The most significant finding is the penetration of hereditary politicians at all the levels of political office: prime minister, cabinet members, and LDP Lower House and all Lower House members from

1953 to 2000. Hereditary politicians accounted for thirteen of the twenty-seven prime ministers since 1945, but seven of the ten prime ministers after 1989 were all hereditary. The percentage of hereditary politicians in the cabinet rose steadily from 10 percent in 1953 to 44 percent in 2001. The percentage of hereditary politicians among Lower House members paralleled the rise among cabinet members, from 6.4 percent in 1953 to 32 percent in 2000 among LDP members and from 13 percent in 1953 to 24 percent in 2000 among all Lower House members.

Our analysis suggests a complex image of the relationship among the University of Tokyo, the bureaucracy, and political office. The stability of *seikai tensin* and the declining (but still high) level of Todai graduates at the cabinet level together with the stability of these two elite features in LDP Lower House membership lends support to elite integration, but integration with changing elite characteristics. The confluence of *seikai tensin*, a Todai education, and being a hereditary politician, found in the early postwar decades, suggests a powerful superimposition of elite characteristics. The more recent separation of these background characteristics for prime ministers and cabinet members and their continued concentration in the MOF for Lower House members suggest the limiting conditions on the elite unity of Todai, the bureaucracy, and political office as it relates to the notion of the iron triangle.

The question is how much integration exists between the bureaucracy and political office. Our analysis suggests an increasing variation of the connection between the bureaucracy and political office at the level of prime minister, including the educational background of prime ministers. At the level of LDP Lower House members and the Lower House overall, however, we find a notable and stable postwar integration (over 20 percent among LDP Lower House members and 15 percent in all Lower House membership). Further, the observed pattern of integration appears to correspond to the percentage of Todai graduates at the three levels of political office we have examined. The percentage of Todai graduates declines for prime ministers, cabinet members, and all Lower House members, but is stable for LDP Lower House members.

The rise of hereditary politicians suggests the emergence of the intergenerational transfer of support organizations based in specific local constituencies. The already high and increasing percentage of hereditary politicians among prime ministers, cabinet members, and LDP Lower House and all Lower House members is a major challenge to pluralist optimism about democracy in Japan. The rise of hereditary politicians is a movement toward competition, merit, and dispersal of power only in the narrowest sense of elite competition—hereditary politicians do not represent diversity as much as they reflect money politics and the integration of the LDP with parochial private-sector interests. The decline of *seikai tensin* at the levels of prime ministers and cabinet members, their increase among LDP Lower House members, and the rise of hereditary politicians suggests a decentralization of politics that patterns close to Frank Schwartz's (1998) notion of neo-pluralists. Relations among Todai, the bureaucracy, and politicians are too decentralized and fragmented for strong models of the iron triangle. Yet these relations are too structured, continuous, and stable to support those who argue that the iron triangle never existed or has long since met its demise.

7 *Amakudari* as a Power Structure

We have examined the main paths of *amakudari*, but our analysis is only a biopsy. The movement of personnel takes place across the boundaries of ministries, firms, public corporations, and political offices and within the private and public sectors. Beyond moves across and within these sectors, there are personnel movements from the central ministries to local governments, industry associations, research institutions and universities. There are also other types of networks, in addition to *amakudari*, that crisscross the boundaries of different political positions, firms, sectors, and ministries. These include policy deliberation councils (*shingikai*) that study policy options, school networks (*gakubatsu*), marriage networks (*keibatsu*), cohort networks, locality networks, and corporate networks (*keiretsu*). These networks, which represent the mechanisms of integration across otherwise analytically distinct spheres of society, are sometimes considered quaint, a primitive form of organization for group-oriented people who have not fully developed the individualistic forms of markets and hierarchies. Be that as it may, it is the network character of Japanese society that is underanalyzed, leaving the foundations of Japanese political economy misunderstood.

In this final chapter, we consider the nature and implications of *amakudari* networks and push the argument, at the risk of exaggeration, to capture the larger topography and meaning of *amakudari*. Our analysis to this point has strived to gather diverse data to assemble the overall pattern and meaning of *amakudari* in Japanese society and its political economy. From a bird's-eye view, it is clear that *amakudari* is not an individual event, although there are clear individual motives. Rather, *amakudari* is a ministry-level phenomenon consciously constructed and reproduced with networks crisscrossing a matrix of institutional spheres. Our thesis is that *amakudari* is a key element of the elite character of Japanese society. *Amakudari* networks are the outcome of the regulatory and public works nature of Japanese society. These *amakudari* processes provide a framework within which other formal institutions are integrated and this integration generates pivotal differences in the organization of the Japanese political economy. *Amakudari* continues because there is benefit for both the bureaucracy and the receiving organizations. A corollary to this is that the interinstitutional fusion created by *amakudari* makes fundamental reforms and restructuring difficult because it is oriented more toward stability and lessens the pressure for change.

We consider three broad functions of *amakudari* in the overall political economy.

1. *Amakudari* is a structure of multiple paths to various societal sectors representing complex network structures. These networks operate as the "arms and legs" and "fingers and toes" of the central bureaucracy and create an interdependence between private and public firms and the political world. *Amakudari* networks are hierarchically organized and cut across formal institutional boundaries providing integration across analytically differentiated institutional spheres.
2. *Amakudari* is cultural and manifests all the characteristics of an institution. It offers a stable set of practices and a homogeneity of cultural categories by providing a degree of continuity and resilience in the face of change. These practices operate across a matrix of organizations and institutional spheres.
3. Beyond structure and culture *amakudari* is an elite power structure. *Amakudari* practices are consciously created and reproduced, manifesting an institutionalized circuit. *Amakudari* is a process for a select group of top bureaucrats and these bureaucrats have been successful in reproducing themselves throughout the postwar era to provide a basis for a power structure.

Amakudari as Multiple Paths

One important contribution of this book is the decomposition of the broad concept *amakudari* into its analytic and empirically accessible components. We distinguish the destinations and sequencing of personnel movements. Our analysis indicates that *amakudari* networks provide a degree of cohesion and integration across diverse institutional spheres. In this sense, *amakudari* networks calibrate a level of fusion stretching across formal institutions of the bureaucracy, private and public sectors, and political offices. In addition, these *amakudari* networks are ministry-based and structured in a hierarchy, with the MOF, MITI, Agriculture, Construction, and Transport dominating all the paths we examined. *Amakudari* (in its broad sense) to top corporate positions involved approximately 800 positions in the private sector and 360 in *tokushu hojin* in 1998 and some 7,000 positions in *zaidan* and *shadan hojin* of which 1,300 were paid positions in 1996.

In chapter 3 we examine *amakudari* (in its narrow sense) to the boards of private firms using incidence and prevalence data. Incidence data show that the annual number of *amakudari* declined significantly after 1986 to only forty in 2000. The prevalence data for 1982–98 indicate a stable distribution of *amakudari* at 2 percent of the directors on the boards of listed private firms. In addition, 28 percent of all listed firms had at least one *amakudari* on their boards in 1994. The prevalence data for the top one hundred private firms in 2000 indicate that 3.3 percent of the directors were *amakudari* and fifty-eight of the firms had at least one *amakudari*. The difference between an overall penetration of 2 percent of all private-sector board positions and 3.3 percent of the board positions among the one hundred largest private firms make it clear that *amakudari* is concentrated among the largest corporations.

Approximately 68 percent of all *amakudari* to the private sector came out of the MOF (including the National Tax Agency), Construction, and the MITI in 1994. The *amakudari* placements were not to second-tier corporations but were disproportionately to the larger, *keiretsu*-affiliated, and expanding sectors of service, banking and insurance, and manufacturing. These two pieces of information indicate which ministries are fused to which parts of the private sector. *Amakudari* provides relations between a handful of ministries and the most powerful corporations in the expanding sectors. Our analysis does not lend full support to a resource-equalization thesis.

The *yokosuberi* path serves to circumvent the limits on *amakudari* (the direct movement to the private sector) imposed by the NPA. In 1998 there were approximately 360 *yokosuberi* on the boards of *tokushu hojin,* accounting for 45 percent of all board positions. This percentage of *yokosuberi* on the boards of public corporations represents strong *prima facie* evidence that the *tokushu hojin* operate under the control of the central ministries. There is, however, a wide variation in the percentage of *yokosuberi* in the different types of *tokushu hojin* and variation in ministry control. We find a high of 72 percent *yokosuberi* on the boards of directors of *kodan* and a low of less than 13 percent on boards of *tokushu kaisha.*

Even though the number of *tokushu hojin* declined from a high of 113 in 1967 to 85 in 1998 to 77 in 2000, the number of board positions in the *tokushu hojin* did not automatically decline. The expanding number of director positions offset the apparent shrinking opportunity for *yokosuberi* placements due to the shrinking number of *tokushu hojin.* Further, of the 6,815 *zaidan* and *shadan hojin,* 2,483 or 36 percent had *yokosuberi* on their boards of directors in 1996. These *yokosuberi* positions accounted for 4.7 percent of all board positions. The number of *yokosuberi* declined in 2000—28.7 percent of *zaidan* and *shadan hojin* had at least one *yokosuberi* director, or 2.8 percent of all board positions. Nevertheless, the sheer number of *yokosuberi* to *zaidan* and *shadan hojin* is huge—7,080 including 1,322 paid board positions in 1996.

Three ministries—the MOF, MITI, and Agriculture—dominated *yokosuberi* to *tokushu hojin.* Agriculture, the MITI, and Transport dominated *yokosuberi* to *zaidan* and *shadan hojin.* Agriculture clearly uses the public sector to place its retirees; it is relatively weak in the private sector. The MITI, on the other hand, uses the private sector and both tracks of the public sector.

Our analysis of *yokosuberi* illustrates how hierarchical networks are expanded. For example, the JNPC, a *tokushu hojin* established by the MITI, brings *yokosuberi* directly to its board of directors from the MITI. In addition, through loans and subsidies, the JNPC controls its subsidiaries and affiliates in the private sector. These private firms, in turn, open their boards to *amakudari* directly from the MITI. Our examination of JNPC suggestes that some *amakudari* board members of private corporations moved there indirectly from the MITI, first stopping on the board of JNPC.

A substantial proportion of *amakudari* and *yokosuberi* take this indirect route, *wataridori* (see chap. 5). Almost one in three *amakudari* on the boards of directors in private firms got there indirectly, moving from the central bureaucracy to public corporations and then to private-sector firms. Similarly, almost one in three *yokosuberi* on the boards of directors in public corporations got there indirectly. These former bureaucrats leave the central bureaucracy for public corporations and then move to another public-sector firm. Although the numbers are interesting, it is the pattern by ministry that is impressive. The MOF and MITI alone account for almost 50 percent of *wataridori* networks. If we add the Ministry of Construction, the three ministries account for almost 69 percent of *wataridori*; if we add the Ministries of Transport and Agriculture the five ministries account for 90 percent. Clearly the MOF and MITI dominate the use of the indirect route.

Chapter 6 examines the prevalence of ex-bureaucrats in high political office (*seikai tensin*) in the central government. Although a dramatic decline of *seikai tensin* and Todai backgrounds occurred in the prime ministership, we find that 33 percent of cabinet members, 15 percent of Lower House members, and 20 percent of LDP Lower House members are *seikai tensin*. Todai background accounts for 20–25 percent of the LDP Lower House members and 20 percent of all Lower House members. There is a sharp rise in the number of people with hereditary political background at all levels of political office.

Taking together all four *amakudari* paths, two important features of the nature and structure of *amakudari* networks are apparent. First, in the 1990s there was a moderate level of cohesion or integration among the bureaucracy, business, and politics along each *amakudari* path. Second, if we look at *amakudari*, *yokosuberi*, and *wataridori*, the MOF and MITI are first-tier superministries in terms of their *amakudari* networks; when we add *seikai tensin*, the MOF clearly distinguishes itself as the dominant ministry in the hierarchy of all four *amakudari* paths.

Amakudari as an Institution

Amakudari (in its broad sense) is more than a pattern of relationships—it is an institution, a stable set of historically constructed practices and patterned relationships, infused with common cultural categories and connecting a matrix of organizations. The shared culture operating across a matrix of organizations is illustrated by the fusion of education and bureaucracy. The fusion between Todai and the top positions of the bureaucracy shapes the cultural categories of top-level bureaucrats and high-level *amakudari* placements. It creates a symbolic category of top bureaucrats and *amakudari* as merit elites and guardians of the national interest. The career connection between Todai and the bureaucracy produces shared socialization and career experiences for top bureaucrats that result in similar orientations toward elitism and nationalism. These common cultural categories, in turn, promote trust among current and retired bureaucrats who are Todai graduates. Their identity as merit elites and the protectors of the nation contributes to the construction of stable sets of practices and relationships. The ministerial promotion systems, with their bias toward Todai graduates, reinforce this shared culture. In other words, *amakudari* creates linkages that are regular, intimate, and embedded. The fusion between Todai and the ministries is partially based on the fact that Todai alums tend to recruit other Todai alums based on their shared socialization, experiences, and orientations presumed to be the correct way of thinking.

Just as ministries develop a standard hierarchy of authority and procedures for the periodic review and redeployment of personnel, so too do *amakudari* practices involve the routinized timing of personnel movements and definitions of appropriate placements by ministry positions. *Amakudari* is a set of practices that are understood as the way things are done. Personnel moves each April illustrate institutionalized practices inside the bureaucracy and across *amakudari* networks. The repeated movement of ex-officials to specific positions in private and public corporations through the different paths of *amakudari* represents one feature of the stable practices of *amakudari*. These categories, practices, and relationships represent the institutionalization of *amakudari* through the ministries and across other formal institutional spheres.

Amakudari connects a matrix of organizations in recognized areas of social life. Just as the institution of medicine includes hospitals, laboratories, and medical teaching colleges, the institution of *amakudari* includes the ministries and agencies of the central bureaucracy and the private and public corporations. Peculiar to *amakudari* as an institution is that it cuts across functional spheres of society that are formally differentiated: government, the private sector, the public sector, the Diet, and the educational sector. *Amakudari* weaves through these differentiated societal institutions. This is precisely why it is so important to define it as an institution cutting across and integrating a matrix of organizations. This feature of *amakudari* counters the characterization of a framework of functions and structures as rigid. The formal institutional boundaries are permeable and are penetrated by *amakudari* networks. This integration is expressed even more strongly in a Japanese characterization of *amakudari* relations as *ichimai-iwa* (literally, one-piece rock), emphasizing that what is solid is the network, not the formal institutional spheres crossed by the network.

Our analysis reveals *amakudari* processes are conscious and calculated strategies of logistical coordination. *Amakudari* placements are conscious, self-interested efforts on the part of bureaucrats and the administrative units of each ministry to gain deferred compensation for fellow bureaucrats and claim sectoral turf for the ministry. These placements create and maintain representatives who define and monitor the boundaries of the ministries' sectors, cultivate policy networks, and represent ministry interests. Similarly, *amakudari* personnel are received by private corporations to increase their capacity to adapt and survive in a regulated economy. The motivation behind *amakudari* results from a combination of the self-interest of individuals and administrative rationality of the ministries and the private corporations.

The historical construction of *amakudari* includes less conscious practical action that is typically involved in institutions. These more taken-for-granted practices occur both within and across *amakudari* networks. For example, a less conscious reproduction of interministry competition occurs once *amakudari* patterns are established. The ministries with initial advantages in *amakudari* tend to use them to reproduce their advantage. They are like first movers in business; advantage, once gained, tends to be less vulnerable to change. In part, this explains the dominance of the MOF across all network paths. The MOF moved quickly to take advantage of opportunities to expand its *amakudari* placements. Once these positions were gained, they took on permanence as placement positions for the MOF.

Amakudari patterns have changed over time, yet these networks demonstrate a continuity and resistance to change. The continuity demonstrates the institutional character of *amakudari*. "Institutions are slow to be established, difficult to change, and powerful shaping forces of any regime." Once established they are "relatively invariant in the face of turnover of individuals and relatively resilient to the idiosyncratic preferences and expectations of individuals" (March and Olson 1987, quoted in Pempel 1998, 23). *Amakudari* patterns are relatively resilient even in an era when they are widely viewed as obstacles to economic recovery.

Amakudari and other horizontal integrating networks result from institutional and cultural features. In the context of discussing elite policy networks, Okimoto (1989, 157) mentions six features of Japanese society that make it conducive to the existence of elite policy networks: (1) a "frame" society, in which consensus, not legalistic codes, is the basis of policy; (2) the Confucian emphasis on human relations; (3) an emphasis on loyalty and trust; (4) social homogeneity; (5) the logistical convenience of Tokyo as the hub of both political and economic activity; and (6) the role of the educational system as the central mechanism for elite selection and social mobility. This combination makes Japan perfectly suited to the informal, elite, nonlegalistic policymaking that is a hallmark of its administrative organization.

Horizontal integrating institutions, such as *amakudari*, operate in the absence of a legalistic, administrative, or contractual basis of coordination. These horizontally integrating institutions provide a functional substitute for legal, administrative, or market mechanisms of coordination and probably operate best in closed systems. They are limited by the extent of the external penetration of the formal institutions of education, the bureaucracy, business, the public sector, and the Diet. Examples include global business competition, Moody's ratings of government and corporate bonds, the removal of corporations from listings on international stock exchanges, international pressure for open trade, and international political pressure for administrative and fiscal reform.

Amakudari as a Power Structure

There are two definitions of social power. For some authors, power is situational and measured by influence over the outcomes of confrontational (conflict) situations. It focuses on behavior in decision making on issues with observable conflicts of interests. This is embodied in the definition of power as the ability of one actor to impose his or her will on another despite resistance. In this sense, situational power is a capacity to act, regarded as being in the same category as electrical power or the power of a motor—a quantitative capacity that may be put to work for a variety of purposes. In contrast, our definition of social power is the structural and observable capacity of political bias in government office and private and public corporations in dominating the terrain of policy decisions. This sense of power is more appropriate for an elite power structure, as seen in the covert exclusion of nonelites from decision making. It is this more covert use of power that makes possible the benign public representation of power as serving the national interest. Social power defined by the structure and capacity of those who dominate the terrain of policy decisions incorporates the issues of control over the policy agenda and the ways potential issues are ushered in or kept out of the policy process (Allison 1971; Colignon 1997; Lukes 1974; Gaventa 1980; Hindess 1996; Roy 1997). Further, this concept of social power includes the exercise of power such that nonelites fail to recognize their real interests, even when these interests are at risk, and consequently make no attempt to defend their interests.

There are three important dimensions involving the roles of *amakudari* in Japan's power structure: (1) *amakudari* is an institution that acts to control strategic locations at the top of powerful institutions and weaves these institutions together; (2) *amakudari* provides symbolic legitimacy and controlling mechanisms of political participation and decision-making processes that might otherwise lead to changes that elites want to avoid; and (3) *amakudari* as an institution resists and lessens pressures for changes, maintaining stability in labor and capital markets. These and other social structures developed to produce stable market relationships.

The idea that *amakudari* networks comprise a power structure becomes more apparent when we move from examining the density of *amakudari* networks to examining the overall pattern of these *amakudari* networks (figure 7.1). The pattern suggests the establishment of different paths emanating from the central ministries and creating an interface between the bureaucracy and the various sectors of society. Regulatory interventions, licensing powers, and surveillance of business life are supplemented by *amakudari* to strategic locations in private-sector corporations. The public sector provides infrastructure, business, educational, medical, and social services in which a complex configuration of interests engage. *Amakudari* to

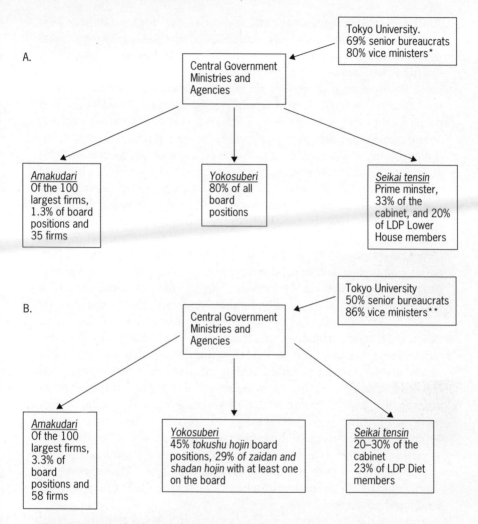

Figure 7.1 Amakudari (A) late 1970s; (B) late 1990s. * indicates 1949–59;
** indicates 1985 (Koh 1989).

political office provides an additional linkage in legislation involving the negotiation of public and private interests.

The ministries operate in an interministry competitive terrain extending across numerous sectors of society. Yet ministries control and even monopolize sectors over which they have regulatory responsibility. Simultaneously, ministries also compete for the talent of new recruits. In other words, *amakudari* is a mechanism of territorial appropriation and personnel incentives—*amakudari* positions claim territory to use as the property of the ministry and *amakudari* provides an economic payoff for years of loyal service at relatively low salaries. Not all central ministries have equal competitive and monopoly power, but there is a relative stability to their ranking over time. *Amakudari* placements and the interministry competition for *amakudari* placements are a special type of appropriation that provides the central ministries the rights to the resulting benefits of *amakudari*. *Amakudari* is used to maintain the prestige and legitimacy of the central bureaucracy and the hierarchical rank of specific ministries (see Stinchcombe 1998, 269, for a similar argument).

When we put together a holistic picture including all *amakudari* paths, we see a substantial density of ex-bureaucrats at various intersections of the whole system. Add to this the likelihood that these individuals act not only in their own personal interests, but also to maximize the interests of their ministry and of the state. When we consider the dispersed locations of ex-bureaucrats throughout diverse sectors and political offices, the idea of structural power allows for the possibility that *amakudari* personnel are oriented to action for collective interests. If *amakudari* serve as coordinator, integrator, intermediary, representative, and mechanism of monitoring, how many amakudari do we need? Structural power operates as the individual occupies a position on a board of directors or political office, which serves to set the expectations and policy choices of that board or those policy committees. *Amakudari* personnel constitute an institutionalized status group that operates with structural power.

A comparison of the game of chess with the Asian game of *go* provides an illustration of differences between situational and structural power. In chess, each piece is moved aggressively to capture and replace the opponent's piece on a certain location on the board. The object is to take the opponent's pieces until the king is captured. This is analogous to situational power. The game of *go* has an entirely different logic, which is analogous to structural power. In *go*, the pieces on the board are moved and placed with the object of making the opponent's moves or choices increasingly limited, not of capturing or replacing the opponent's pieces (Rosen and Usui 1994).[1]

The board in *go* consists of a grid of nineteen lines by nineteen lines, on which black and white pieces are placed at the intersections during play. The number of pieces, or "stones," is 361 and equals the number of intersections. The two players alternate placing one stone on each turn. The stones are not removed by direct confrontation (unlike chess) but are removed only if the opponent succeeds in encircling them. The goals of the game are to eliminate as many of the opponent's stones as possible and to control territory. A smaller number of stones can be effective if deployed strategically. It is generally understood that the skillful player slowly works from the edge of the board toward the center, gradually circling and countercircling the stones of the opponent. Head-on battles and similar direct strategic moves, which are popular in Western military doctrine, athletic events, corporate strategy, and games such as chess, are alien to the logic of *go*. The preferred type of attack is indirect, nonlinear, and discontinuous. Beginners often concentrate their stones toward the center of the board and immediately pounce on the opponent when they attack, only to be easily defeated by the experienced player (see Swedberg 2001).

One of the fascinating features of the *go* game analogy is its application to social power in the Japanese context. Some authors believe the number of players and who "wins" in a situation of negotiations or direct confrontations are measures of power (Calder 1993; Richardson 1997; Schwartz 1998). There is a long literature that takes this perspective. This assumes that aggregate numbers are the only ones that count and that the only proof of the effectiveness of *amakudari* is who wins in direct face-to-face negotiations. But the game of *go* reminds us that a group that sits on the boards of directors of almost 30 percent of listed private firms and 58 percent of the one hundred largest private firms, occupies 40–50 percent of the board positions in large and powerful *tokushu hojin* and close to 30 percent of board positions in *zaidan* and *shadan hojin*, and account for 20 percent of LDP Lower House seats and 33 percent of cabinet positions provides an argument for the importance of structural power. Ex-bureaucrats' presence on these boards and in these offices provides a basis for a framework of expectations about and limitations of policy choices. Because actors have been placed in the strategic locations, there need be no direct confrontation over policy or even promotion. Having ex-bureaucrats on the board of directors and having political representation provide the basis for controlling the degrees of freedom (or framework of expectations and choices in policymaking), limiting the choices that can be made in corporate and public policy.

Our definition of *amakudari* as part of an elite power structure is "a structure in which powerful people are committed to some value or interest"[2] (Stinchcombe 1968, 107). These people are powerful because they occupy the pinnacles of powerful institutions, maintain relations among these institutions, and reproduce themselves by controlling the selection of elite succession and general instruments of communication and socialization. "By selection, socialization, controlling conditions of incumbency, and hero worship, succeeding generations of power-holders tend to regenerate the same institutions" (Stinchcombe 1968, 111). Thus, there is compelling reason for the top of the bureaucracy to have a preponderance of Todai graduates and to fill key political offices and board positions in the private and public sectors with these top bureaucrats.

Our *amakudari* network–mapping approach is particularly resonant with structural social power because it focuses on behavioral patterns and locations. Another feature of a power structure is the control of information and skillful use of symbols in creating the illusion of change. Elites shape the consciousness of nonelites by defining what is an appropriate policy option. The availability of policy choices is rooted in the overall configuration of *amakudari* placements throughout Japanese society. For example, Krauss (2000, 269–70) illustrates how the media offer little in the way of the framing of real political alternatives. Japanese Broadcasting Corporation (NHK) networks are partly funded by the government and occupy the dominant position in the media industry. The executive ranks of NHK are filled with *amakudari* personnel from the MPT and such linkages between MPT and top corporate positions exist throughout the major corporations in the media industry (Nakano 1998). The recognition of widespread *amakudari* in the top ranks of Japanese media suggests that the media function to pacify nonelites, while legitimating the state and the elite power structure in the eyes of the general public. The media directly contribute to the insulation of elites and to absence of challenges from nonelites in the way in which information is released. The central ministries, local governments, police, corporate headquarters, and unions all disseminate information to journalists of the major media organizations at *kisha* (reporters') clubs. Club membership is not open to the minor presses (or to foreign journalists until the late 1990s). Journalists who report "disagreeable" information are excluded from the club. Because they cannot risk being excluded from the club, journalists often agree not to report on sensitive issues.

Elections, political parties, the Diet, and other forms of political participation are, in part symbolic, providing the forms of democratic participation without its content. For example, political quiescence is induced in the public through the symbolic reassurance that "something is being done"—reforms thus appear to be more symbolic than substantive. The electoral reform of 1994 (after the LDP's defeat in 1993) raised widespread optimism for ending money politics and correcting the discrepancy in the value of votes that existed between rural and urban areas. But the discrepancy still remains after the reform, and the LDP reemerged as the dominant party in a controlling coalition in 1996. In the economy, most sectors are still highly regulated, and Japan remains a producer- rather than consumer-oriented economy.

Another feature of an elite power structure is the removal or blunting of instruments of change that might bring changes elites do not want. This is nowhere more apparent than in the lack of laws to protect citizens' rights. There are "no environmental-assessment regulations, no product liability laws, no lender liability law, few rules on insider trading or other forms of market manipulation, few testing protocols for new medicines, and no cost-benefit analysis of gigantic building schemes" (Carlile and Tilton 1998, 10). Japan's judiciary is not independent and dares not rule against the government, the police has broad powers to imprison, and 95 percent of lawsuits against the government end in rulings against the plaintiffs (Kerr 2001, 56–57). Similar to the bureaucracy, the Japanese judiciary reveals a homogeneity of career backgrounds and a uniform outlook. Unlike U.S. judges, who begin their careers as lawyers representing varying interests, Japanese judges enter the judiciary at the outset of their careers, are trained together, and remain within the institution until retirement. Thus, the quality of the Japanese judiciary is even and its outlook is uniform. Consequently, the courts have the ability to maintain the status quo and protect elite interests rather than the interests of individual citizens. Also, Japanese citizens are more comfortable relying on experts in making major decisions. Legally trained experts, for example, are preferred to the Anglo-American jury system, and controversial high-profile jury decisions in the United

States seem to confirm to many Japanese that their system is preferable (Rosen and Usui 1994, 40).

The elite control of information is a key feature of a power structure. In reference to business, bureaucracy, and parliament, "the lack of reliable data is the single most significant difference between Japanese democracy and those of the West. . . . Banks and securities firms routinely falsify financial information at the direction of the Ministry of Finance" (Kerr 2001, 104, 137–38). In chapter 4 we discuss how the accounting methods of the *tokushu hojin* and other public corporations deviate from the standards used in the private sector and how such practices obscure business operations and the use of public funds among public corporations. Ministry regulation illustrates another feature of symbolic politics of the elite power structure. Our discussion with officials at the MCA indicated that "deregulation" did not mean a reduction in the number of regulations but the creation of additional regulations to repeal previous regulations. The official intent may be clear in government information, but the real intent may well be disguised. Similarly, the NPA's official report on *amakudari* shows how elites control information. As we discuss in chapters 1 and 3, the NPA is presumed to monitor and report the annual number of *amakudari* to the private sector. The number reported has precipitously declined since the mid-1990s, which has led many researchers to assume that *amakudari* is dead—a presumption this book contests. In reality, the NPA is neither equipped nor mandated to conduct an exhaustive review of *amakudari* personnel.

Another feature of the power structure stems from FILP (*zaito*) and the laws that are written and interpreted by the bureaucracy. Many operations in the public sector are hidden from public scrutiny. As we discuss in chapter 4, the law provides for capital investment by the national government. When it is set up, a public corporation may be insulated from many of the mechanisms of parliamentary supervision. For example, the transfer of FILP funds to *tokushu hojin* is not included in the government budget submitted to the Diet, providing the controlling ministries and public corporations with considerable policymaking freedom. Thus, the allocation process for FILP is more dispersed and decentralized than the regular national budget. This measure of independence from the Diet also generates criticisms about public corporations. With rising government deficits, the public sector has been subjected to a series of reforms and reorganizations since the 1970s. Reform proposals under the Koizumi cabinet attempted to change few of the funding mechanisms for *tokushu hojin*. Despite the degree of financial mismanagement in many *tokushu hojin*, no ministry officials, ex-bureaucrats, business executives, or politicians have been held accountable. Instead, past reforms of *tokushu hojin* have been limited to mergers or the reclassification of one type of public organization into another. As we discuss in chapter 4, the reform of FILP (*zaito*) might not fundamentally change their operation or their alignment between the ministries and private sector.

Amakudari as a power structure functions to modify change and maintain stability. The patterns and contents of *amakudari* networks are important for the operations of the markets in terms of coordination among institutions and the pacification of nonelites. Societies have rules, both formal and informal, about organizing economic activities. The norms embedded in these networks of *amakudari* relationships further specify the appropriate social relations among the government, the public firms, and the private firms. The *amakudari* networks provide a basis for defining the governance structures of public and private firms, how the organization should operate, and how interactions among firms should be structured (e.g., the convoy system). Both of these features, network of *amakudari* and the informal norms they embody, suggest that the purpose of *amakudari* is to produce stable market outcomes (i.e. survival) for the firms that use them. In other words, *amakudari* and their networks address the effectiveness (as opposed to the efficiency) of the firms. These networks are thought to be effective if a given set of organizations survives. However, it is more common to view *amakudari* as a pathological institution inhibiting free market forces and efforts for administrative reform and market deregulation. The essence of this view rests with free market economics oriented to organizational efficiencies. Our position is agnostic about the optimal allocation of resources and personnel—elite power structures are neither inherently good nor bad.

Our argument is not that there is an elite centralized monolithic structure to the absolute exclusion of nonelites with direct unilateral domination of all policy decisions in every sector of Japanese society.[3] We argue that just as the knee-jerk explanation of the Japanese political economy as a power structure is an exaggeration and cuts off reasoned examination, so too does the wholesale dismissal of the idea of a power structure. The concept of a power elite does not imply that all aspects of a society are controlled by a very few or that large-scale changes in a society can be created or stopped even by the most organized and self-conscious power elite. An elite power structure involving the major institutional hierarchies of society merely participates in the decisions of national consequence that are made; it does not control history (Domhoff and Dye 1987, 9). The evidence for our position is a circumstantial pattern of change and continuity (resistance to change) with *amakudari* providing a mechanism of appropriation, monopoly, and legitimacy for the major ministries. We have no smoking gun, no eyewitness, but we do have motive and opportunity, and *amakudari* provides the weapon. Our evidence should be judged not on the criminal law criteria of "beyond a reasonable doubt" but on the civil law criteria of "probability."

Difficulties of Reform: Scandals and Legitimacy

The discussion of two types of social power illustrates different points of view on Japan's current problems. One group believes that the verdict is overwhelming—Japan's success has soured. Japan emerged from World War II to become the second largest economy in the world by the 1970s only to stagnate through the 1990s. So deep is the pessimism that commentators suggest Japan is moving from being an irrelevance to a liability to the rest of the industrial world (*Economist*, February 2002, 16). Various scholars and commentators attribute this stagnation to the growing irrelevance of the institutions that gave distinctive recognition to the Japanese version of capitalism and its cooperative elite institutions. For example, Alex Kerr goes so far as to state that "an indurated bureaucracy is Japan's single most severe and intractable problem, responsible for bringing the nation to the brink of disaster in the 1990s. . . . at present the old LDP stalwarts are firmly back in power, beholden as before to bureaucrats and large business" (2001, 359, 361). Further indicating the elite character of the obstacles to reform, Kerr points out "the Japanese bureaucratic system has never relied on public approval for its legitimacy and power; it works in a separate dimension, far above and removed from the democratic process" (van Wolferen, quoted in Kerr 2001, 361). This elite character of Japanese society is not new; it has its roots at least back to the Tokugawa era (1603–1867).[4]

During the past two decades, the financial fortunes of Japan and the United States have reversed. Optimism for free-market capitalism has increased dramatically with the overwhelming U.S. dominance in the global markets. So too has faith in the stock market increased as the most efficient means of allocating capital and improving national competitiveness. This belief has reinforced the sovereignty of shareholders in corporate governance at the expense of other stakeholders. What counts most is increasing earning or raising corporate stock prices. Shedding redundant workers is seen as evidence that a corporation is committed to focusing on the bottom line. Those who call for a wholesale change in the rules of how the Japanese do business contend that the changes Japan has gone through so far are not sweeping enough to destroy the old system (Katz, 1998). Old institutions and mechanisms of co-ordinating the economy such as *amakudari* networks should be eliminated.[5]

A second view suggests that the complaints about the lack of change with reforms on the part of the first group are based on an inability to see Japan holistically, as *sui generis* Japanese capitalism, an emphasis on the liability of the Japanese system—or both. The second group sees Japan as a relational system, pointing to the institutional embeddedness of the firms, the market, and the state as constituting interdependent parts and operating differently from Anglo-Saxon style capitalism. The strength of Japanese society is its ability to maintain a sense of social cohesion, stability, and personal well being. The society depends on compromising parties showing that they work together for the whole group. This is illustrated by institutions like lifetime employment, which is embedded in relations of cross-shareholding within the enterprise groups, and the balanced cooperation and competition within industries and cooperative government-industry relations. In the words of Ronald Dore, Japan's economic structure operates with "a dense web of obligation-loaded relational, as opposed to contractual-liability-only arm's-length transacting, a structure which does much of its business in customer markets, not auction markets" (Dore 2001b, 7).

This systemic nature of Japanese society resists attempts to change its relational aspects. Thus, after so much speculation on the demise of lifetime employment, most changes in employment patterns have come from attrition, voluntary retirement, movement of workers to subsidiaries and affiliates, and bankruptcy—and not the outright dismissal of redundant workers. After lengthy discussions of a merit pay and promotion system less geared to seniority, most firms outside of the financial sector have adopted a merit pay scale that has changed wages only a few percentage points. Calls for changes in corporate governance led to changes in the size of corporate boards of directors but no clear shareholder representation. Changes in cross-shareholding appear to be more a response to short term crisis book-keeping than to a dramatic change in the system. Japan legalized the payment of directors and senior managers with stock options in 1997, but most firms that have adopted the scheme have made them more a symbolic than a substantial part of directors' compensation (Dore 2001b). Deregulation designed to lower consumer costs has limited impact, except in a few industries like domestic airlines and gasoline distribution (Dore 2001b, Dedoussis 2001, Tatsumichi 2001). Now add to this list the number of attempts to reform or even eliminate *amakudari* as illustrative of frustrated reform. Even though much discussion has centered on changing the promotion system within the bureaucracy, reassessment of remuneration, postponement of retirement age for civil servants, restraint on *amakudari*, or creation of a job bank for civil servants, no practical proposal is in sight to replace the old system. Our book demonstrates a pattern of resilience in the *amakudari* networks, even in the face of efforts to reform and antagonistic public opinion.

What makes Japanese style stakeholder capitalism systemic is its inherent relational character which embeds it in society. The relational character of the Japanese political economy rests on institutional complementarity, institutional interlocks, and elite interdependence. These features are underpinned by motivational consistency. "Similar behavioral dispositions are called for in a variety of situations: primarily the acceptance of certain basic oblig-ations imposed on one as a member of Japanese society, and secon-darily the willingness to take on further obligations by entering into long-term commitments which seriously limit one's options to shift to another employer, another supplier, another bank" (Dore 2001b, 6). This systemness circumscribes efforts to reform and restructure its institutions. Any attempt to change one institution will be met by resistance from other institutions with which it is interdependent. This interdependence is both an asset and a liability. The interde-pendence makes each institution resilient, yet inhibits its ability to act and change quickly.

Most commentators agree there is a kind of paralysis in the institutions, albeit for different reasons. They claim there is an unwillingness or inability to fundamentally restructure Japanese institutions (Katz 1998; Gao 2000; Dore 2001b; Kerr 2001; van Wolferen 1989). A few authors note that Japan has averted the banking and financial crisis (by injecting $550 billion in 1997) and is moving in the right direction, though only slowly (Patrick 2001; Washio 2002). This situation has created boycotts of the system by the Japanese people on two fronts, leading to the precariousness of some of Japan's institutions including the bureaucracy and *amakudari*. The real issue is a confidence problem, lack of consumer spending, a paradox of frugality, or a demand deficiency problem. Consumers are saving and not spending given the lack of confidence in Japanese institutions and the fear and uncertainty for the future. In addition, there have been major scandals—such as Daiwa, *jusen* (housing loan corporations), HIV (Green Cross), and mad cow disease—involving the mishandling of taxpayer money, bureaucratic incompetence, collusion, and a lack of transparency. These and other recent scandals exposed the bureaucracy and *amakudari* to accusations of mismanagement and corruption. In each case public sentiment favored punishing the principals for violating the public trust. But instead of dismissal and prosecution, the ministries attempted to cover up the issue and provide early retirement and *amakudari* for those bureaucrats involved in the scandal. They eroded the public trust and, more generally, undermined the legitimacy of Japan's institutions.[6]

Amakudari is not without its vulnerabilities. The Achilles' heel of Japanese institutions is the erosion of public trust, which led to boycotts of participation and assent on the part of the public. We are seeing a withdrawal of the public from participation in and support of institutions like consumer markets and central ministries. The boycott of the public creates a precarious condition for Japan's elite institutions. The power and prestige of the ministries depend on the perceived legitimacy of the central ministries. The ministries organize networks of collective action (*amakudari*), create networks of talent (Todai graduates), and socialize bureaucrats to perform successfully. They maintain the vitality of those networks by beating out the alternative networks to which the most talented students might go to start their careers. A career as a bureaucrat with its power and prestige is defended as preferable to alternative career choices, even at a lower salary than one might receive in other occupations. Yet the relation between ministry organization and opportunity is precarious because the ministries must maintain their ability to recruit the most talented students and they must be able to appropriate the benefits of a bureaucratic career (*amakudari*). They are only successful as long as the institutional integrity of the bureaucracy and *amakudari* (the connections among education, the bureaucracy, and *amakudari*) continues to pay off. The erosion of the legitimacy of a bureaucratic career and the rank of any specific ministry occurs if the field changes. Change may occur when career incentives (such as *amakudari*) disappear, where legitimacy of the bureaucratic career is withdrawn, or when alternative career paths offer more power, prestige, and economic returns than the ministries.

Japan is in the midst of a crisis of the legitimacy of its institutions—particularly the bureaucracy and its personnel extension in *amakudari*. The institutions cannot lead without their perceived legitimacy and people's confidence in their abilities to effectively manage the affairs of the nation and to discipline any of its members who jeopardize the perceived interest of the nation. Corrupt officials must be held accountable and be purged to maintain the public's faith in the bureaucracy.

It has long been noted that the nature of Japanese society provides opportunities for some insiders to exploit resources. The Japanese public has tolerated corruption among politicians and businesspersons as unfortunate imperfections in the overall society. However, "if they occur among the bureaucracy, they signal the need for quick surgery and reconstitution of the system" (Johnson, 1982: 317). Public trust is the currency of the bureaucracy. The way the scandals have been handled by the ministries has left the lingering impression that the bureaucracy is more protective of itself and its industrial interests than those of the public.

We contend that Japan is changing, but in a slow and incremental way. It is oriented more toward continuity than quick change and efficiency, as our analysis of *amakudari* shows. *Amakudari* has been under intense media and political pressure since the middle of the 1990s, yet it has not disappeared or declined as much as one might expect and as some have stated. *Amakudari* relational patterns are the hidden fabric of the relational society, with a tradition of legitimacy accorded elites and few legal mechanisms for nonelites to challenge institutional patterns. Elite interdependence, institutional interlocks, and institutional complementarity maintain these *amakudari* patterns. *Amakudari* networks are anchored in the interdependence of politicians, bureaucrats, business interests, and the underlying and supporting webs of norms, values, and orientations. You could hardly expect *amakudari* to continue without extralegal regulation and informal norms that are enforced through mutual webs of obligations.

The contribution of this book is the illustration of how deeply Japan's institutions are fused, consciously maintained, or even manipulated by elites and how difficult it is to induce fundamental changes from within. So far, without a clear consensus and strong leadership for reform, Japan has chosen to muddle through by maintaining an emphasis on stability with a pattern of continuing reforms with small changes instead of a wholehearted embrace of efficiency-oriented policies.

Japan's economy is circumscribed within myriad social features such as laws, regulations, formal rules, and informal norms. These social features are administered by a configuration of interlocking social institutions, which provide Japan with its distinct variation in the form of markets and capitalism. The old institutions and mechanisms of coordination rooted in the *amakudari* networks act to shape and modify concrete reform plans. *Amakudari*, in turn, coordinates other institutions that administer Japanese markets or Japanese capitalism. The logic of *amakudari* and other social institutions is oriented toward stability and encourages organizational survival and effectiveness, not necessarily efficiency. This is why only incremental change occurs despite so many attempts at reform.

Amakudari is a central thread in the Japanese power structure, which has been in the background of the dynamics of the Japanese economy. Certain courses of action are unavailable because of existing bureaucracy-legislature-business rules and understandings of appropriate policy. The organization of the economy is governed by this general set of rules. These rules and understandings allow private firms and politicians to survive. The dominance of these institutional elites means that those rules tend to reflect their interests, values, and orientations. These interests, values, and orientations underpin and bolster the institutional interlocks. In this way, *amakudari* representing the fabric of the power structure represents a key, historically constructed feature of Japanese society.

Appendix

Interview Cover Letter

We used the following letter soliciting interviews with *amakudari* officials and key informants, including journalists and associates of *amakudari* officials.

Dear ———:

We have been studying the retirement paths of bureaucrats to private companies, government-related organizations, public corporations, and political positions in Japan. We began this research two years ago and published several articles. This year we wish to gather more detailed, practical information on the *amakudari* process by interviewing ex-bureaucrats and corporate and ministry people who are familiar with the process.

We are not expecting to obtain sensitive information or data. We are not going to publish the entire content of interviews. Names and company/ministry affiliations will not be revealed. We are seeking the inside information that might enrich our analysis of data we collected over the past two years. As social scientists, we want to produce statistical demonstrations of complex issues. Interviews will provide us with more contextual nuance.

Compared to two years ago when we came to Japan, we now have difficulties finding people. *Amakudari* has had negative media exposure and people are not willing to talk on the subject. We are indifferent in evaluating *amakudari* as good or bad. Instead, we want to add a human touch or live stories to our dry, statistical analysis of *amakudari*.

For your information, we include our short biographies and a list of interview questions. If you know someone who may provide us with frank, open views on any question on our list or other issues of *amakudari*, it will be greatly appreciated. If it is more convenient, interviews can be done over the telephone.

Chikako Usui
Visiting Researcher

Tokyo University

Richard A. Colignon
Fulbright Lecturer to Tokyo
University &
Kyoritsu Women's University

Questions on Reemployment of Civil Servants (*Amakudari*)

We used the following questions for our in-depth interviews with *amakudari* officials and key informants, including journalists and associates of *amakudari* officials.

Process of making arrangements for *amakudari*

Question: How are inquiries made? What is the routine procedure? Who decides who moves and when, where, and what position to move?

Question: How does *amakudari* to a private company differ from *amakudari* to a government-related organization (e.g., *tokushu hojin*) or public organization (*zaidan* or *shadan hojin*)? Who decides who goes to a government-related organization? or to a *zaidan hojin*?

Ties

Question: How are the ties between ministries and ex-bureaucrats maintained? What do ministries/agencies and retired bureaucrats do to stay in contact? What do retired bureaucrats do to retain their value for successive *amakudari* positions? How do they get the most-updated ministry/agency information?

Receiving *amakudari*

We hear company's attitudes toward *amakudari* are changing. Some say that private companies are hesitant to accept *amakudari* because bureaucrats lack flexibility in making adjustments (to a new business environment). However, bureaucrats who possess distinctive talents, technical skills, foreign-language facility, international diplomacy experience, or international business knowledge/experiences are always in demand. Also, some companies seek retiring bureaucrats to act as brokers for the receiving firm. These ex-bureaucrats are expected to bring government contracts to the company. Some journalists suggest deregulation has decreased the need for *amakudari*. Some others point to ongoing corporate restructuring/downsizing as reducing *amakudari*. Many companies are cutting costs, including the number of *amakudari*.

Question: Which of these views is true in your experience?

Shukko, haken, chuzai, and amakudari

Question: In your opinion, will there be an increase in the use of *shukko*, *haken*, or *chuzai* by the bureaucracy in the near future?

Question: Why is personnel exchange—sending out and receiving—so deeply rooted in Japanese organizations? Why does business rely on such a system? What do you think?

Notes

Chapter 1. *Amakudari* and the Political Economy of Japan

1. The bubble economy refers to an asset price bubble that began in the late 1980s. Land and stock prices collapsed in 1990 and the economy has suffered from highly anemic growth in the 1990s. The bubble began as Japan attempted to fight off the 1986 recession caused by the sudden increase in the value of the yen associated with the international Plaza Accord in 1985 (see Aggarwal 2002).

2. Japan is often depicted as a society dominated by vested interests or the alliance of the three power sources, which some have called the iron triangle. It includes the politicians (especially the LDP politicians), the bureaucracy, and the large corporations. The concept of iron triangle fell out of favor with the rise of pluralist interpretations of Japan's political economy in the 1980s and 1990s (see later). However, the slow pace of Japan's reforms in economy and government structures has bred frustration and the iron triangle has been resurrected as the explanation for Japan's lack of change (see Colignon and Usui 2001; Uchida 1993; Hyland 1997; Wanner 2000; Rothacher 1993; Mulgen 1997).

3. *Amakudari* has been criticized as one of the root causes of collusion and corruption in Japan's iron triangle. A bureaucrat who descends into a corporate world, for example, essentially coordinates with his old ministry and lobbies for his company. Because his junior colleagues at the ministry are looking forward to their own *amakudari*, they often oblige their senior friend with his request for the release of valuable information, a government permit, or friendly legislation. Or when something goes wrong with the company, the *amakudari* official lobbies for special favors or protection from the ministry. Characterizing *amakudari* as a cause of collusion and corruption, however, distorts the meaning and significance of *amakudari* to Japan's political economy. The label "corruption," for example, suggests *amakudari* is pathology even though it is the rule. The label "collusion" suggests *amakudari* is something to eliminate. The scandals are not merely the tip of the iceberg; they are exaggerations of a standard form.

4. Unlike the Japanese case, French job training is also broader—typically French bureaucrats are attached to other government agencies, public corporations, banks, and the private sector as part of their career training. Japanese bureaucrats spend their entire career in one ministry. (See Suleiman 1974, 1978; Birnbaum 1982; van Wolfren 1989, 155–57.)

5. In fact, the Japanese public has been familiar with the term *amakudari* but less informed about its nature and influence on society until the 1990s. Because of the lack of transparency and the difficulty of getting inside information, very few scholars studied *amakudari*. Ironically, more publications on *amakudari* came

out in the 1990s when bureaucrats were linked with collusion and corruption scandals.

6. On January 6, 2001, the central ministries and agencies were reorganized into ten ministries and some 10 agencies. The idea was to strengthen cabinet functions and streamline the overgrown ministries and agencies. It created the new structure consisting of: Ministry of Environment (*Kankyo Sho*); Ministry of Land, Infrastructure, and Transport (*Kokudo Kotsu Sho*); Ministry of Economy, Trade, and Industry (*Keizai Sangyo Sho*); Ministry of Agriculture, Forestry, and Fisheries (*Norin Suisan Sho*); Ministry of Health, Labor, and Welfare (*Kosei Rodo Sho*); Ministry of Education, Culture, Sports, Science, and Technology (*Monbu Kagaku Sho*); Ministry of Finance (*Zaimu Sho*); Ministry of Foreign Affairs (*Gaimu Sho*); Ministry of Justice (*Homu Sho*); Ministry of Public Management, Home Affairs, Posts, and Telecommunications (*Somu Sho*); Japan Defense Agency (*Boei Cho*); Postal Service Agency (*Yusei Jigyo Cho*); National Police Agency (*Keisatsu Cho*); Financial Service Agency (*Kinyu Cho*); Fire and Disaster Management Agency (*Shobo Cho*); Agency for National Resources and Energy (*Shigen Enerugi Cho*); Japan Patent Office (*Tokkyo Cho*); Small and Medium Enterprise Agency (*Chosho Kigyo Cho*); Japan Meteorological Agency (*Kisho Cho*); and Japan Coast Guard Agency (*Kiajo Hoan Cho*) (Nihon Seikei Shinbunsha, 2001, p. 450).

7. The number of public employees serving the central government (*kokka komuin*) was approximately 1,160,000 in 1998. The general category (*ippanshoku*) accounted for approximately 70 percent of this total. This general category includes administrative servants who have passed the type I examination (approximately 230,000), college professors (approximately 70,000), doctors (approximately 60,000), and tax specialists (approximately 54,000). As a comparison, the number of public employees serving the local government was 3,280,000 (NPA 1998, app., pp. 7, 9).

8. Even though the number of elite-track bureaucrats is small, there are others in the bureaucracy who reach the level of section chief or above, including those on the technical track and tax specialists. This explains why there are approximately 3,000 bureaucrats who leave the bureaucracy early.

9. Okimoto (1989, 152) and Keehn (1990, 1021) go further, contending that informality in Japanese government-business relations represent "organizational strategies crucial to the functioning and performance of bureaucracy and government in Japan." (Keehn 1990: 1021)

10. For exceptions, see Haley (1987); Richardson (1997); Broadbent (1998).

11. Pempel argued that "the long term secular shifts taking place in Japanese policy making involve an increased autonomy for Japanese business, a relative decrease in the hegemonic powers of bureaucratic agencies, and a rise in the influence of the LDP and its parliamentary members" (1987, 152).

12. Richardson contends that Japanese politics is and has been "democratic, pluralistic and decentralized" (1997, 260). The era of LDP rule was one of intense pluralism, and politics in the current coalition government remains "highly pluralistic" with some interinstitutional relationships "replaced by frequently renegotiated understandings" (264).

13. Okimoto contends that "reemployment of higher civil servants in high posts within the private sector (*amakudari*) is perhaps the best unobtrusive indicator of relative bureaucratic power [relative strength of a ministry vis-à-vis other ministries]" (1988, 319).

14. A few studies measure the degree of ministry influence by the number of *amakudari* going to different segments of society. Some authors use the number of ex-

bureaucrats in political office (*seikai tensin*) as indicative of ministry power (Lockwood 1965; Pempel 1987). Van Wolferen (1989, 115) counts the number of public corporations controlled by each ministry (by *yokosuberi*) as indicative of ministry influence. Ishizawa (1995) focuses on the indirect path of *wataridori*—how ex-bureaucrats from MOF move to banks and then on to private companies—as indicative of the influence of the MOF in the private sector.

15. For example, Van Wolferen (1989) contends that the MOF has the unofficial job of protecting the system against the excesses of special relationships (*jinmyaku*). To accomplish this oversight protection, the MOF uses the negotiation over shares of the national budget to discipline ministries it judges to be too close to interest groups or politicians. The MOF also maintains indirect control over other ministries through its right to monitor budgetary and other financial accounts of ministries and agencies. Also, the MOF controls the NPA (through *shukko*, "temporary loan"), especially in divisions that handle salary and benefits for bureaucrats (Kawakita 1989). Another monitoring mechanism used by the MOF is the placement of its personnel—the MOF sends its bureaucrats to the positions of vice minister or director general in other agencies, a practice described as "colonization" (Kawakita 1989, 138). Through its policing powers, the MOF can monitor or sanction politicians; for example, the MOF arrested Kanemaru Shin in 1993 not by pursuing charges of bribery or illegal political contributions, but by pursuing charges of tax evasion (Kawakita 1989). The MOF uses its taxing and policing power to increase its *amakudari* network; the *amakudari* of numerous MOF officials to brewery industries may be attributed to the alcohol-related taxes it controls (Ishizawa 1995, 90). The MOF also uses an indirect *amakudari* structure to shape and guide the private sector. It is customary for a main bank to send its personnel to the companies to which it gives loans. Banks receive *amakudari* bureaucrats and also send personnel to private companies. In other words, there is a pyramid-shaped *amakudari* structure from the MOF to banks and from banks to private companies (Ishizawa 1995, 138–39).

16. The Home Ministry (*Naimu Sho*) was created in 1873. Its responsibilities involved the management of social order and welfare. It spun off the Ministry of Agriculture and Commerce (*Nogyo Shomu Sho*) in 1881 (from which the Ministry of International Trade and Industry came in 1949), the Ministry of Telecommunications (*Teishin Sho*) in 1883 (from which the Ministry of Transport (*Unyu Sho*) came in 1943), and the Ministry of Health and Welfare (*Kosei Sho*) in 1925. It was dismantled and reorganized by the Occupation in 1946–47, which divided it into the Ministry of Labor (*Rodo Sho*), the Ministry of Construction (*Kensetsu Sho*), the National Police Agency (*Keisatsu Cho*), and the Ministry of Home Affairs (*Jichi Sho*). The Ministry of Home Affairs was downgraded to the Agency of Home Affairs (*Jichi Cho*) in 1954 but was returned to its original ministry status in 1960 (Funaki, 1997, 69; Muramatsu and Pempel, 1995, 178–79).

17. In the Ministry of Construction, there are approximately one hundred bureaucrats (at the rank of section chief or above) leaving the ministry annually. The reemployment of these bureaucrats is 100 percent. In 1994, for example, of those one hundred leaving the ministry, only eleven (approximately 10 percent) were subject to NPA inspection and approval. The remaining eighty-nine bureaucrats did not take positions in the private enterprises regulated by the Ministry of Construction. Instead, these bureaucrats took positions in the private sector not regulated by Construction and in public enterprises (Cho 1995, 32). We expect a considerable variation among ministries and agencies in terms of the *amakudari* routes of relatively high-ranking bureaucrats. A comparison of such data for each

ministry and agency would lead us to a more definitive conclusion about the nature of *amakudari*.

18. It is instructive to review estimates of such incidents given by Cho (1995, 33, fig. 1-3). From 1988 to 1994, the total number of *amakudari* inspected and approved by the NPA ranged from 246 to 203. The number of *amakudari* among those at the level of section chief or above ranged from 86 to 55. To put it differently, during the seven years Cho examines, we calculate that *amakudari* by those at the level of section chief or above constituted approximately 22 percent (in 1989) to 36 percent (in 1992). In other words, only one-fifth to one-third of the *amakudari* cases published in the NPA annual reports are *amakudari* of relatively high-ranking bureaucrats. The remaining cases are clearly *amakudari*, in that bureaucrats are taking positions in profit-making enterprises that their ministries/agencies regulated, but they are *amakudari* by noncareer bureaucrats and *amakudari* by career bureaucrats below the section-chief level. The NPA reports are not *amakudari* reports of all high-ranking elite bureaucrats.

19. The number of *tokushu hojin* was 87 in 1998. The number of *zaidan* and *shadan hojiin* was 26,089 in 1996. The number of other types of public organizations is unknown.

20. The concept "power elite" does not imply that all aspects of a society are controlled by very few or that large-scale changes in a society can be created and stopped even by the most organized and self-conscious of power elites. For Mills, and other power structure researchers, the power elite of major institutional hierarchies merely make the decisions of national consequence; they do not control history (Domhoff and Dye 1987, 9).

Chapter 2. *Amakudari* as an Institution

1. The Home Ministry (Naimusho) was abolished in 1947 by the Supreme Commander of the Allied Powers (SCAP) and its functions were divided among the prefectural governments and other ministries of the national government, especially the Prime Minister's Office. The Ministry of Health and Welfare (1938; reorganized 1948), the Ministry of Labor (1947), and the Ministry of Construction (1948) were each created out of functions previously exercised by the Home Ministry. Sixty percent of the bureaucratic purges by SCAP were in the Home Ministry (Kubota 1969, 98, 105, 111).

2. The remaining postretirement movements included positions at educational and research institutions, industry associations, appointments to local government office, and self-employment such as consulting.

3. According to Kubota's analysis of 1,353 high-ranking bureaucrats who held posts of section chief or above between 1949 and 1959, nearly 10 percent came from prominent families. In those days, prominent families constituted less than 0.55 percent of the population; thus, children of elite backgrounds supplied a disproportionately large number of higher civil servants (Kubota 1969, 53).

4. Koh (1989) presents survey data of attitudes toward country and society by youth from Japan, the United Kingdom, Germany, the United States, and France that suggests increasing individualist and self-interested attitudes among Japan's youth. Japanese youth rank lowest in expressing a willingness "to sacrifice their own interests for their country" and "willingness to work on behalf of society" (Koh 1989, 156–57). For Koh (1989) these results indicate that individuals in Japan are increasingly self-centered. We think there is an alternative interpretation.

These attitudes are consistent with a mass-elite society, in which the general population is disinterested in country and society. In contrast, countries where there is a high proportion of interest and commitment to society are precisely those where attitudes are most self-centered and most consistent with pluralist participatory democracy.

5. Prior to 1919, there were eight higher schools (*kouto gakko*) and the most prestigious was the First Higher School, or Ichiko. The prewar higher schools were patterned after the upper level of the German *Gymnasium* and the French *lycée* (Kubota 1969, 60). Some Japanese pronounce the First Higher School "Ikko." However, our interviewees who attended the First Higher School and those who attended Todai call the First Higher School Ichiko.

6. According to Kubota, higher school enrollment was 4 percent in 1919 and 6 percent in 1929. In addition, between 1949 and 1959, Ichiko graduates accounted for 24 percent of vice ministers, 25 percent of seretariats and bureau chiefs, 21 percent of division chiefs, and 15 percent of section chiefs (1969, 66).

7. The term *gakubatsu* implies clannishness among graduates of the same school and is often used to mean a Todai clique at large or Todai graduates from Ichiko. It refers to a strong in-group feeling to the exclusion of graduates from other schools. The extraordinary concentration of Todai graduates in the bureaucracy and the processes of recruitment, training, promotion, and *amakudari* do support the importance of group identity and *gakubatsu* in providing stability in the administrative machinery and its relations with the rest of society.

8. All examinations have multiple stages: multiple-choice tests of general and specialized knowledge, and then essay tests of generalized and specialized knowledge.

9. In 1987 this group consisted of 227,725 or 46.8 percent of all people covered by the seventeen salary schedules (Koh 1989, 136, 70–71).

10. Civil servants with administrative salaries at the rank of 9 or below, postal service employees, forestry employees (e.g., mountain rangers), and assistant public prosecutors whose positions are not equivalent to bureaucrats possessing the rank of section chief at a central ministry/agency are not subject to NPA inspection as long as they do not take board-of-director positions after retirement. Civil servants who work in courts are also subject to this rule; however, civil servants who work for the Defense Agency are subject to the legislative prohibition (the same stipulation applies, but the director general of the Defense Agency approves *amakudari*, not the NPA).

11. The reorganization of the bureaucracy effective January 2001 brought a much smaller bureaucracy consisting of ten ministries and some ten agencies plus the Cabinet Office. For example, the Ministry of Finance (Okura Sho) was broken into two: the Ministry of Finance (Zaimu Sho) and the Financial Service Agency (Kinyu Cho). The Ministry of Education and the Science and Technology Agency merged into a new ministry, the Ministry of Education, Culture, Sports, Science, and Technology. The Ministry of Labor and the Ministry of Health and Welfare merged into a new entity, the Ministry of Health, Labor, and Welfare. The Ministry of Construction, the Ministry of Transport, the National Land Agency, and the Hokkaido Development Agency were collapsed into the new Ministry of Land, Infrastructure, and Transport. The Environment Agency was upgraded to ministry status as the Ministry of Environment. The MITI was changed to the Ministry of Economy, Trade, and Industry (METI).

12. Some ministries perform better than others. They organize networks of collective action (*amakudari*) and create networks of supplies of talent (Todai graduates). This means ministries maintain the competencies of those networks by

beating out alternative networks in which customers (corporate boards and offices) and the most talented students may start their careers. However, the relationship between ministry organization and opportunity is a precarious appropriation. Ministries appropriate benefits (*amakudari*) through competition as long as the opportunity continues to pay off. The ministry's rank erodes if the field changes and the opportunity no longer pays or if competitors develop competitive competencies so that the monopoly is no longer defensible.

Chapter 3. *Amakudari*: Movement to the Private Sector

1. According to Cho (1995), the *Nikkei Weekly* (the Japanese equivalent of the *Wall Street Journal*) for the years 1975–94 published 601 articles on *amakudari*. These were essentially neutral reportings of the facts of some bureaucrat retiring to take a position in the private sector; almost none of these articles contained suggestions of wrongdoing or were critical of the practice. During the same twenty-year period, there were more than 17,000 news articles reporting collusion, bribery, and suspicion of wrongdoing. Of these 17,000 stories, Cho found that only 19 reported both *amakudari* and charges or suspicion of wrongdoing.

2. The number of *amakudari* in 2001 reported by the NPA increased to sixty-nine from forty in 2000. The increase was attributed to the reorganization of the bureaucracy which took place in January 2001 and the NPA's ending calls for self-restraint of *amakudari* by ministries ("Amakudari stages comeback after seven years of restraint" *The Japan Times*, March 30, 2002. http://www.japantimes.co.jp, accessed on 9/27/02).

3. Johnson (1982) noted the relative decline of the MITI, along with the rise of the MOF based on NPA data for 1963–73. Okimoto (1988) reported the eclipse of the MITI's dominance based on 1976 NPA data. Thus, both authors treat *amakudari* as a measure of ministry influence (Usui and Colignon 1995).

4. Interpretations vary on which ministries were the most important and powerful. Kerbo and McKinstry (1995) suggest these are the Ministries of Justice, Finance, and Foreign Affairs and the MITI. Okimoto's (1988) survey of twenty-one government officials indicates the Ministry of Foreign Affairs was only "fairly influential" and does not mention the Ministry of Justice. In contrast, the Ministry of Foreign Affairs was very weak based on our behavioral (as opposed to reputational) measure of influence and power (i.e., *amakudari*). Given the nature of expertise, however, it is not surprising to find weak linkages between these ministries and private industry. We expect bureaucrats from the Ministries of Justice and Foreign Affairs to take postretirement careers in the public and academic spheres or to pursue a business that is not arranged through *amakudari* (e.g., consulting).

5. Okimoto (1988, 320) includes the Ministry of Health and Welfare among the ministries considered powerful by their *amakudari* placements in 1976; however, 1976 was an aberration in a much more modest overall pattern of placements for that ministry.

6. The resource dependency model has several internal contradictions. One pertinent to *amakudari* is the conception of the organization as market weak, yet politically capable of influencing the placement of retired government personnel. The external control of organizations by their environment is the primary idea of resource dependency; yet rather than focusing on how an organization adapts its internal structure to the environment, the resource dependency model

emphasizes the malleability of the environment and how organizations influence it. In the case of *amakudari*, the weaker the organization is vis-à-vis the
market, the more effective it is presumed to be in acquiring this resource from
the government (Cho 1995; Colignon and Usui 1997).

7. As Calder expresses the resource dependency logic: "Smaller and weaker organizations have striven harder than their larger and more powerful counterparts
to influence the process or resource allocation by political means, precisely
because their concerns have been more intense than those of better-placed competitors" (1989, 381).

8. Calder contends that "a disproportionately large share of retired bureaucrats
move to non-Tokyo-based corporations, particularly those of Kansai, thus
enhancing the position of such corporations at the expense of Tokyo-based
firms and promoting geographical decentralization of econopolitical power
across Japan" (1989, 387).

9. There are several definitions of *keiretsu* (enterprise groups). There are two types
of *keiretsu*: vertical and horizontal (intermarket or *kigyo* group). Companies of
a specific enterprise group are characterized by affiliation, long-term relationships, multiplex transactions, extended networks, and symbolic significance.
Dodwell Marketing Consultants (1994) identifies six major *keiretsu*—Mitsui,
Mitsubishi, Sumitomo, Fuji, Sanwa, and Dai-Ichi Kangyo—and two medium horizontal (intermarket or *kigyo* group) *keiretsu*—IBJ and Tokai. Major vertical
keiretsu include Hitachi, Toyota, Matsushita, and NTT.

10. "In a political economy traditionally dependent on credit, with corporate debt-
equity ratios among the highest in the industrialized world, no private firms are
more powerful than the major banks and trading companies, particularly those
standing at the head of major industrial groups. . . . The largest banks, securities
firms, and trading companies traditionally do not make a practice of hiring
bureaucrats, especially to fill top executive positions" (Calder 1989, 383).

11. However, Kubota's (1969, 56) analysis of *amakudari* between 1949 and 1959
found the MITI, Transportation, MPT, and Agriculture more likely to send their
retirees to *keiretsu*-affiliated firms.

12. In contrast, Okimoto (1989, 162) says *amakudari* placements reflect the leading
growth sectors of the economy, which suggests that the industries experiencing
the most growth are the ones likely to receive *amakudari*.

13. The Kanto region includes Tokyo, Kanagawa, Saitama, Chiba, Ibaraki, Tochigi,
and Gunma.

14. The BOJ is not a central ministry but a quasi-public corporation (see chap. 4).
However, a significant percentage of personnel coming from the BOJ originated
in the MOF.

15. Ministry regulation essentially involves rules of procedures that constrain the
operation of the private sector. This is considered a key lever of control of the
private sector by the ministries. The general presumption is that more regulation by a ministry means more control of the relevant industries. The greater
the regulation, the more likely that private-sector corporations will hire *amakudari* to help them interpret these ministry regulations. Conversely, as deregulation proceeds in certain industries, there is less need for *amakudari* to interpret
regulations.

16. *Amakudari* has been implicated in the compromise of the government oversight
agencies (e.g., Administrative Management Agency) charged with the regulation
of private business and public enterprises because of their reliance on recommendations from influential ministries (Johnson 1975, 7). Further, *amakudari*
has been implicated in bid rigging in the construction industry (Arakawa 1993).

Chapter 4. *Yokosuberi* and Public Corporations

1. Each year, a total of approximately 3,000 high-ranking bureaucrats (those reaching section chief or above) leave their ministries and agencies early. Of these 3,000, approximately 1,300 take positions at research institutions and universities. We focus on the remaining 1,700.

2. Public corporations have an advantage over government operation in that they perform with more flexibility in financial and personnel management compared with the direct operations of the national government. Efficient management can be effected under special arrangements for such corporations (e.g., flexibility in the use of funds, self-procurement of funds, flexibility in contract procedure, and autonomy in employment). Further, public corporations may use local public entities or private sources for finance and personnel. Independence from the national government can be assured (e.g., in promoting academic activities or research on labor relations). Public corporations have several advantages over private corporations when the provision of continuous and stable services is required, when the amount of capital required for operations cannot be obtained from private financial sources alone due to the high risks involved or the small prospects of profits, or when the operations must be conducted from a fair and impartial standpoint (Colignon and Usui 2000).

3. In general, detailed business operations are prescribed in the operation procedure documents, which must be approved by the ministers that oversee the public corporation. Compensation for services (fees, loan interest rates, etc.) must be authorized by the supervising ministers. Some public corporations' capital is financed by the national government. (Capital investment by the national government is provided for by law and is limited to public corporations and authorized corporations.) In addition, they may also receive loans (from postal saving funds) and some are permitted to issue bonds. In most cases, the profits gained by the public corporations through their business operations are held as reserve funds. Sometimes a part of or the entire profit is paid to the national government or is paid as dividends to investors with the approval of the supervising ministers.

4. The dispersal of FILP funds in 1993 was as follows: housing, 29.5 percent; improvement of living environment,16.6 percent; small and medium-size enterprises, 14.6 percent; road construction, 9.9 percent; transportation and communications, 7.9 percent; trade and economic cooperation, 5.8 percent; social and welfare facilities, 3.8 percent; industrial technology, 3.5 percent; local development, 2.7 percent; agriculture, forestry, and fisheries, 2.5 percent; educational facilities, 1.8 percent; and preservation of land and disaster restoration, 1.5 percent (IPMS Group, 1994, 104).

5. To become a nonprofit organization (*hi-eri hojin* or *koeki hojin*), an organization must satisfy three conditions: its activities must have merit for public purposes, it must carry out nonprofit-seeking activities, and it must receive a permit from the appropriate central government ministry or a local government office (*chiho jichitai*) (Hayashi 1997, 4). These three requirements have not been uniformly enforced in the twentieth century, thus creating variation in public corporations. Hayashi and Iriyama (1997, 5) note that the third requirement, government permission, contributes to the easier establishment of nonprofit-seeking quasi-governmental entities (i.e., organizations with public merit established by governmental organizations) than of nonprofit-seeking entities initiated by private organizations and citizens.

6. To reduce government debts, the administrative reform of 1996 included the reorganization of the central government ministries and agencies. It transformed

national hospitals, museums, and research institutions into *dokuritsu gyosei hojin*. Originally, *dokuritsu gyosei hojin* were to function like private firms and were required to submit management plans of 3–5 years. However, many *dokuritsu gyosei hojin* are involved in education, research and development, and cultural promotion and are not profitable ventures. Consequently, they remain dependent on government subsidies, as do *tokushu hojin*. In other words, government capital contributions, subsidies, and loans from FILP continue to these organizations. In addition, observers argue that some *tokushu hojin* have been converted to *dokuritsu gyosei hojin* simply to give an appearance of the reform. They are concerned with the lack of oversight of these new organizations, noting the high number of *amakudari* to *dokuritsu gyosei hojin* (*Asahi Shinbun*, 20 December 2001, "The Same Problem Under a Different Name.").

7. For example, the data in Organization for Economic Cooperation and Development ([OECD] 1997) show that government employment expressed as the percentage of total employment was 6.0 percent in Japan, 12.7 percent in the Netherlands, 14 percent in Switzerland and the United States, 14.4 percent in the United Kingdom, 16.1 percent in Italy, 16.6 percent in Australia, 19.4 percent in Belgium, 19.6 percent in Canada, 22.1 percent in New Zealand, 22.4 percent in Austria, 24.8 percent in Finland, 30.5 percent in Denmark, 30.6 percent in Norway, and 32 percent in Sweden.

8. The calculation of 6.5% of GDP in 2001 was made by the authors. According to the Japan Information network (www.jinjapan.org, accessed in 9/19/02), Japan's GDP for 2000 was $4.65 trillion. Using the exchange rate of $1 = ¥106.9 as of January 2000 reported in *NIPPON2000: Business Facts and Figures* (JETRO, 2000: i), we converted the 2000 GDP dollar figure into yen and divided ¥32 trillion (2000 FILP) by the 2000 GDP expressed in yen. Matsubara states "FLIP exceeded ¥400 trillion (400 cho yen), which was 1.5 times the combined capital of major private banks operating in Japan" (1995, 34). However, his figure of ¥400 trillion must be an error. The more likely figure is ¥40 trillion. FLIP was ¥26.8 trillion for fiscal year 2002, down 17.7 percent from the previous year (*Japan Times*, 25 December 2001).

9. This was a recommendation, agreement, or decision made by the cabinet (*kakugi kettei*), not a Diet decision. Newspaper reports in English on "government decisions" are often unclear about whether they refer to cabinet decisions or the Diet decisions to adopt particular cabinet proposals. Unless it is approved by the Diet, no decision or plan is final.

10. Seiroren (the Organization of Government-Related Labor Unions) has taken on the political goal of reducing *yokosuberi* to *tokushu hojin*. Seiroren stopped its publication of data on *tokushu hojin* in 1994 because of media attention and because its publications were being used recklessly by the media in their attempt to abolish *tokushu hojin*, which was not what Seiroren had intended.

11. Johnson (1978, 112) gives the example of the Japan Highway Public Corporation. The Ministry of Construction is the controlling ministry dominating seven of the twelve positions on the board. The MOF has one position, because the corporation needs financial support from that ministry. Because highways are a part of the transportation system, the Ministry of Transport has claim to one position.

12. Until the publication of reports by Hayashi and Katayama (1995) and Hayashi and Iriyama (1997), there was virtually no systematic account of *zaidan* and *shadan hojin* in Japan.

13. To determine whether a company was carrying out governmental functions, Hayashi and Iriyama (1997, 50) checked to see who gave the capital to start the company, the sources of operating money, and the present and previous positions of the company directors. According to Hayashi (1997, 20), of a total of 25,216 *zaidan* and *shadan hojin* in 1994, 7,689 (or 30 percent) were *shitei hojin* carrying out administrative functions on behalf of the government. The remaining 17,527 were general *zaidan* and *shadan hojin*. Although the 7,689 *shitei hojin* carried out government activities, this does not necessarily mean they were controlled or supervised by specific government ministries. This issue of control is contingent and ambiguous. For organizations carrying out governmental activities, it is often local governmental offices, rather than central government or private companies, that contribute start-up funds (capital) as well as operating costs. In addition, directors on the board may be unpaid (nonregular *riji*). For example, the current governor of a prefecture and retirees from local government may make up the board of directors. For these organizations, the function is often local and the board of directors may be unpaid.

14. As part of an administrative reform, the cabinet approved a set of criteria for the disclosure of administrative information in 1991 (IPMS Group 1994, 94). The public disclosure of business operations of public corporations was then mandated December 1, 2000 (Management and Coordination Ministry 2001, app., 64); however, the cabinet actually recommended the disclosure of business operations by the middle of 2001.

15. The first administrative reform (*gyosei kaikaku*) began in 1981–83, the second in 1987–90, and the third in 1990–93. The government promoted these reforms in accordance with recommendations to the prime minister by the Provisional Commission for Administrative Reform (popularly known as *rincho*). In 1985, three *tokushu hojin*—JNR, NTT, and Japan Tobacco—were broken up and reorganized toward privatization. In addition, JAL was fully privatized (IPMS Group 1994, 4, 80). The original proposal of the second administrative reform had included the reorganization of thirty-four *tokushu hojin*, but the bureaucracy successfully blocked it (Matsubara 1995, 4).

16. The public debt is projected to increase to ¥63 trillion by March 2003, equal to 140 percent of GDP (*Japan Times*, 25 December 2001).

17. There are conflicting reports on the exact amount of the debts or bad loans. For example, the *Daily Yomiuri* reported that JNPC accumulated ¥1 trillion in bad loans.

18. JNPC's investment funds (out of which it provides initial capital or loans to private firms) come from taxes on petroleum and crude oil.

19. With the reorganization of ministries and agencies that took place on January 6, 2001, the Ministry of Home Affairs, MPT, and Management and Coordination Agency were joined together into the MMC (or Ministry of Public Mangement). Initially the plan was that the MPT's three enterprises (*yusei san jigyo*)—mail services, postal life insurance, and postal savings—would be transformed by 2003 into public corporations or would be privatized. At the time of reorganization, this idea was dropped due to opposition from influential members of the LDP. The idea is still under discussion by the Koizumi cabinet.

Chapter 5. *Wataridori* and Private and Public Corporations

1. Evans defines *amakudari* as part of an "informal network" of "carefully institutionalized" "ties" in which Japanese bureaucrats "end up in key positions . . .

not only in private corporations, but also in the industrial associations, and quasi-governmental organizations" (1995, 49–50).

2. According to Granovetter there are two forms of embeddedness: relational and structural. "The structural aspect is especially crucial to keep in mind because it is easy to slip into 'dyadic atomization,' a kind of reductionism, as if relations among pairs of people (or other units) mattered but not the way these pairs are themselves embedded in higher order structures as in, for example, the treatment of husbands and wives by Gary Becker (1981) or of employers and employees by Harvey Leibenstein (1976). This focus on dyadic atomized or direct relations makes it impossible to see the central role in *outcomes of network cohesion and fragmentation*" (1990, 98–99; emphasis added).

3. Granovetter warns against viewing relationships as having no history. "In ongoing relations, human beings do not start fresh each day, but carry the baggage of previous interactions into each new one. Built into our cognitive equipment is a remarkable capacity, depressingly little studied, to file away the details and especially the emotional tone of past relations for long periods, so that even when one has not had dealings with a certain person for many years, a reactivation of the relationship does not start from scratch, but from some set of previously attained common understandings and feelings. It follows that the characteristics of structure of relations also result from processes over time, and can rarely be understood except as accretions of these processes" (1990, 98–99).

4. We disagree with the use of "informal" to describe *amakudari* in both of the term's two senses—not codified and spontaneous and unconscious. Although no one has found written evidence to disprove the first, we believe such evidence exists, and our data disproves the second (Colignon and Usui 1999).

5. "Bounded rationality" simply means something is rational within the information limits of its structural location.

6. The personnel moving from public corporations to private firms are not perceived to have the socialization or human and social capital of civil servants from the central ministries (Koh 1989), and our analysis shows that they do not benefit from the reemployment apparatus of the central ministries. The Japanese media, however, often treat the movement of these personnel, originating from public corporations, as *amakudari*.

7. This is an interesting hypothesis. It may be contradicted when sequential *watari-dori* move up in rank to insure their seniority within the same corporation.

8. *Daihyo* includes the chairman of the board, *riji*, *shacho* (president), *sosai*, and *todari*. *Fuku daihyo* includes the vice chairman, vice *sosai*, and vice *shacho*.

Chapter 6. *Seikai Tensin*: Movement to the Political World

1. Authors refer to this personnel movement as "ex-bureaucrats becoming politicians" or as a form of *amakudari* (Thayer 1969; Johnson 1974; Curtis 1988; Okimoto 1989; Schwartz 1998). Johnson characterizes *seikai tensin* as the retirement path that was historically open only to those "who served in choice national or regional posts that are particularly suitable for building general political support" (1974, 954).

2. "Iron triangle" has been used to mean: (1) the high level of integration and coordination among bureaucrats, businesspersons, and politicians; (2) that bureaucrats are first among equals; or (3) and industrial and social policy is dominated by this group to the exclusion of other groups (e.g., Uchida 1993). See also chapter 1.

3. The Diet consists of the Lower House (or the House of Representatives) with 500 seats and the Upper House (or the House of Councillors) with 247 seats (Nihon Seikei Shinbunsha 2000, 366–67).

4. A guided democracy places a heavy premium on the virtue and wisdom of the ruling elite. Bureaucratic power was enhanced by entry of the bureaucrats into political parties, eventually (1908 election) making up one of two key elements in the ruling parties, the other being "pure politicians" (Scalapino 1968, 264–65).

5. The fragmentation in the LDP parallels fragmentation in the bureaucracy. The organization of the Japanese bureaucracy into twelve ministries and over thirty agencies represents both formal and substantive cleavages. These organizational designations overlay or correspond to distinct interests in society and in the LDP.

6. Curtis (1988) and Rothacher (1993) agree on the decline of *seikai tensin* as a function of the fortunes of a faction whose strategy was to recruit ex-bureaucrats to its ranks. They differ, however, on the genealogy of the faction. Rothacher (1993, 19) traces the Miyazawa faction back to Shigeru Yoshida through six generations of leaders (Yoshida, Ikeda, Shigesaburo Maeo, Ohira, Suzuki, and Miyazawa). Curtis (1988, 81) sees a five-generation lineage starting with Ikeda.

7. This stricter enforcement of the seniority system is premised on an implicit requirement that politicians who achieve high office have extensive and diverse experience. A prime minister must rise in the party hierarchy and the LDP's promotion ladder is very much geared toward garnering experience in virtually all aspects of national politics. Thus, by the time a prime minister starts office, he will have spent more than ten terms or approximately 25–30 years in the Diet and served in a number of important government and party posts. On the government side, he will have had experience on Diet committees and in a number of cabinet posts, as well as more informally as a *zoku giin* (elected office holder). Thus, prime ministers have experience handling legislation in the Diet and are fairly well versed in important economic and foreign policy issues; on the party side, prime ministers have experience as faction leaders and as top party executives in intraparty and interparty relations.

8. The sense of inheritance is different from a political position directly inherited, as in the House of Lords in the United Kingdom. Instead, the key ingredients leading to a successful election are passed through the family.

9. We do not count Nakasone as a *seikai tensin* politician because he left the Home Ministry after only six years.

10. Shigeru Yoshida is counted once, although he occupied two prime ministerships.

11. Some authors contend that some cabinet positions are more important or prestigious (e.g., MOF, MITI, Foreign Affairs, Justice) (Kerbo 2000; Rothacher 1993), but there does not appear to be a pattern when we look at these six cabinets (see table 6.2).

12. For *seikai tensin*, our estimates are lower than other sources because our definition of *seikai tensin* is more restrictive. We counted the number of officials who moved to political office after reaching the rank of section chief or after serving at least fifteen years in the bureaucracy. Newspaper sources count everyone from bureaucracy as *seikai tensin*, even those who leave it after a few years, which leads to a higher count.

13. As Bourdieu and Wacquant point out, "Indeed, it seems to me that, when you take a close look at what goes on inside what we call the "state" you immediately annul most of the scholastic problems that scholars, armchair Marxists and other speculative sociologists, keep raising about the state. . . . In fact, what we encounter, concretely, is an ensemble of administrative or bureaucratic fields (they often take the empirical form of commissions, bureaus, and boards) within

which agents and categories of agents, governmental and nongovernmental, struggle over this peculiar form of authority" (1992, 111).

Chapter 7. *Amakudari* as a Power Structure

1. Boorman (1969) illustrates how the metaphor of game illuminates different types of social power. Boorman's basic argument is that the Chinese game of *wei-ch'I* (elsewhere known as *go*) inspired the military strategy of Mao Zedong and therefore can help to explain the strategy of control and domination by the Chinese Communist Party.

2. Furthermore, "the key to institutionalizing a value is to concentrate power in the hands of those who believe in that value. It can be arranged that they should believe in it by surrounding powerful roles with rewards and punishments that make it in their interest to believe in the value. Whatever values or interests are defended by the various power centers of a society or group are said to be institutionalized in that group" (Stinchcombe 1968, 107–8).

3. Although this characterization of an elite power structure appears to be a caricature, it is surprising how often critics use these exaggerated dimensions as the basis of their criticisms (see Pempel 1987, 152) and the characterization of hegemonic powers implied in the idea of Japan Inc. and Samuels's criticism of bureaucratic dominance and the presumption of a monolithic and consensual inter-institutional ruling elite implicit in the concept of the 'developmental state' (1987). Critics tend to focus on: (a) the formal differentiation of the state and society, arguing that scholars using the managerial model to analyze Japan tend to ignore autonomy, competition, and conflict among the bureaucracy, business interests, and political parties (i.e., the LDP); (b) the internal fragmentation, conflicts, and competition within the bureaucracy, LDP, and business community, for example, the vertical administration (*tatewari gyosei*) of the central bureaucracy, factions within the LDP, and conflict between global and domestic-oriented business interests; or (c) the inclusion of nonelite groups in policy initiation and formation as evidence for the weakness of the managerial model in explaining Japanese state-society relations.

4. Barrington Moore's analysis of class relations and state autonomy emerging out of the Tokugawa era reveals Japan as an elite society with an elite institutional predisposition. He concluded that the oligarchic structure, internal solidarity, and effective vertical ties with higher authority all survived with very little change in the transition to a modern economy (Moore 1966, 312). Militarism united the upper classes as a way to modernize without changing substantial elements of the rural feudal structure (442). A coalition of agricultural, commercial, and industrial elites rationalized the political order by creating a strong central government and a uniform administrative system and legal codes. The parliament served to maintain the political power of the agricultural elites. The agricultural elites preserved the feudal structure and strengthened the commitment of agricultural people to the centralized elite authority structure. This elite political leadership and powerful bureaucracy, including agencies of control and manipulation, provided government with autonomy from society.

5. In a climate where optimism for the American-style shareholder capitalism ran strong, the wisdom of a tight-knit stakeholder form of capitalism is blamed for Japan's current economic problems. However, the burst of the U.S. technology bubble and the accounting scandals at some high profile corporations may only

reinforce the Japanese perception of the American economic model as dangerous and may mute some of the strident critics of Japan's economy.

6. Hugh Patrick points out "Mishandling the *jusen* problem created public distrust of the authorities; taxpayer monies were perceived as being used to bail out rich bankers and mismanaged but politically protected agricultural credit cooperatives" (Patrick 2001, 20). What is extraordinary in the Japanese banking and financial crises is that its problem has persisted so long, and became worse in late 1997 when the impending systemic crisis led to the injection of an unprecedented 60 trillion yen (about $550 billion) to finance this bailout of the banking system (Patrick 2001, 21).

References

Abegglen, James. 1970. "Economic Growth of Japan." *Scientific American* 22(3): 31–37.

Aggarwal, Raj. 2002. "Bubble Economy." In *Encyclopedia of Japanese Business and Management*, edited by Allan Bird, 51–54. London: Routledge.

Alford, Robert, and Roger Friedland. 1985. *Powers of Theory: Capitalism, the State, and Democracy*. Cambridge, UK: Cambridge University Press.

Allinson, Gary. 1989. "Politics in Contemporary Japan: Pluralist Scholarship in the Conservative Era." *Journal of Asian Studies* 48(2): 324–32.

——. 1993. "Citizenship, Fragmentation, and the Negotiated Polity." In *Political Dynamics in Contemporary Japan*, edited by Gary Allinson and Yasunori Sone, 17–49. Ithaca: Cornell University Press.

Allison, Graham T. 1971. *Essence of Decision: Explaining the Cuban Missile Crisis*. Boston: Little & Brown.

Arakawa, Hirotada. 1993. *Hashimoto Rutaro*. Tokyo: Toyokeizai Shinposha.

Asahi Shinbun. 2002. "The Same Problem under Different Name." http://infoweb.asahi.com/english/politics (date accessed, 3/27/02).

Asahi Shinbunsha. 1970. *Jiminto*. Tokyo: Asahi Shinbunsha.

Becker, Gary S. 1981. *A Treatise on the Family*. Cambridge, Mass.: Harvard University Press.

Birnbaum, Pierre. 1982. *The Heights of Power: An Essay on the Power Elite in France*, Translated by Arthur Goldhammer. Chicago: University of Chicago Press.

Boorman, Scott. 1969. *The Protracted Game: A Wei-ch'i Interpretation of Maoist Revolutionary Strategy*. New York: Oxford University Press 1969.

Bourdieu, Pierre, and Loïc J. D. Wacquant. 1992. *An Invitation to Refelxive Sociology*. Chicago: University of Chicago Press.

Broadbent, Jeffrey. 1998. *Environmental Politics in Japan: Networks of Power and Protest*. Cambridge, UK: Cambridge University Press.

Calder, Kent. 1988. *Crisis and Compensation: Public Policy and Political Stability in Japan, 1949–1986*. Princeton: Princeton University Press.

——. 1989. "Elites in an Equalizing Role: Ex-Bureaucrats as Coordinators and Intermediaries in the Japanese Government-Business Relationship." *Comparative Politics* 21(4): 379–403.

——. 1993. *Strategic Capitalism: Private Business and Public Purpose in Japanese Industrial Finance*. Princeton: Princeton University Press.

Carlile, Lonny. 1998. "The Politics of Administrative Reform." In *Is Japan Really Changing Its Ways? Regulatory Reform and the Japanese Economy*, edited by Lonny Carlile and Mark Tilton, 76–110. Washington, D.C.: Brookings Institute Press.

Carlile, Lonny, and Mark Tilton. 1998. "Is Japan Really Changing?" In *Is Japan Really Changing Its Ways? Regulatory Reform and the Japanese Economy*, edited by Lonny Carlile and Mark Tilton, 197–218. Washington, D.C.: Brookings Institute Press.

Cho, Kyu Chul. 1995. Nihon no seifu-kigyo kankei to seifu shigen douin no osmotic networker to shite no amakudari (The Relationship between the Japanese Bureaucracy and Business Enterprises: *Amakudari* as "Osmotic" Networkers in the Mobilization of Public Resources). Ph.D. diss., Tsukuba University.

Colignon, Richard A. 1997. *Power Plays: Critical Events in the Institutionalization of the Tennessee Valley Authority*. Albany: State University of New York Press.

——. 2002. "Amakudari." In *Encyclopedia of Japanese Business and Management*, edited by Allan Bird, 20–23. London: Routledge.

Colignon, Richard A., and Chikako Usui. 1997. The Permeability of the Japanese Political Economy: Amakudari. Paper presented at 10th Annual Conference of the Association of Japanese Business Studies, June 13–15, Washington, D.C.

——. 1999. "Serial Retirement of Administrative Elites: Wataridori." In *The 1999 Best Papers Proceedings*, edited by Christopher B. Meek and Sane J. Schvaneveldt, 43–60. Chesterfield, Mo.: Association of Japanese Business Studies.

——. 2000. "Hidden Aspects of Japan's Central Bureaucracy: Yokosuberi (Sideslip) and Public Corporations." In *The 2000 Best Papers Proceedings*, 39–56. Chesterfield, Mo.: Association of Japanese Business Studies.

——. 2001. "The Resilience of Japan's Iron Triangle: Amakudari." *Asian Survey* 41(5): 865–95.

Cottingham-Streater, Paige, and Weston Konishi. 1999. "From Okurasho to Zaimusho: Prospects for Administrative Reform in Japan." *Business Insight Japan* 5(October): 1–6.

Curtis, Gerald. 1988. *The Japanese Way of Politics*. New York: Columbia University Press.

Cutts, Robert. 1997. *An Empire of Schools: Japan's Universities and the Molding of a National Power Elite*. Armonk, N.Y.: M. E. Sharpe.

Dedoussis, Vagelis. 2001. "Keiretsu and Management Practices in Japan: Resilience amid Change."
Http://www.china_biz.org/Lectures/BUS0301/Keiretsu_in_Japan.pdf. Accessed 10/21/02.

Dodwell Marketing Consultants. 1973. *Industrial Groupings in Japan.* Tokyo: Dodwell.

——. 1982. *Industrial Groupings in Japan.* Tokyo: Dodwell.

——. 1990. *Industrial Groupings in Japan: The Anatomy of the Keiretsu 1990/91.* 9th ed. Tokyo: Dodwell.

——. 1992. *Industrial Groupings in Japan: The Anatomy of the Keiretsu 1992/93.* 10th ed. Tokyo: Dodwell.

——. 1994. *Industrial Groupings in Japan: The Anatomy of the Keiretsu 1994/95.* 11th ed. Tokyo: Dodwell.

Domhoff, G. William, and Thomas Dye. 1987. *Power Elite and Organizations.* Beverly Hills: Sage Publications.

Dore, Ronald. 1983. "Goodwill and the Spirit of Market Capitalism." *British Journal of Sociology* 34: 459–82.

——. 2000. *Stock Market Capitalism: Welfare Capitalism: Japan and Germany versus the Anglo-Saxons.* New York: Oxford University Press.

——. 2001a. "Response to Book Review on Ronald Dore's *Stock Market Capitalsim: Welfare Capitalism.*" Available at http://www.glocom.org/debates/200112_dore_res/, accessed 3/27/02.

——. 2001b. "Will Global Capitalism be Anglo-Saxon Capitalism?" Http://www.dea.unibo.it/~narduzzo/SeminariDEA/Papers/dore.pdf. Accessed 10/22/02.

do Rosario, Louise. 1993. "No Jobs for the Boys: Japanese System of Hiring Retired Officials Loses Favor." *Far Eastern Economic Review* 15(April): 55.

Evans, Peter. 1995. *Embedded Autonomy: States and Industrial Transformation.* Princeton: Princeton University Press.

Farrell, William R. 1999. *Crisis and Opportunity in a Changing Japan.* Westport: Quorum Books.

Fukui, Haruhiro. 1977. "Studies in Policymaking: A Review of the Literature." In *Policymaking in Contemporary Japan*, edited by T. J. Pempel, 22–63. Ithaca: Cornell University Press.

——. 1987. "Too Many Captains in Japan's Internationalization: Travails at the Foreign Ministry." In *The Trade Crisis: How Will Japan Respond?* edited by Kenneth B. Pyle. 153–75. Seattle: The Society for Japanese Studies.

Funaki, Haruhito, ed. 1997. *Gyosei no shikumi* [Structures of government administration]. Tokyo: Kanki Shuppan.

Gao, Bai. 2001. *Japan's Economic Challenge.* Cambridge, UK: Cambridge University Press.

References

Garon, Sheldon. 1987. *The State and Labor in Modern Japan.* Berkeley: University of California Press.

Gaventa, John. 1980. *Power and Powerlessness: Quiescence and Rebellion in an Appalachian Valley.* Urbana: University of Illnois Press.

Gikai Seido Kenkyukai. 1996. *Rekidai kokkai giin meikan.* Tokyo: J. P. Tsushinsha.

Granovetter, Mark. 1990. "The Old and the New Economic Sociology: A History and an Agenda." In *Beyond the Marketplace: Rethinking Economy and Society,* edited by Roger Friedland and A. F. Robertson, 89–112. New York: Aldine.

Gyosei Kanri Kenkyu Center. 1996. *Data Book: Nihon no gyosei '96–97.* Tokyo: Zaimu Kyoiku Shuppan.

Haley, John O. 1987. "Governance by Negotiation: A Reappraisal of Bureaucratic Power in Japan." In *The Trade Crisis: How Will Japan Respond?* edited by Kenneth B. Pyle, 177–91. Seattle: Society for Japanese Studies.

———. 1991. *Authority without Power: Law and the Japanese Paradox.* New York: Oxford University Press.

———. 1995. "Japan's Postwar Civil Service: The Legal Framework." In *The Japanese Civil Service and Economic Development: Catalysists of Change,* edited by Hyung-Ki Kim, Michio Muramatsu, T. J. Pempel, and Kozo Yamamura, 77–101. Oxford: Clarendon Press.

Hall, Richard H. 1991. *Organizations: Structures, Processes, and Outcomes.* 5th ed. Englewood Cliffs: Prentice Hall.

Hamilton, Gary, and Nicole Biggart. 1988. "Market, Culture, and Authority: A Comparative Analysis of Management and Organization in the Far East." *American Journal of Sociology* (supp.) 94: S52–S94.

Hayashi, Chikio, ed. 1997. *Genzai nihon no hi-eiri hojin* [Present conditions of nonprofit organizations in Japan]. Tokyo: Sasagawa Heiwa Zaidan.

Hayashi, Chikio, and Akira Iriyama.1997. *Koeki hojin no jitsuzo* [Reality of Japanese public corporations]. Tokyo. Diamondsha.

Hayashi, Chikio, and Shoichi Katayama. 1995. *Nihon no zaidan to shadan* [*Zaidan* and *Shadan* Corporations in Japan]. Tokyo. Sasagawa Heiwa Zaidan

Hindess, Barry. 1996. *Discourses of Power: From Hobbes to Foucault.* Cambridge, Mass.: Blackwell.

Hirch, Paul, Stuaet Michaels, and Roy Freeidman. 1987. "Dirty Hands versus Clean Models: Is Sociology in Danger of Being Seduced by Economics?" *Theory and Society* 16(3): 317–36.

Hyland, Jason. 1997. "The Japanese Way–With Japan at Political Crossroads, Insider Unveils Guide to Bureaucracy's Elite, Powerful 'Mandarins.'" *American Foreign Service Journal* (February): 1–5.

Inoki, Takenori. 1995. "Japanese Bureaucrats at Retirement: The Mobility of Human Resources from Central Government to Public Corporations." In *The Japanese Civil Service and Economic Development: Catalysts of Change*, edited by Hyung-Ki Kim, Michio Muramatsu, T. J. Pempel, and Kozo Yamamura, 213–34. Oxford: Clarendon Press.

Inoguchi, Takashi, and Tomoaki Iwai. 1987. *Zoku giin no kenkyu: Jiminto seiken o gyujiru shuyakutachi* (An Analysis of Zoku Politicians and Their Control of the LDP). Tokyo: Nihon Keizai Shinbunsha.

IPMS Group. 1994. *Kasumigasei Data Handbook*. Tokyo: The Japan Times.

Ishizawa, Yasuharu. 1995. *The MOF*. Tokyo: Chuo Koronsha.

Ito, Mitsuyoshi. 1995. "Administrative Reform." In *The Japanese Civil Service and Economic Development: Catalysts of Change*, edited by Hyung-Ki Kim, Michio Muramatsu, T. J. Pempel, and Kozo Yamamura, 235–60. Oxford: Clarendon Press.

Ito, Terry. 1996. *Owarai Okura-sho gokuhi joho* (Funny Secret Tales of the Ministry of Finance). Tokyo: Asuka Shinsha.

Iwami, Takao, ed. 2001. *Kozokaikaku no subete ga yoku wakaru hon* (A guide to the Current Structural Reform). Tokyo: Chukei shuppan.

Iwase, Tatsuya. 1997. "Project Company: Gosen okuen no yami." In *Tokushu hojin no himitsu* (Unknown facts about Tokushu Hojin), edited by Shinji Ishii, 105–17. Tokyo: Takarajimasha.

Japan Company Handbook. Annual. Tokyo: Toyo Keizai, Inc.

Johnson, Chalmers. 1974. "The Reemployment of Retired Government Bureaucrats in Japanese Big Business." *Asian Survey* 14(11): 953–65.

———. 1975. "Japan: Who Governs? An Essay on Official Bureaucracy." *Journal of Japanese Studies* 2: 1–28.

———. 1978. *Japan's Public Policy Companies*. Washington, D.C.: American Enterprise Institute.

———. 1982. *MITI and the Japanese Miracle: The Growth of Industrial Policy, 1925–1975*. Stanford: Stanford University Press.

J. P. Tsushinsha. 1996. *Saishin rekidai naikaku soran*. Tokyo: J. P. Tsushinsha.

Katz, Richard. 1998. *Japan: The System That Soured*. Armonk, N.Y.: M. E. Sharpe.

Kawakita, Takao. 1989. *Okurasho* (The Ministry of Finance). Tokyo: Kodansha.

Keehn, Edward. 1990. "Managing Interests in the Japanese Bureaucracy: Informality and Discretion." *Asian Survey* 30(11): 1021–37.

Kerbo, Harold. 2000. *Social Stratification and Inequality: Class Conflict in Historical and Comparative Perspective*. 4th ed. Boston: McGraw Hill.

Kerbo, Harold, and John A. McKinstry. 1995. *Who Rules Japan? The Inner Circles of Economic and Political Power*. Westport: Praeger.

Kerr, Alex. 2001. *Dogs and Demons: Tales from the Dark Side of Japan*. New York: Hill and Wang.

Koh, Byung Chul. 1989. *Japan's Administrative Elite*. Berkeley: University of California Press.

Krauss, Ellis S. 2000. *Broadcasting Politics in Japan: NHK and Television News*. Ithaca: Cornell University Press.

Kubota, Akira. 1969. *Higher Civil Servants in Postwar Japan*. Princeton: Princeton University Press.

Kuribayashi, Yoshimitsu. 1990. *MOF shukei kyoku* (The Budget Bureau of the Ministry of Finance). Tokyo: Kodansha.

Leibenstein, Harvey. 1976. *Beyond Economic Man: A New Foundation for Microeconomics*. Cambridge, Mass.: Harvard University Press.

Lie, John. 1996. "Sociology of Contemporary Japan," *Current Sociology* 44(1): 1–101.

Lincoln, James, Michael Gerlach, and Peggy Takahashi. 1992. "Keiretsu Networks in the Japanese Economy: A Dyad Analysis of Intercorporate Ties." *American Sociological Review* 57(5): 561–85.

Lockwood, William. 1965. "Japan's New Capitalism." In *The State and Economic Enterprise in Japan*, edited by William Lockwood, 447–522. Princeton: Princeton University Press.

Lukes, Steven. 1974. *Power: A Radical View*. London: Macmillan.

Mabuchi, Masaru. 1995. "Financing Japanesene Industry: The Interplay between the Financial and Industrial Bureaucracies." In *The Japanese Civil Service and Economic Development: Catalysts of Change*, edited by Hyung-Ki Kim, Michio Muramatsu, T. J. Pempel, and Kozo Yamamura, 288–310. Oxford: Clarendon Press.

——. 1997. *Okura-sho wa naze oitsumeraretanoka* (Why Was the MOF Hunted Down?). Tokyo: Chuo Shinsho.

Management and Coordination Agency. 1995. *Kisei kanwa suishin no jokyo* (An Update on Deregulation). Tokyo: Okurasho Printing Office.

——. 1996. *Tokushu hojin soran* (Directory of Tokyu hojin). Tokyo: Government Printing Office.

March, James, and Johan Olsen. 1989. *Rediscovering Institutions: The Organizational Basis of Politics*. New York: The Free Press.

Masumi, Junnosuke. 1995. *Contemporary Politics in Japan*. Translated by Lonny E. Carlile. Berkeley: University of California Press.

Matsubara, Satoru. 1995. *Tokushu hojin kaikaku* (Tokushu hojin Reform). Tokyo: Nihon Hyoronsha.

Mills, C. Wright. 1956. *The Power Elite*. Oxford: Oxford University Press.

Ministry of Labor. 1990. *Rodo hakusho* (White Paper on Labor). Tokyo: Government Printing Office.

——. 1995. *Rodo hakusho* (White Paper on Labor). Tokyo: Government Printing Office.

Ministry of Management and Coordination. 2001. *Koeki hojin hakusho* (White Paper on Public Corporations). Tokyo: Zaimusho Printing Office.

Miyajima, Hideaki. 1998. "The Impact of Deregulation on Corporate Governance and Finance." In *Is Japan Really Changing Its Ways? Regulatory Reform and the Japanese Economy*, edited by Lonny Carlile and Mark Tilton, 33–75. Washington, D.C.: Brookings Institution.

Moore, Barrington. 1966. *Social Origins of Dictatorship and Democracy: Lord and Peasants in the Making of the Modern World*. Boston: Beacon Press.

Mulgen, Aurelia G. 1997. "The Politics of Deregulation and Japanese Agriculture." In *The Politics of Economic Reform in Japan: Collected Papers, Pacific Economic Papers*, edited by T. J. Pempel, Aurelia G. Mulgen, Purnenda Jain, Keiko Tabusa, and Hayden Lesbirel. Pacific Economic Papers, no. 270. Canberra: Australian-Japan Research Centre, Asia Pacific School of Economics and Management.

Muramatsu, Michio. 1981. *Sengo Nihon no kanryosei* (Japanese Bureaucracy in the Post-WWII Era). Tokyo: Toyo Keizai Shinposha.

——. 1994. *Nihon no gyosei* (Public Administration in Japan). Tokyo: Chuo Koronsha.

——. 1997. "Post-War Politics in Japan: Bureaucracy versus the Party/Parties in Power." In *State and Administration in Japan and Germany*, edited by Michio Muramatsu and Frieder Naschold, 13–37. New York: Walter de Gruyter.

Muramatsu, Michio, and Ellis Krauss. 1984. "Bureaucrats and Politicians in Policy Making: The Case of Japan" *American Political Science Review* 78(1): 126–46.

Nakano, Koichi. 1998. "Becoming a Policy Ministry: The Organization and Amakudari of the Ministry of Posts and Telecommunications." *Journal of Japanese Studies* 24(1): 95–117.

National Personnel Authority (NPA). 1998. *Komuin jinji kanri no kaikaku* (Reforming the National Personnel Management). Tokyo: Okurasho Printing Office.

——. 1963–2001. *Eiri kigyo eno shushoku no shonin ni kansusu nenji hokokusho* (Annual Report on the Approval of Re-Employment by Private Enterprises). Tokyo: National Personnel Authority.

Nichigai Associates. 1990. *Japanese Statesmen*. Tokyo: Nichigai Associates, Inc.

——. 1999. *Modern Japanese Statesmen*. Tokyo: Nichigai Associates, Inc.

Nihon Keizai Shinbunsha. 1997. *Kaisha nenkan* [Annual Corporation reports]. Tokyo: Nihon Keizai Shinbunsha.

——. 2000. *Kaisha nenkan* [Annual Corporation reports]. Tokyo: Nihon Keizai Shinbunsha.

——. 1963, 1995. *Kaisha sokan* (NIKKEI Annual Corporation Reports). Tokyo: Nihon Keizai Shinbunsha.

——. 1963, 1964, 1995. *Kaisha sokan: Mijojo Kaishaban* (NIKKEI Annual Corporation Reports (Unlisted Firms)). Tokyo: Nihon Keizai Shinbunsha.

——. 2001. *Kensho: Tokushu hojin kaikaku* (A Study of Tokushu hojin Reform). Tokyo: Nihon Keizai Shinbunsha.

Nihon Seikei Shibunsha. Annual. *Kokkai benran* (A Directory of the Diet). Tokyo: Nihon Seikei Shinbunsha.

NIPPON 2000: Business Facts and Figures. Tokyo: JETRO, 2000.

Noguchi, Yukio. 1995. "The Role of Fiscal Investment and Loan Program in Postwar Japanese Economic Growth." In *Japanese Civil Service and Economic Development: Catalysts of Change,* edited by Hyung-Ki Kim, Michio Muramatsu, T. J. Pempel, and Kozo Yamamura, 261–87. Oxford: Clarendon.

Norville, Elizabeth. 1998. "The 'Illiberal' Roots of Japanese Financial Regulation." In *Is Japan Really Changing Its Ways? Regulatory Reform and the Japanese Economy,* edited by Lonny Carlile and Mark Tilton, 111–41. Washington, D.C.: Brookings Institution.

Okimoto, Daniel. 1988. "Political Inclusivity: The Domestic Structure of Trade." In *The Political Economy of Japan.* Vol. 2, *The Changing International Context,* edited by Takashi Inoguchi and Daniel Okimoto, 304–55. Stanford: Stanford University Press.

——. 1989. *Between MITI and the Market: Japanese Industrial Policy for High Technology.* Stanford: Stanford University Press.

Organization for Economic Cooperation and Development (OECD). 1997. *Statistics for Industrial Societies.* Paris: OECD.

Park, Yung. 1986. *Bureaucrats and Ministers in Contemporary Japanese Government.* Berkeley: University of California Press.

Patrick, Hugh, and Henry Rosovsky. 1976. "Japan's Economic Performance: An Overview." In *Asia's New Giant,* edited by Hugh Patrick and Henry Rosovosky, 1–61. Washington, D.C.: The Brookings Institution.

——. 2001. "From Cozy Regulation to Competitive Markets: The Regime Shift of Japan's Financial System." Center on Japanese Economy and Business, Columbia Business School, Working Paper No. 186 (30 pp).

Pempel, T. J. 1987. "The Unbundling of 'Japan, Inc.': The Changing Dynamics of Japanese Policy Formation." In *The Trade Crisis: How Will Japan Respond?* edited by Kenneth B. Pyle, 117–52. Seattle: Society for Japanese Studies.

——. 1998. *Regime Shift: Comparative Dynamics of the Japanese Economy.* Ithaca: Cornell University Press.

Pempel T. J., and Michio Muramatsu. 1995. "The Japanese Bureaucracy and Economic Development." In *The Japanese Civil Service and Economic Development: Catalysts of Change,* edited by Hyung-Ki Kim, Michio Muramatsu, T. J. Pempel, and Kozo Yamamura, 19–76. Oxford: Clarendon Press.

Polsby, Nelson. 1963. *Community Power and Political Theory*. New Haven: Yale University Press.

Powell, Walter, and Paul DiMaggio. 1991. *The New Institutionalism in Organizational Analysis*. Chicago: University of Chicago Press.

Prestowitz, Clyde V., Jr. 1988. *Trading Places: How We Allowed Japan to Take the Lead*. New York: Basic Books.

Prime Minister's Office. 1990. *Nihon no tokei* (Statistics of Japan). Tokyo: Government Printing Office.

——. 1998. *White Paper on Public Corporations*. Tokyo: Government Printing Office.

Richardson, Bradley. 1997. *Japanese Democracy: Power, Coordination, and Performance*. New Haven: Yale University Press.

Roethlisberger, Fritz J., and William Dickson. 1939. *Management and the Worker*. Cambridge, Mass.: Harvard University Press.

Rosen, Dan, and Chikako Usui. 1994. "The Social Structure of Japanese Intellectual Property Law." *UCLA Pacific Basin Law Journal* 13(1): 32–69.

Rothacher, Albrecht. 1993. *The Japanese Power Elite*. New York: St. Martin's Press.

Roy, William. 1997. *Socializing Capital: The Rise of the Large Industrial Corporation in America*. Princeton: Princeton University Press.

Samuels, Richard. 1987. *The Business of the Japanese State: Energy Markets in Comparative and Historical Perspective*. Ithaca: Cornell University Press.

Sato, Seizaburo, and Tetsuhisa Matsuzaki. 1986. *Jiminto seiken* (LDP Rule). Tokyo: Chuo Koronsha.

Saxonhouse, Gary. 1982. "Evolving Comparative Advantage and Japan's Imports of Manufactures." In *Policy and Trade Issues of the Japanese Economy: American and Japanese Perspectives*, edited by Kozo Yamamura, 237–69. Seattle: University of Washington Press.

Scalapino, Robert. 1968. "Elections and Political Modernization in Prewar Japan." In *Political Development in Modern Japan*, edited by Robert Ward, 249–92. Princeton: Princeton University Press.

Scalapino, Robert, and Junnosuke Masumi. 1962. *Gendai Nihon no seito to seiji* (Party and Politics in Contemporay Japan). Tokyo: Iwanami Shoten.

Schaede, Ulrike. 1995. "The 'Old Boy' Network and Government-Business Relationships in Japan." *Journal of Japanese Studies* 21(2): 293–317.

Schlesinger, Jacob. 1997. *Shadow Shoguns: The Rise and Fall of Japan's Postwar Political Machine*. New York: Simon and Schuster.

Schneider, Ben Ross. 1993. "The Career Connection: A Comparative Analysis of Bureaucratic Preferences and Insulation." *Comparative Politics* 25(April): 331–50.

Schoppa, Leonard. 1991. "*Zoku* Power and LDP Power: A Case Study of the *Zoku* Role in Education Policy." *Journal of Japanese Studies* 17(1): 79–106.

Schwartz, Frank. 1998. *Advice and Consent: The Politics of Consultation in Japan.* New York: Cambridge University Press.

Scott, W. Richard. 1992. *Organizations: Rational, Natural, and Open Systems.* 3rd ed. Edgewood Cliffs: Prentice Hall.

Seifu Kankei Hojin Rodo Kumiai Rengo (Seiroren). 1977. *Amakudari jittai chosa hokokusho* (Report on the Conditions of *Amakudari*). Tokyo: Seiroren.

———. 1992. *Seiroren amakudari hakusho* (Seiroren White Paper on *Amakudari*). Tokyo: Seiroren.

———. 1994. Seiroren *Amakudari hakusho* (Seiroren white paper on *Amakudari*). Tokyo: Seiroren.

Seifu Kankei Tokushu Hojin Rodo Kumiai Kyogikai (Seirokyo). 1974. *Amakudari hakusho* (White Paper on *Amakudari*). Tokyo: Seirokyo.

———. 1982. *Seirokyo amakudari hakusho* (Seirokyo White paper on *Amakudari*). Tokyo: Seirokyo.

———. 1983. *Seirokyo amakudari hakusho* (Seirokyo White Paper on *Amakudari*). Tokyo: Seirokyo.

Selznick, Philip. 1948. "Foundations for a Theory of Organizations." *American Sociological Review* 13: 23–35.

———. 1949. *TVA and the Grass Roots.* New York: Harper and Row.

Shibata, Tokue. 1993. *Japan's Public Sector: How the Government Is Financed.* Tokyo: University of Tokyo Press.

Smelser, Neil and Richard Swedberg. 1994, "The Sociological Perspective" 1994. In *The Handbook of Economic Sociology,* edited by Neil Smelser and Richard Swedberg, 3–26. Princeton: Princeton University Press.

Stark, David. 1996. "Recombinant Property in East European Capitalism." *American Journal of Sociology* 101(4): 993–1027.

Stinchcombe, Arthur L. 1968. *Constructing Social Theories.* New York: Harcourt, Brace, and World.

———. 1998. "Monopolistic Competition as a Mechanism: Corporations, Universities, and Nation-State in Competitive Fields." In *Social Mechanisms,* edited by Peter Hedstom and Richard Swedberg, 267–305. New York: Cambridge University Press.

Suleiman, Ezra N. 1974. *Politics, Power and Bureaucracy in France.* Princeton: Princeton University Press.

———. 1978. *Elites in French Society.* Princeton.: Princeton University Press.

Swedberg, Richard. 2001. "Sociology and Game Theory: Contemporary and Historical Perspectives." *Theory and Society* 30(3): 301–35.

Tatsumichi, Shingo. 2001. "How Advanced is Japan's Personnel Management in the IT Industry?" JIL News and Information. Tokyo: The Japan Institute of Labor, April. http://www.jil.go.jp/bulletin/year/2001/vol40-04/06.htm (accessed 9/27/02).

Thayer, Nathaniel. 1969. *How Conservatives Rule Japan*. Princeton: Princeton University Press.

Toyo Keizai Shinbunsha. Annual. *Kokkai benran* (Diet Members) Tokyo: Toyo Keizai Shinbunsha.

Toyo Keizai Shinposha. 1984–2000. *Kigyo keiretsu soran* (Conglomerate Corporations). Tokyo: Toyo Keizai Shinposha.

Toyo Keizai Shinposha. 1995. *Seikai kancho jinjiroku*. Tokyo: Toyo Keizai Shinposha.

——. 2000. *Seikai kancho jinjiroku*. Tokyo: Toyo Keizai Shinposha.

Tsujinaka, Yutaka. 1990. "Kokusai Kankei eno seiji approach." In *Kokusai Kankei Nyumon* (Introduction to International Relations), edited by Hideo Sato, 145–70. Tokyo: University of Tokyo Press.

Uchida, Kenzo. 1989. *Gendai Nihon no hoshu seiji* (Conservative Rule in Contemporary Japan). Tokyo: Iwanami Shoten.

Uchida, Michio. 1993. "The Dictatorship of the Bureaucracy." *Tokyo Business* (November): 6–9.

Usui, Chikako, and Richard A. Colignon. 1995. "Government Elites and Amakudari in Japan, 1963–1992." *Asian Survey* 35(7): 682–98.

——. 1996. "Corporate Restructuring: Converging World Pattern or Societally Specific Embeddedness?" *The Sociological Quarterly* 37(4): 551–578.

van Wolferen, Karel. 1989. *The Enigma of Japanese Power*. New York: Alfred Knopf.

Wanner, Barbara. 2000. *Economic Problems, Political Changes: Challenge Japan's Cozy Business-Government Ties*. Japan Economic Institute of America, Washington, D.C., no. 22A, 9 June.

Washio, Tomoharu. 2002. "A New Business Environment in Japan." A paper presented at the 15th Annual Meeting of the Association of the Japanese Business Studies, St. Louis, Missouri, June 6–9.

Who's Who in Japanese Government. 1988. Tokyo: International Cultural Association, Japan.

Zuker, Lynne. 1977. "The Role of Institutionalization in Cultural Persistence." *American Sociological Review* 42: 726–42.

Zukin, Sharon, and Paul DiMaggio. 1990. "Introduction." In *Structures of Capital: The Social Organization of the Economy*, edited by Sharon Zukin and Paul DiMaggio, 1–36. New York: Cambridge University Press.

Index

Abegglen, James, 12, 32
Administrative reforms, 45, 47–48,
    192 n.6, 195 n.11, 200 n.19,
    200 nn.14–15
  of public corporations, 83, 105, 107–9
Agriculture, Ministry of (MOA), 53
  amakudari to private sector from, 64,
    67, 68
  seikai tensin and, 157–58, 161
  wataridori from, 168
  yokosuberi from, 167
Alford, Robert, 28, 136
Allinson, Gary, 136, 137, 138
Allison, Graham T., 172
Amakudari, 3–7, 29–31, 164–85
  defined, 2, 20, 29
  analogy to game of go, 174–76
  causes of, 38–43
  cohesion within, 15–17
  corporate hostages and, 42
  corruption and, 191 n.3, 197 n.16
  cultural homogeneity of, 37–38, 165,
    168–71
  dimensions of, 172
  as elite power structure, 14–15, 165,
    171–80, 173
  extent of control, 176–78
  FILP and, 178–79
  lack of transparency, 191–92 n.5
  legislative restrictions to, 43–49
  legitimacy crisis of, 183–84
  media and, 58, 176–77, 196 n.1,
    201 n.6
  ministry motives for, 39–40, 43
  ministry stratification in, 17–18
  multiple paths of, 7, 10–11, 12,
    19–20, 31, 165–68
  organization and coordination of,
    49–56, 170

political economy and, 12–14
resilience of, 55–56
resistance to change, 2–3, 18–19,
    170–71, 179–80, 182
restriction of, 48–49
sectionalism by ministry, 39, 54–55,
    174
See also Amakudari, to private
    sector; Seikai tensin; Wataridori;
    Yokosuberi
Amakudari, to private sector, 57–81,
    116–17
  centrality of, 64, 66
  compared to yokosuberi, 103–5, 104
  concentration of, 66–68, 166
  by ministry, 60, 61, 63–68, 65, 104
  regulation and, 75–80, 78, 79,
    197 n.15
  resource dependency and, 68–75, 70,
    71, 72, 73, 80
  trends, 58–63, 59, 60, 61, 62
  See also Amakudari
Arakawa, Hirotada, 197 n.16
Asahi Shinbun, 153, 154, 198–99 n.6
Asahi Shinbunsha, 154
Ashida, Hitoshi, 144

Banking system, bailout of, 204 n.6
Bank of Japan (BOJ), 74–75, 197 n.14
Biggart, Nicole, 2
Boorman, Scott, 203 n.1
Bourdieu, Pierre, 202–3 n.13
Broadbent, Jeffrey, 137
Bubble economy, 191 n.1
Bureaucracy
  cultural homogeneity of, 31–38
  education of, 32–34
  examinations for entry into, 34–35,
    195 n.8

217

Bureaucracy *(continued)*
  legislative restrictions on, 46
  promotion within, 35–36
  reorganization of, 48, 192 n.6,
    195 n.11, 200 n.19, 200 nn.14–15
  retirement from, 36–37

Cabinet
  background of members of, *152*
  hereditary politicians representation
    in, 149–50, *152*, 161–62
  seikai tensin and, 149–50, *150–51,*
    152, 160
  Todai representation in, 149, 152,
    161, 168
Calder, Kent, 16–17, 31, 175, 197 n.10
  on notion of iron triangle, 16–17,
    136, 137
  on resource dependency, 41, 68,
    197 nn.7–8
Carlile, Lonny, 2, 15, 48, 76, 177
Cheney, Richard B., 5
"Cherry Blossoms Received in the Jade
  Sake Cup" (song), 33
Cho, Kyu Chul, 16, 22, 26, 54, 193–
  94 nn.17–18
  on causes of *amakudari,* 40, 42, 50,
    197 n.6
  on *kanbocho,* 52, 128
  on legislative constraints to
    amakudari, 44, 45, 47
  on media coverage of *amakudari,*
    196 n.1
  on ministry stratification in
    amakudari networks, 17
  on *wataridori,* 113
Civil servants. *See* Public employees
Civil Servants Law, 103, 44–45
Civil service. *See* Bureaucracy
Colignon, Richard A., 2, 30, 172,
  197 n.6
Construction, Ministry of (MOC)
  amakudari from, 53, 193 n.17
  amakudari to private sector from, 59,
    64, 66–67, 68
  seikai tensin and, 157, 161
  wataridori from, 168
Corporations. *See* Private corporations;
  Public corporations
Cottingham-Streater, Paige, 2
Curtis, Gerald, 137, 140, 141, 143,
  201 n.1, 202 n.6
Cutts, Robert, 34, 74

Daily Yomiuri (newspaper), 200 n.17
Dedoussis, Vagelis, 182
Deferred compensation, 40
Deregulation, 85–86, 178, 182
  See also Regulation
Dickson, William, 114
Diet, 202 n.3
  legislative restrictions to *amakudari,*
    45–47
  movement of personnel, 135
  See also Lower House
DiMaggio, Paul, 37, 114
Dodge Line, 45
Dodwell Marketing Consultants, 24,
  72, 197 n.9
Dokuritsu gyosei hojin (independent
  administrative organizations), 86,
  198–99 n.6
  See also Public corporations
Domhoff, G. William, 180, 194 n.20
Dore, Ronald, 2, 181, 182, 183
do Rosario, Louise, 75
Dye, Thomas, 180, 194 n.20

Economic reforms
  deregulation, 85–86, 178, 182
  obstacles to, 1–3, 180–83
Economist (magazine), 180
Election Law, 1962 amendment, 45
Electoral reform (1994), 177
Electric Power Development Company,
  88
Elite integration, 136, 162, 168–69
Embeddedness, structural, 37, *119,* 133,
  201 n.2
Employment, lifetime, 181–82
Evans, Peter, 63, 113, 136, 200–1 n.1
Examinations, civil service, 34–35,
  195 n.8

Faction leadership, changes in, 140–41
Farrell, William R., 75
FILP. *See* Fiscal Investment and Loan
  Program
Finance, Ministry of (MOF), 17, 18,
  170
  amakudari from, 51–52, 53, 54
  amakudari to private sector from, 59,
    64, 66–67, 68, 74–75
  falsification of financial information,
    178
  FILP and, 85
  powers of, 76, 193 n.15

seikai tensin and, 156–57, 158, 160, 161
wataridori from, 168
yokosuberi from, 167
See also National Tax Administration Agency
Financial compensation
for *wataridori*, 130–33, *131*
for *yokosuberi*, 130
Fiscal Investment and Loan Program (FILP), 84–85, 87–88, 105, 178–79, 198n.4
reform of, 108
France, 5, 191n.4
Friedland, Roger, 28, 136
Fukuda, Takeo, 140, 144, 145
Fukui, Haruhiro, 16, 32, 136, 137
Funaki, Haruhito, 4, 15, 17, 35, 113, 193n.16
Fundraising, political, 141

Gakubatsu (school-based cliques), 33–34, 195n.7
Gao, Bai, 183
Garon, Sheldon, 18, 30
Gaventa, John, 172
Gerlach, Michael, 2
Go (game), 174–75, 203n.1
Government Employee Act, 46
Granovetter, Mark, 113, 201nn.2–3
Gyosei Kanri Kenkyu Center, 9, 35, 86–87

Haley, John O., 13, 32, 44
Hall, Richard H., 41
Hamilton, Gary, 2
Hashimoto, Ryutaro, 48, 143
Hata, Tsutomu, 143
Hayashi, Chikio
on nonprofit organizations, 198n.5
on public corporations, 83, 87, *87*, 88, *89*
on *zaidan* and *shadan hojin*, 26, 200n.13
Hereditary politicians, 142–43, 147–48, 162–63
representation in Cabinet, 149–50, *152*, 161–62
representation in Lower House, *153*, 154, *154*, 161–62
representation in prime ministership, 161–62
Hindess, Barry, 172

Hokkaido Takushoku Bank, 76
Home Affairs, Ministry of, 157–58, 161, 193n.16
See also Management and Coordination, Ministry of
Home Ministry, 193n.16, 194n.1
Hoover commission, 44, 45
Horiuchi, Mitsuo, 107
Hyland, Jason, 19

Ichiko (elite higher school), 32–33, 195nn.5–6
Ikeda, Hayato, 140, 144, 148, 149
Inoguchi, Takashi, 139–40
Inoki, Takenori, 26, 30, 37, 40, 47
on *wataridori*, 113, 126, 130
International Trade and Industry, Ministry of (MITI)
amakudari from, 39–40, 52–53, 54
amakudari to private sector from, 64, 66–67
JNPC and, 106–7, 167
seikai tensin and, 157–58, 161
wataridori from, 168
yokosuberi from, 167
IPMS Group, 103, 198n.4, 200nn.14–15, 202n.3
Iriyama, Akira, 26, 87, *87*, 89, 198n.5, 200n.13
Iron triangle, 16–17, 74, 80, 135, 136, 137, 191n.2, 201n.2
Ishigaki, Kazuo, 107
Ishizawa, Yasuharu, 17, 51, 52, 126, 139, 193n.15
Ito, Mitsuyoshi, 17
Iwai, Tomoaki, 139–40
Iwami, Takao, 105
Iwase, Tatsuya, 106

Japan, Inc., 12–13, 40
Japan Airline Corporation (JAL), 88
Japan Broadcasting Corporation (NHK), 176
Japan Company Handbook, 70
Japanese National Railways (JNR), 47, 88, 91
Japan National Highway Corporation, 88, 105
Japan National Railway (JNR), 47, 48, 200n.15
Japan National Petroleum Company (JNPC), 83, 105–7, 167, 200nn.17–18

Japan Times, 82, 196 n.2, 200 n.16
Japan Tobacco, 200 n.15
Japan Tobacco Public Corporation, 47,
    88
JNPC. See Japan National Petroleum
    Corporation
JNR. *See* Japan National Railway
Johnson, Chalmers, 12, 13, 31, 84,
    196 n.3
    on causes of *amakudari*, 38, 40
    on corruption, 184, 197 n.16
    on *kanbocho*, 50–51, 128
    on regulation, 45, 75
    on *seikai tensin*, 136, 137, 201 n.1
    on *wataridori*, 113
    on *yokosuberi*, 92–93, 94–95,
        199 n.11
    J. P. Tsushinsha, 146, 147
Judiciary, 177–78

Kaisha nenkan (Nihon Keizai
    Shinbunsha), 25, 57–58
Kanbocho (*amakudari* placement
    officer), 50–51, 52, 53, 128
Kansai Airport Corporation, 105
Kata-tataki (tap on the shoulder), 7
Katz, Richard, 181, 183
Kawakita, Takao, 17, 137, 193 n.15
Keehn, Edward, 84, 139, 192 n.9
Keiretsu affiliations, 4, 197 n.9
    resource dependency and, 69, 71,
        71–72, 72
Kerbo, Harold, 34, 137, 196 n.4
Kerr, Alex, 177, 178, 180, 183
Kigyo keiretsu soran (Toyo Keizai
    Shinposha), 24, 57–58
Kishi, Nobusuke, 144, 148
Koh, Byung Chul, 36, 194 n.4, 195 n.9,
    201 n.6
    on civil service examinations, 34,
        35
    on cultural homogeneity of elite, 15,
        32
Koizumi, Junichiro, 105, 143, 149–50
Kokkai benran (Nihon Seikei
    Shinbunsha), 27
Konishi, Weston, 2
Kono, Yohei, 143
Krauss, Ellis, 137, 176
Kubota, Akira, 18, 30, 31, 44,
    194 n.1
    on causes of *amakudari*, 40

on elitism of bureaucracy, 34, 36,
    194 n.3, 195 nn.5–6
on *keiretsu* affiliated firms, 197 n.11
Kuribayashi, Yoshimitsu, 51

Labor organizations, conflict with
    wataridori, 130, 132, 133
Liberal Democratic Party (LDP), 1, 137,
    140, 177, 202 n.5
    enforcement of seniority system,
        141–43, 145–47, 202 n.7
    See also Policy Affairs Research
        Council; *Zoku* politicians
Liberal Democratic Party (LDP), Lower
    House members
    background of newly elected, *155*
    seikai tensin and, 152, *153*, 156–58,
        157, 159–60, 160
Lifetime employment, 181–82
Lincoln, James, 2
Lockwood, William, 12, 15, 16, 32,
    193 n.14
Lower House
    background of newly elected
        members, *155*
    educational background of members,
        152, *153*, 154
    hereditary politicians representation
        in, *153*, 154, *154*, 161–62
    seikai tensin and, 151–52, *153*, *154*,
        154–58, *155*, *157*, *158*, *159–60*,
        160–61
    Todai representation in, 152, *153*,
        154, *154*, 161, 168
    See also Diet
Lukes, Steven, 172

Mabiki (thinning out), 7
Mabuchi, Masaru, 18, 40, 138
Management and Coordination,
    Ministry of (MCM), *87*, 103,
        200 n.14
    See also Management and
        Coordination Agency
Management and Coordination Agency
    (MCA), 26, *78, 99*
    tokushu hojin and, 88, 98
    on *yokosuberi*, 94, *100*, 103
    See also Management and
        Coordination, Ministry of
March, James, 170–71
Masumi, Junnosuke, *153*

Matsubara, Satoru, 87, 88, 89, 200 n.15
Matsuzaki, Tetsuhisa, 138, 139, 140, 142
MCA. *See* Management and Coordination Agency
McKinstry, John A., 196 n.4
Media, 58, 176–77, 196 n.1, 201 n.6
Mills, C. Wright, 6, 28, 194 n.20
Minkatsu (private-sector vitality), 47–48
MITI. *See* International Trade and Industry, Ministry of
Miyajima, Hideaki, 2
Miyazawa, Kiichi, 140, 143, 144, 145
MCM. *See* Management and Coordination, Ministry of
MOA. *See* Agriculture, Ministry of
MOC. *See* Construction, Ministry of
MOF. *See* Finance, Ministry of
Moore, Barrington, 203 n.4
MOT. *See* Transport, Ministry of
MPT. *See* Posts and Telecommunications, Ministry of
Mulgen, Aurelia G., 3, 74, 76
Muramatsu, Michio, 4, 37, 39, 45, 50, 137, 193 n.16
on civil service examinations, 34, 35

Nagaoka, Minoru, 52
Nakano, Koichi, 176
National Mobilization Order (1941), 31
National Personnel Authority (NPA), 10, 47, *104*, 178, 192 n.7
on *amakudari* to private sector, 57–58, *65*, 70, 71, 72, *104*
creation of, 22, 44–45, 45–46, 49
limitations of reports from, 22–23, 63, 82, 194 n.18
MOF control of, 193 n.15
National Tax Agency, 59, 64, 66, 67, 68
See also Finance, Ministry of
Nemawashi (convention of negotiation), 43
NHK (Japan Broadcasting Corporation), 176
Nichigai Associates, *146*, *147*, *150–51*, *153*, *154*, *155*
Nihon Keizai Shinbunsha (publishing firm), 25, 27, 88, 106
on *amakudari* to private sector, 62, 70, 72
on *tokushu hojin*, 105, 108, 109

Nihon Seikei Shinbunsha (publishing firm), 192 n.6
on background of Cabinet members, *150–51*
on background of prime ministers, *146*, *147*
on Lower House members, *153*, *154*, *155*, *157*, *158*
Nikkei Weekly (newspaper), 196 n.1
Nippon Telegraph and Telephone Corporation (NTT), 47, 48, 88, 200 n.15
Noguchi, Yukio, 85, 88
Nonprofit organizations, 198 n.5
Norville, Elizabeth, 2, 76
NPA. *See* National Personnel Authority
NTT. *See* Nippon Telegraph and Telephone Corporation

Obuchi, Keizo, 143
OECD (Organization for Economic Cooperation and Development), 199 n.7
Ohira, Masayoshi, 140, 144, 145, 148
Okimoto, Daniel, 13, 17, 171, 192 n.9
on *amakudari* to private sector, 63, 192 n.13, 197 n.12
on indicators of ministry influence, 196 nn.3–5
on *seikai tensin*, 201 n.1
on *wataridori*, 114
Olson, Johan, 170–71
Organization for Economic Cooperation and Development (OECD), 199 n.7
Ozawa, Ichiro, 143

Pantouflage, 5, 191 n.4
PARC. *See* Policy Affairs Research Council
Park, Yung, 138
Patrick, Hugh, 12, 183, 204 n.6
Pempel, T. J., 4, 50, 136, 192 n.11, 193 n.14, 193 n.16
on cultural homogeneity of elite, 35, 37
on ministry stratification, 17
on political pluralism, 13, 16
Policy Affairs Research Council (PARC), 138
See also Liberal Democratic Party
Political economy, *amakudari* and, 12–14

Posts and Telecommunications,
Ministry of (MPT), 53, 64
See also Management and
Coordination, Ministry of
Powell, Walter, 114
Power, 174–75
See also Social power
Power elite, concept of, 194 n.20
Prestowitz, Clyde V., Jr., 4, 16, 17
on causes of amakudari, 40, 42
on iron triangle, 74, 80
Prime ministership
educational background and, 148–49
hereditary politicians representation
in, 161–62
seikai tensin and, 144–49, 146, 147,
160
Todai representation in, 148–49, 161,
168
Prime Minister's Office, 26, 73, 98, 99,
100, 102
Private corporations
interest in amakudari, 41–43
See also Amakudari, to private sector
Public corporations, 198 n.2
categories of, 25, 86, 87
employees of, 86–87
funding of, 87–88 (See also Fiscal
Investment and Loan Program)
rationale for, 83–86
yokosuberi to, 82–83
See also Dokuritsu gyosei hojin;
Tokushu hojin; Tokushu kaisha;
Yokosuberi; Zaidan and shadan
hojin
Public debt, 200 n.16
Public employees
classification of, 10, 34–35, 47
number of, 8–9, 86–87, 192 n.7
as percentage of total employment by
nation, 199 n.7
Public trust, 183, 184, 204 n.6

Regulation, 75–80, 78, 79, 85–86,
197 n.15
Resource compensation, 39–40
Resource dependency, 41, 197 nn.7–8
amakudari to private sector and,
68–75, 70, 71, 72, 73, 80
company location and, 69, 71, 71
company size and, 68–71, 70, 71
industry type and, 69, 72–74, 73

internal contradictions of, 196–97 n.6
keiretsu affiliations and, 69, 71,
71–72, 72
Richardson, Bradley, 18, 68, 139, 175,
192 n.12
on seikai tensin, 136, 137, 138
Roethlisberger, Fritz J., 114
Rosen, Dan, 174, 177–78
Rosovsky, Henry, 12
Rothacher, Albrecht, 137, 141, 142–43,
150, 202 n.6
Roy, William, 172

Samuels, Richard, 4, 13, 136, 137
Sato, Eisaku, 46, 140, 144, 145, 148
Sato, Seizaburo, 138, 139, 140, 142
Saxonhouse, Gary, 12
Scalapino, Robert, 136, 153, 202 n.4
Schaede, Ulrike, 25, 62, 74, 75
Schneider, Ben Ross, 15, 32, 36
Schoppa, Leonard, 138
Schwartz, Frank, 136, 137, 163, 175,
201 n.1
Scott, W. Richard, 29, 41
Seikai kancho jinjiroku (Toyo Keizai
Shinposha), 24–25, 57–58
Seikai tensin (movement to political
office), 11, 18, 20, 21, 30, 135–63,
201 n.1
to Cabinet, 149–50, 150–51, 152,
160
decline of, 138–44
literature on, 136–38
prime ministership and, 144–49, 146,
147, 160
zoku politicians and, 160
See also Amakudari
Seikai tensin (movement to political
office), to Lower House, 151–52
educational background of members,
152, 153, 154, 154, 155
by ministry, 156–58, 157, 158,
159–60, 160
Seiroren, 25–26, 199 n.10
on financial compensation for
wataridori, 130, 131, 131, 132
on wataridori, 113, 121, 122, 132
on yokosuberi, 90, 92, 96
Selznick, Philip, 114
Shadan hojin. See Zaidan and shadan
hojin
Shibata, Tokue, 88

Shidehara, Kijuro, 144
Shin, Kanemaru, 193 n.15
Social power
  definitions of, 171–72
  See also Power
Stark, David, 2
Stinchcombe, Arthur L., 19, 50, 176,
  203 n.2
Structural embeddedness, 37, *119*, 133,
  201 n.2
Swedberg, Richard, 175

Takahashi, Peggy, 2
Takeuchi, Michio, 52
Tanaka effect, 141
Tanimura, Hiroshi, 52
Tatsumichi, Shingo, 182
Thayer, Nathaniel, 201 n.1
Tilton, Mark, 2, 15, 76, 177
Todai, 15, 32, 34, 35, 36
  representation in Cabinet, 149, 152,
    161, 168
  representation in Lower House, 152,
    153, 154, *154*, 161, 168
  representation in prime ministership,
    148–49, 161, 168
Tokushu hojin, 86, 88–97, 103–4
  classes of, 88
  number of, 194 n.19
  reform of, 105, 107–9
  scale by ministry, *89*, 89–90
  wataridori to, 118–21, *120*, 132
  yokosuberi to, 90, 90–91, 92, 93–95,
    104
  See also Public corporations
Tokushu hojin soran (Management and
  Coordination Agency), 26
Tokushu kaisha, 91
  See also Public corporations
Toyo Keizai Shinposha (publishing
  firm), 24–25, 57–58
  on *amakudari* to private sector, *65*,
    104, *116–17*, *124*
  on *amakudari* to private sector by
    ministry, *60*, *61*, *62*
  on background of newly elected
    Lower House members, *155*
  on *wataridori*, *116–17*, *120*, *124*
  on *yokosuberi*, *104*
Transaction cost and contingency
  theories, 41–42
Transport, Ministry of (MOT), 53

amakudari to private sector from, 59,
  64, 66, 67
wataridori from, 168
yokosuberi from, 167
Tsujinaka, Yutaka, 42

Uchida, Roan, 30, 138, 142, 150, *153*
United States
  consumer interest strength in, 15
  global economic dominance of, 181
  judiciary of, 177–78
  power structure of, 5
Uno, Sosuke, 148
Usui, Chikako, 2, 174, 197 n.6
  on judiciary, 177–78
  on Lower House, *153*, *154*

van Wolferen, Karel, 7, 180, 183,
  193 n.14
  on power of MOF, 17, 18, 193 n.15

Wacquant, Loïc J. D., 202–3 n.13
Wanner, Barbara, 74, 76
Washio, Tomoharu, 183
Wataridori distance, 126–27
Wataridori (migratory bird), 11, 20, 21,
  112–34, 167–68
  conflict with labor organizations,
    130, 132, 133
  creation of, 46
  financial compensation for, 130–33,
    131
  indirect routes of, 114–15, *116–17*,
    118–21, *120*
  literature on, 113–14
  organization and coordination of,
    113–14, 127–30
  to private sector, *116–17*
  rank of ex-bureaucrats and, 125–27
  structure by ministry, 121–25, *122*,
    124
  tokushu hojin and, 118–21, *120*, *122*
  See also Amakudari
Who's Who in Japanese Government,
  8–9
World War II, 31

Yamaichi Securities Company, 76
Yokosuberi (sideslip), 11, 20–21, 46, 85,
  130, 166–67
  compared to *amakudari* to private
    sector, 103–5, *104*

Yokosuberi (sideslip) *(continued)*
by ministry, 93–95, *94, 96, 97*
regulation and, 85–86
to *tokushu hojin,* 90, 90–91, *92,*
93–95, *94, 96, 118*
to *zaidan* and *shaban hojin* by
ministry, *100,* 100–103, *102*
See also Amakudari; Public
corporations
Yoshida, Shigeru, 140, 144, 145, 149,
150
Yoshida School, 140–41

Zaidan and *shadan hojin,* 86, 97–103,
104

establishment of, 98–99, *99*
number of, 97–98, 194n.19
yokosuberi to by ministry, *100,*
100–3, 102, 104
See also Public corporations
Zaisei toushi. See Fiscal Investment
and Loan Program
Zaito. See Fiscal Investment and Loan
Program
Zaito bonds, 108–9
Zaito kikansai (private loans
guaranteed by government), 108–9
Zoku politicians, 18, 137–40, 160
See also Liberal Democratic Party
Zukin, Sharon, 37, 114